The Unknown Distance

The Unknown Distance

From Consciousness to Conscience

Goethe to Camus

Edward Engelberg

Harvard University Press
Cambridge, Massachusetts
1972

© 1972 by the President and Fellows of Harvard College
All rights reserved
Library of Congress Card Catalog Number 74-188974
SBN 674-92965-9
Printed in the United States of America

. . . The lowest depth that the light of our Consciousness can visit even with a doubtful Glimmering, is still at an unknown distance from the Ground . . .

—Coleridge

For Elaine

Preface

The advantages of exploring great writers are obvious: they stimulate and enrich; and one may assume a wider audience. But, equally obvious, there are disadvantages as well, chief among them the responsibility placed on the author. It is an exhilarating experience to confront so much greatness: Goethe, Wordsworth, Mann, Nietzsche, James—a veritable parthenon. Assuredly, then, I have the proper respect for my subject. It has, of course, been impossible to cite all the scholarship; nor do I think that essential. I have tried to avoid repeating the obvious; it should be clear that all the authors and their works are discussed from a very special point of view. Far from evading that fact I want to stress it.

The choice of works, though hardly arbitrary, is limited by personal accessibility, taste, and space. Many works have lent themselves to my topic, and to choose among them has not been easy. Yet rather than skim superficially over too many works, I have allowed myself some room to develop my ideas by limiting, as much as possible, the number of works discussed at length.

On the subject of Conscience and Consciousness as I explore it very little has been written that I found useful. Chapter I, note 1, lists some of the help I have found. A large book like James H. Breasted's *The Dawn of Conscience* (1933) was interesting and speculative, but it was not pointed in my direction. On the other hand, Austin Warren's *The New England Conscience*, especially the first chapter, was directly related, and I have made use of what I could learn there. M. H. Abrams's new study, *Natural Supernaturalism, Tradition and Revolution in Romantic Literature,* appeared too late for me to make use of here, but its treatment of Wordsworth, Hegel, and others is clearly relevant to my own undertaking. Also, as I write this preface, a new collection of essays edited by Harold Bloom entitled *Romanticism and Consciousness* has been published. The table of contents reassures me that some of Geoffrey Hartman's important work has already been used with benefit in various chapters. A book like Erich Neumann's *The Origins and History of Consciousness* was far too specialized to be of use. My chief sources, outside of literature, have come from philosophy. I have not intended to use philosophy as a method, or an approach, to guide me through literature. But in philosophers I have found, for obvious reasons, a wide concern with Conscience-Consciousness; and most of the writers with whom I am concerned here were well read in philosophy. Direct influence is never crucial; indirectly, however, philosophy perhaps more than any other extraliterary discipline, save the other arts, has exerted a powerful influence upon poets from Dante to T. S. Eliot, from Shakespeare to Valéry, from Goethe to Tolstoy. Philosophy often disputes what literature presents. It is in that spirit that the amateur can make use of philosophy in the discussion of literature; and in that spirit I have used it in this book.

Conscience and Consciousness are complex terms that cannot be reduced to a single definition; they are always used in the *specific* context of this book, and both terms are clearly limited and defined by the progress of the argument.

Some of the translations from the German are my own, either because no translations existed or a particular passage crucial to my point did not satisfy. Otherwise I have used the best and most accessible editions available, and in the case of all translations I have collated with the original.

In order to spare the reader too many footnotes I have not used page numbers in my discussion of well-known works of fiction, though I have indicated which edition was consulted. For plays,

Act and Scene are given; for poetry, line numbers have been provided wherever it seemed necessary, and, when appropriate, editions have been cited.

It is a pleasure to be able to dedicate this book to my wife without having to express thanks for help in proofreading, typing, and long hours of toil: she has given me far more than that over the years—faith and attention. I could not ask for more.

E. E.

January 21, 1971
Lexington, Mass.

Acknowledgments

It is always a pleasure to acknowledge debts to colleagues who have read one's work in draft and suggested enrichments, but this time I have for the most part spared my colleagues from possible complicity. For one thing, there were too many expert voices; and valuable and well-meaning as they would have been, they might have succeeded in persuading me not to undertake the whole venture—which some might still feel would have been the better part of valor. Several colleagues, however, have provided helpful details: Murray Sachs, Stephen Gendzier, Karen Klein, David Wiesen, and to them I express my thanks. Special help from Mr. Roger Hooper is acknowledged elsewhere. My deep gratitude goes to Harry Zohn who so cheerfully and generously gave me books from his library and little valuable hints whenever I needed them, and to Robert Szulkin who read my chapter on Hegel and Dostoevsky.

I am indebted in more ways than I can express to Austin Warren whose friendship I have valued for so many years. It is not merely the obvious stimulus of his own work on "conscience" which fueled my own; to have been a friend and colleague for so many years was a privilege, and during those years when we both shared so many thoughts at the University of Michigan, I came to know a man who truly possessed, in the manner men once defined it, a conscience.

I must express my appreciation to Professor Ralph Freedman

for his sensitive and sympathetic reading of my manuscript. His suggestions at every turn improved this book. Although the usual disclaimer of not holding him responsible for shortcomings is certainly in order, so is the pleasant conviction that his generous recommendations, whenever I followed them, have added considerably to strengthening my argument.

I would also like to take this opportunity to thank Peter Diamondopoulos of Brandeis who, when he was Dean of Faculty, expressed not only an interest in my work but activated that interest by graciously providing funds needed in the preparation of this book. I wish to thank Bernard Levinson for expediting the delivery of those funds once they were authorized. To Brandeis University I express gratitude for providing Harvard University Press with some supplementary funds toward publication and I thank Eugene Black, Acting Dean of Faculty, for his efforts in obtaining those funds. Many thanks to Naneen Wendler and to Claire Grant for typing and retyping many pages with good cheer. The staff of the Brandeis Library was always helpful in times of crises and I wish to thank the many persons who have been gracious in their assistance. Harvard University Press has extended me many courtesies.

Thanks are also due the following publishers for permission to reprint passages from the works indicated:

Mr. M. B. Yeats and Macmillan & Co. Ltd. with The Macmillan Co.: From "The Choice," "The Statues," "A Dialogue of Self and Soul," and "Leda and The Swan," *The Collected Poems of W. B. Yeats,* copyright, 1933; copyright renewal 1956 by Georgie Yeats.

Alfred A. Knopf, Inc.; Martin Secker & Warburg Ltd.; Schocken Books Inc.: From *The Trial* by Franz Kafka, tr. Willa and Edwin Muir and E. M. Butler, copyright © 1937, 1956, copyright renewal 1964.

Alfred A. Knopf, Inc.: Translations of some passages from *Altes und Neues,* by Thomas Mann. (S. Fischer Verlag)

Alfred A. Knopf, Inc.: From *Buddenbrooks,* by Thomas Mann, translated by H. T. Lowe-Porter, copyright, 1924, renewal copyright, 1952.

Alfred A. Knopf, Inc.: From *The Fall,* by Albert Camus, translated by Justin O'Brien, copyright, 1956.

Alfred A. Knopf, Inc.: From "Sunday Morning" by Wallace Stevens from *The Collected Poems of Wallace Stevens,* by Wallace Stevens, copyright, 1950.

The Macmillan Company: From "Notes from The Underground," *White Nights and Other Stories* by Fyodor Dostoevsky, translated by Constance Garnett.

Doubleday & Co., Inc.: From *Peer Gynt* by Henrik Ibsen, translated by Michael Meyer, copyright © 1963 by Michael Meyer. Reprinted by permission of Doubleday & Company, Inc.

W. W. Norton & Co., Inc.: From *Werther* by Goethe, translated by Harry Steinhauer, copyright © 1970 by W. W. Norton & Company, Inc.

J. M. Dent & Sons, Ltd. and the Trustees of the Joseph Conrad Estate: From *Lord Jim* by Joseph Conrad.

Harvard University Press: From Emily Dickinson, "One Need Not Be A Chamber" reprinted by permission of the publishers and the Trustees of Amherst College from Thomas H. Johnson, Editor, *The Poems of Emily Dickinson,* Cambridge, Mass.: The Belknap Press of Harvard University Press, copyright 1951, 1955, by The President and Fellows of Harvard College.

Jonathan Cape Ltd. and the Estate of Robert Frost; Holt, Rinehart and Winston, Inc.: From "Neither Out Far Nor In Deep," *The Poetry of Robert Frost,* edited by Edward Connery Latham.

Holt, Rinehart and Winston, Inc.: From *Steppenwolf* by Hermann Hesse, translated by Basil Creighton, revised by Walter Sorell, copyright 1929.

Farrar, Straus & Giroux: Translated from some passages of Hermann Hesse's review of Kafka's *The Trial* published in *Die Neue Rundschau.*

Wayne State University Press: Reprinted from "James and Arnold: Conscience and Consciousness in a Victorian 'Künstlerroman'," *Criticism,* vol. 10, no. 2, Spring 1968, by Edward Engelberg, by permission of the Wayne State University Press.

Sigmund Freud Copyrights Ltd., The Institute of Psycho-Analysis and The Hogarth Press for permission to quote from *The Standard Edition of the Complete Psychological Works of Sigmund Freud,* revised and edited by James Strachey.

Contents

The Unknown Distance

Introduction

Introduction

Since the first chapter introduces the specific problems of this study, this introduction seems an appropriate place to set down some generalizations. Ideally all arguments proceed by assertion, exploration, and conclusion. What I assert is that, by slow degrees, the words and concepts, Conscience and Consciousness, have drifted apart from their once nearly identical meaning. This occurred most dramatically in England and Germany, where two distinct words have existed for some time; for this reason almost the entire book deals with English (or American) and German authors. Also, it seems clear that the division between Conscience and Consciousness reached a critical point sometime in the latter part of the eighteenth century and in the nineteenth century. However, such separations became untenable almost as quickly as they were proposed.

So much may be termed assertion; exploration is explicit in the discussions of the works themselves. I attempt no distinctions between literary analysis and what may be classified as extraliterary discussion. To speak bluntly, I have written of a subject that has long occupied my mind, and I have put on paper my thoughts using freely whatever I found justifiable for advancing what I had to say. Having made no claim of using a particular critical method,

I can be held responsible only for choosing not to use one. Frankly, for certain purposes, I have come to distrust methods.

My conclusions are implicit in my explorations and the assertions from which they proceed. The argument advances towards the conviction that the Consciousness of Conscience is the only solution—however risky—that men can find, provided they want to speak either of the one or the other. That is to say men cannot possess a Conscience (whatever they may mean by it), or anything else, without having a full awareness, a full Consciousness first. Because Conscience was for so long linked to and made synonymous with bad conscience—sin and guilt—there was, understandably, a movement to dispense with it. This was part of what has been repeatedly called the reorientation of values coming to full crisis from one end to the other of the nineteenth century. I should like to suggest that the causes of this turning against sin and guilt were more complicated than a mere revolt against existing value systems indicates. One factor that strikes anyone familiar with the nineteenth century is its love of dialectics and dualisms. Not since the medieval disputers have poets, philosophers, even painters, sculptors and composers indulged so lavishly in establishing sometimes neat, sometimes untidy balances.[1]

Some of the dualisms were the old ones in new dress: life and death, good and evil, body and soul; but some, like the *Doppelgänger*, Apollonian versus Dionysian, "naïve" versus "sentimental," achieved psychological and historical subtleties that were not possible before. The dualism, and sometimes the dialetic, between Conscience and Consciousness served many as the seesaw between what they conceived of as antagonistic civilizations, the Hellenic, full of open and joyful awareness, or Consciousness, versus the Christian, weighed down by the sense of sin, by Conscience. Well into the twentieth century Greek and Christian are opposed. From Blake to Nietzsche and beyond, dualisms operated on nearly every level, culminating, according to Thomas Mann's vision of modern culture, in the contrapuntal music that Mann described through his Faust-hero, the composer Adrian Leverkühn, in *Doktor Faustus*. Indeed Mann, one of the last of the great nineteenth-century writers (as were Yeats, Joyce, and Proust),[2] had earlier created the master dialecticians in *The Magic Mountain,* Settembrini and Naphta. In staging the duel of these dualists—despite his protestations, Naphta, the Jesuit Marxist, is a dualist—Mann has ironically annihilated his dialectic. The suicide of Naphta and the departure of the hero leave his *Humaniste manqué,* Settembrini, without a world. And *The Magic Mountain,* on at least one level, is the allegory of the death of dialectics and dualisms.

Arthur O. Lovejoy writes in *The Revolt against Dualism,* first published in 1929, "The last quarter-century, it may fairly confidently be predicted, will have for future historians of philosophy a distinctive interest and instructiveness as the Age of the Great Revolt Against Dualism; though it is possible that they prefer to describe this uprising as a phase of a wider Revolt of the Twentieth century against the Seventeenth." Lovejoy's book concerns the modern rejection of the Cartesian dualism, among others; and he ascribes the motives for this revolt to the current hope of an "eventual unifiability of our understanding of things" and to the "continuity and fundamental homogeneity of nature," motives which today appear as operative, if not more so, than in 1929.[3] The argument of Lovejoy's book, then, is about philosophy and epistemology, and it concerns a revolt against dualisms quite different, on the surface at least, from the ones I have suggested. For I believe that dualism not only survived but thrived in the nineteenth century in some of the areas I have indicated, though it is true that even in the postulation of a dualism the men of the nineteenth century were more apt to look for a Hegelian synthesis, "a unifiability of our understanding of things," than to keep opposing forces in the severed state characteristic of the seventeenth-century dualism which Lovejoy has in mind. Still, however more subtle the nineteenth-century dualism may at times have been, there remained the essential divisive effect. In the case of Conscience and Consciousness, that effect took the shape of moral, theological, and psychic consequences of crucial importance, for one of the questions raised was, radically put: Could Conscience really be considered as a bad cultural habit of Hebraic-Christian civilization and therefore a false and dispensable idea from which, indeed, we were obliged now to wean ourselves?

Austin Warren, who has studied the New England Conscience, writes: "Of the varieties of conscience, it seems easiest to say, with the elder Henry James, that there is no such thing as a " 'good' conscience: the function of conscience is always to convict us of sin." In the same vein, "the chief functions of conscience" are "self-castigation, repentance, the determination to lead a new life"; these, one must keep in mind, are the household views of the Christian Conscience of New England and, one might add, of Old England, too, from a certain point onward. But Warren would not, like Henry James, Sr., deny us a good conscience, which he compares to good health: a human being may, he argues, be free of mortal sin as he may be free of mortal pain. Any preoccupation with conscience exclusively bad becomes a "sick conscience"— "rigid, inflexible"; with an excessive, distorted, and pragmatic view of conscience as "scrupulosity," this sort of Conscience is the New England version of Conscience "in its pathology." In giving "undue predominance" to relentless "self-examination and discipline," it will tend to rule out of existence what Warren recognizes (with the poets) as lamentable, even impossible to rule out of any healthy life: "pleasure, graciousness, joy, love." Basic to man, however, Warren argues, is a sensible middle way between all conscience and no conscience: "Always to be taking one's spiritual pulse is neurotic; to refuse ever to take it—or, better, have it taken—is moral stupidity and arrogance."[4] But to allow, in effect, a good as well as a bad Conscience may ultimately, and beneficially, be a way of having them cancel each other out.

The present book took shape some time ago, certainly long before we became conscious of how deeply enmeshed we were in the conflicts that have divided us this past decade. Our psychedelic world (it has surely passed the stage where we can patronize it by calling it a "subculture"), which the media have brightened considerably, has offered us some perplexing questions. In the words of some of its own adherents and proponents, this world has embarked on new dimensions for the mind: it is dedicated to "mind-expansion," to a new "consciousness." It is irresponsible to call this "escapist"; besides, it is clearly more than that. Yet one may suggest that it is a world hell-bent on getting away from self-consciousness as we know it; perhaps that is why it finds safety in vast communal rites, political, musical, or pharmaceutical. The brave new world searches again for Consciousness without Conscience; it is a symptom of a profound revolution, and no one should be foolish enough to ignore it. After the second World War there was an exhaustive guilt-catharsis; the inevitable lunge away from the stench of that war, the almost panicky surge away from guilt association, began long before acid and speed became consumer goods. Today's lotus-eaters are not new, though their sheer numbers are undoubtedly greater, their lotus far more powerful. That the same people who often sing for peace, picket napalm-makers, and grab at our collective and personal conscience are also sometimes the most consistent and eager bathers in Lethe is no paradox. Come to think of it, the origins of this apparent paradox is perhaps what this book is all about.

I have tried to organize this study in some chronological order without slavishly adhering to date-sequences, since on occasion the comparative aspect involves writers who were, relatively speaking, far apart in time; instances are the chapters on Poe and Mann, *Werther* and *The Prelude*. Other chapters deal with development—from Arnold to Conrad, from Schopenhauer to Freud. Still, taken as a whole, the book begins with the Romantics and concludes with three twentieth-century writers: my intention is to steer a forward course with certain excursions that look before and after.

The opening chapter examines the words Conscience and Consciousness from an etymological and a historical-philosophical view. My assumption is that these two aspects are intertwined and neither the one nor the other alone would suffice to tell the whole story. I also make some attempts to present an overture of leit-motifs: the problem of knowledge and value; the origins of judgment; the theme of egotism.

The titles of the chapters that follow are intended to be clues to their content. Consciousness has its price and its inherent risks; these aspects are the subject of the second and third chapters, and the pairings were chosen to reveal contrasting as well as comparative strategies of coping with the problem. Manfred's Conscience and Faust's Consciousness are the twin-headed engine of Romanticism: each hero emerges as an archetype, a point of reference. Werther's idyl-making and Wordsworth's romantic realism also point to two opposing solutions to the burden and exhilaration of Consciousness: one leads to annihilation; the other to accommodation. Dostoevsky's Underground Man fully opens the issue of freedom and its contingencies, and the "disease" of Consciousness when it becomes, inevitably, obsessive self-consciousness. Hegel's views on the "beautiful soul" and the "unhappy consciousness" I found particularly apposite here and preparatory to my chapter on Schopenhauer, Nietzsche, and Freud. Peer Gynt was yet another, and somewhat different, example of *amour de soi* transformed into *amour-propre*.

Mann and Poe, the subject of the fifth chapter, explore the relationship of Will and Consciousness, and *Buddenbrooks* is a paradigm of the nineteenth century. In this *Familienroman,* Mann conjugates the decline, through successive generations, not merely of a family but of Will itself. The term "tyranny" seemed best to describe what gave rise to and mobilized, from Arnold to James, a rebelliousness against an overbearing Conscience. James's early work (as his late) preoccupied itself with one question perhaps above any other: How could Conscience, if it were not to remain a tyrannical and destructive force, become a noble and redeeming act of Consciousness? Conrad's psychological analysis of the "romantic conscience" in *Lord Jim* brings the story to a conclusion at the point where we can recognize the overreaction against Conscience by replacing that tyranny with another, the tyranny of a Consciousness that deals with the shadow rather than the substance.

Although I recognize the difficulties of dealing with such eclectic figures as Schopenhauer, Nietzsche, and Freud, their analysis of the problem could not be evaded; in the end I found the light they shed worth the risks of not doing justice to their complexities. Furthermore, this chapter prepares for the final chapter in which I submit, in effect, that by the first quarter of this century we had arrived at a point of crisis. This crisis was inherent in Faust and

Manfred: the insistence of Conscience that it have its say in man's "trial." Between Kafka, Hesse, Camus and the present there is time not accounted for, and in the conclusion I attempt to bring us up to date and to pose some questions which have not yet been explored but are ready to be taken up where I leave off.

I. Conscience and Consciousness: Dualism or Unity?

Just so, conscience is not something to be acquired, and there is no duty to provide oneself with a conscience; but insofar as every man is a moral being, he has it originally within him.

—Kant

Etymology

Originally, conscience did not primarily mean either good or bad, though both adjectives became associated with the word very early in its linguistic history. It is clear that in German, English, and in the Romance languages, conscience and consciousness are intimately related, the latter word growing out of the former. As philosophy and psychology became increasingly subtle and preoccupied themselves with exceptional energy about theories of the mind, conscience needed to find a permanent home, a place where it might be said to reside. That place became, inevitably, consciousness. Also, as already suggested, in German and English the division of the two words resulted in the division, or attempted division, of what they implied. It might be reasonably argued that otherwise a new word need not have been created; nevertheless, as I plan to show, the terms resisted separation. Consciousness was a relatively late term and in such languages as German and English, where it attained the status of a separate term, its growth out of conscience and its repeated identity with it can be traced to this day. Although we are often unaware of it, we still use the two words interchangeably.[1]

For instance, in English we speak commonly, now more than ever, of having (or not having), say, a "social consciousness"; we mean, of course, a "social conscience," a responsibility or obligation to be aware. When Joyce has Stephen Dedalus write into his Diary at the conclusion of *A Portrait of the Artist as a Young Man,* "I go to encounter for the millionth time the reality of experience and to forge in the smithy of my soul the uncreated conscience of my race," he means the uncreated consciousness of his race, its identity and awareness of itself. In German law one is asked to bear witness, *nach bestem Wissen und Gewissen,* to the best of his knowledge and his conscience. The favorite French phrase *la crise de la conscience,*[2] is deliberately ambiguous, pointing to both conscience and consciousness in a language that has but one word for both meanings; only context can determine precise shades of emphasis. As long ago as 1527 the Spanish writer Bartolome de las Casas, writing his *Historias de las Indias* to arouse the conscience of Spaniards by pointing to the evils of colonial exploitation, suggested that his countrymen become *"ser conscios"* (conscious) of such iniquities.[3] Italo Svevo's best-known work is entitled in Italian *La Coscienza di Zeno (The Conscience of Zeno),* the consciousness of Zeno. When Milton wrote in "To Cyriack Skinner, Upon His Blindness" (1655?) about "The conscience, friend, to have lost them [eyes] overpli'd/In liberty's defence," he obviously meant consciousness. Examples like this abound in many languages, and I have suggested merely a few spanning several languages and several centuries. In the following pages and again in the sixth chapter, I examine some cases in more detail; for the present the history of the two words needs more precise probing.

To pursue the etymological niceties of conscience and consciousness is no mere exercise in tracing the vagaries of language, especially in the case of English and German. Both languages, at least in common usage, sometimes behave as if they had forgotten the near identity of the two words which once in fact existed. This does not contradict the earlier remark that the terms are still used interchangeably, for we do so unawares; and, in many instances, particularly with the advent of psychoanalysis and the existential metaphysics of such philosophers as Heidegger and Jaspers, consciousness has tended to carve out for itself very definite areas of meanings. Yet precisely some of those writers who sought to make the cleavage official before the twentieth century, Schopenhauer, Arnold, and Nietzsche, were in the very process of creating the dualism demonstrating the unity they were splitting in half. There are parts of Arnold's "Hebraism and Hellenism" (1868-1869) and Nietzsche's *Genealogy of Morals* (1887) which advocate not only a divorce between conscience and consciousness but an opposition between them, perhaps even a dialectic. Implicit in the plea to divide is, of course, the admission that unity exists. Hegel, Schopenhauer, and, later, Freud recognized this most clearly. Presently I want to establish the developing historical landscape of actual usage of conscience and consciousness in English and German, relying strictly on etymological scholarship. The literary and doctrinal works I subsequently examine throughout this book are the enlarged illustrations of that scholarship.

In English, conscience has enjoyed a rich history from early Middle English to modern English. *The Oxford English Dictionary*[4] says that "In M[iddle] E[nglish], *conscience* took the place of the earlier term INWIT in all its senses." That may be somewhat misleading, although Skeat and Mayhew, in their *Concise Dictionary of Middle English,* define Inwyt/inwit as "Conscience, Consciousness." Inwit is familiar to many because of Joyce's motif-use in *Ulysses* of a title of a fourteenth-century work called *Ayenbite of Inwyt,* or *Pricke of Conscience* (1340), by Michel, Dan of Northgate, which is a translation of a French work by Father Lorens, *Les sommes des vices et des vertues* (1279).[5] For Joyce, "inwit" certainly meant conscience; in Middle English it seems to have been used either in place of or in conjunction with conscience. One instance in the famous *Ancrene Riwle* (c. 1230?) makes a particularly subtle distinction: "Inwið us seluen ure ahne concience. Þ is, ure inwit. forwi ðande hire seluen wiþe fur of sunne." The translation, fairly literal, has been rendered, "within ourselves our own conscience, that is, our mind [inwit] reproaching itself with the fire of remorse for sin."[6] In Middle English inwit seems more generally to refer to "mind," while conscience—taken from Latin and sometimes, in the *Ancrene Riwle,* as elsewhere, spelled in Latin—begins to take on the more common connotations. In any case, the *MED* offers as its fourth definition of inwit: "Inward awareness of right or wrong, conscience." The first definition, however, is "Mind, reason, intellect, comprehension, understanding," that is, what in essence we later come to call consciousness. In Anglo-Saxon, inwit is used often, meaning "deceit," "guile," and similar terms. If one were to expect to find conscience in the form of inwit, it would be in the *Blicking Homilies* (10th century), but the only use of inwit there refers to the traditional meanings ("deceit," "guile"). The *MED* itself declares that inwit, as used in Middle English, is a compound of "in" and "wit." When the Anglo-Saxon texts wished to refer to conscience they used "ingeþanc," defined as "thought, thinking, cognition, intent, mind, heart, conscience." Its relation to the modern German *innere Gedanken* (inner thoughts) is clear. The Anglo-Saxon "inwit," therefore, seems to have no semantic connection with the Middle English "inwit," which meant literally "inner knowledge," from which the transition to conscience is logical and remains intact to modern times. The Anglo-Saxon "witan," to have knowledge, may possibly have exerted an influence on the Middle English transition to "inwit."

In the *MED* the word "conscience" (also *consience, conciens, conscientia*) is defined, in its first definition, as "the mind or heart as the seat of thought, feeling, and desire; attitude of mind, feelings." "The faculty of knowing what is right . . . awareness of right and wrong; consciousness of having done something good or bad," "the moral sense," is the second definition and here sin and guilt are associated with "conscience." "Conscience gret" is defined as "full awareness," "conscience sure" as "strong conviction." It should be emphasized that these two meanings of conscience—the "mind or heart as the seat of feeling" and "awareness of right and wrong"—were concurrently in use partly because consciousness, according to the *OED*, first makes an independent appearance in the seventeenth century. In early use "consciousness" meant *"consciousness to oneself,"* "internal knowledge or conviction; knowledge as to which one has a testimony within oneself; esp. of one's own innocence, guilt, deficiencies, etc." It can already be seen from these early definitions that the two words were close

relatives, consciousness evolving from conscience as the latter became increasingly associated with good or bad, that is, with moral
definitions.

The first definition of conscience in the *OED* reads: "inward
knowledge, consciousness; inmost thought, mind"; under this, "inward knowledge or consciousness; internal conviction" is marked
"*Obs.*". Ironically, a quotation from Swinburne, in 1869, "The
conscience of this sharpens and exasperates the temper of his
will," seems to use the word in that obsolete meaning of "internal
conviction." In any case it is the latest entry under the general
heading "Inward knowledge, consciousness." The year 1869 saw
the publication of Arnold's *Culture and Anarchy,* in which, in the
now famous essay, "Hebraism and Hellenism," Arnold sought to
establish entirely new ground for both conscience and consciousness.

As the *OED* points out, English adapted conscience from Latin;
so did the Romance languages: Spanish, *conciencia;* Italian, *coscienza;* and French, of course, simply *conscience.* The *OED*
renders the Latin *conscientia* as "privity of knowledge (with
another), knowledge within oneself, consciousness, conscience."
The word is formed from "*con*-together + *scire* to know; thus
conscire alii, to know along with another, to be privy with another
to a matter, thence, *conscire sibi* to know with oneself only, to
know within one's own mind." This emphasis on knowledge is
important, as the remainder of the discussion will shortly make
clear. It is evident that conscious(ness) has the same roots as the
Latin *con* plus *scire;* to be "conscious," used in English earlier
than the noun consciousness, meant, again from the Latin, "*con-
sci-us* knowing something with others, knowing in oneself, privy
to"; the *OED* also notes that in Italian, since the sixteenth century, *conscio* may mean "privy, accessary, guilty," clearly showing its relationship to conscience.

The second meaning for conscience in the *OED* is the more
familiar: "consciousness of right and wrong," but we should note
"consciousness" already concedes that one must have it even to
define the state of possessing conscience: Conscience is something
of which one is conscious. One further interesting note on etymology in the *OED* explains how conscience became individualized:

being originally a "noun of condition or function" it had no plural, that is, "a man or a people had *more* or *less* conscience." But "gradually [conscience came] to be thought of as an individual entity . . . of which each man possessed *one* . . . So *my conscience, your conscience,* was understood to mean no longer our respective shares or amounts of the common quality *conscience,* but to be two distinct individual *consciences,* mine and yours." No doubt this development parallels certain attitudes in theology which are beyond my scope here, but the idea is suggestive as one follows how some of the writers I discuss use the concept of conscience.

In German, as Hegel, Schopenhauer, Nietzsche, and Freud have noted, the cognates are obvious: Conscience is *Gewissen;* knowledge is *Wissen;* to be certain (with conviction) is to be *gewiss;* and consciousness is *Bewusstsein.* Like English, however, German has for a long time possessed two words, and it was this linguistic opportunity that men seized, either to divide or to unite, the words and their meanings; and, as I have noted, sometimes the same men, at different times, did both.

The German *Gewissen*[7] has had an equally instructive etymological evolution. Schopenhauer commented that its origin lay with both "the Latin *conscientia* . . . and the Greek word "συνείδyis [syneidesis]," which means conscience-consciousness.[8] Dictionaries since his time have made these and further connections. The Gothic *miþwissei* literally "with knowledge," was a direct translation of *con scientia.* This became *gewizzeni* (also *giwizzani* and *gawizani*), again from Latin but beginning to resemble the modern German. Around 1000 the Monk of St. Gallen, Notker "Teutonicus," used *gewizzen* as a translation of the Latin *conscius,* "so that Conscience originally also meant consciousness in the religious-moral sense." Luther used *Gewissen* as an entity of which one must be conscious. As in English so in German, *Bewusstsein* (consciousness) makes a late appearance, particularly in its psychological sense. However, it seems to have had a more direct and purposeful relation to consciousness in German than in English. In philosophic meanings it had meant merely a "knowledge of"—guilt, bad deeds. But Christian Wolff (1679-1754) took the older *Gewissen,* equated it with the more modern and added

Bewusstsein, thereby insisting on its psychological rather than its moral connotations of both the older and the newer *Gewissen.* Thus it appears he made the first definite division, but kept close relationships intact. This occurred earlier than any English entry noted in the *OED.* The same entry also notes that Schlegel, in translating Hamlet's soliloquy as *"so macht Gewissen Feige aus uns allen"* (Thus conscience does make cowards of us all), still used conscience "where Consciousness is meant."[9] That reference to *Hamlet* is worth pursuing. Here is the relevant passage of the most famous soliloquy in English:

> Who would fardels bear,
> To grunt and sweat under a weary life,
> But that the dread of something after death,
> The undiscovered country from whose bourn
> No traveller returns, puzzles the will,
> And makes us rather bear those ills we have
> Than fly to others that we know not of?
> *Thus conscience does make cowards of us all;*
> And thus the native hue of resolution
> Is sicklied o'er with the pale cast of thought,
> And enterprises of great pitch and moment
> With this regard their currents turn awry
> And lose the name of action. (III, i, 76-87)

I have quoted at length to permit context to emerge, for, without certain words around my italicized line, it is difficult to see what the argument may be all about. Note first that Hamlet does in fact use the word "conscience" in the singular and plural sense: there is clearly a reference to a quality in which all men have a share, and a personal reduction by Hamlet himself, in effect a confession that *his* conscience makes *him* a coward at *this* point in *his* life. It is impossible to list all the commentary on Hamlet's use of the word "conscience" here, but in John Munro's edition of *The London Shakespeare* (1958) from which I have quoted, the Note is interesting and I give it in part: "Some have interpreted this [the passage on conscience] in a moral sense. Onions glosses as 'sense of right and wrong.' . . . The reference to thought . . . shows that a wider meaning is intended . . . in this passage the meaning is meditative reflection." The trend since Kittredge, who supports the "moral sense" ("A less probable interpretation takes *conscience* to mean 'that of which we are conscious' ")[10] has on the whole been in the other direction. And this shift in the commentary on so famous a passage tells much about a wider shift in sensibility, one which attempts once more to bring the concepts of conscience "as that of which we are conscious" into focus.

Although I have no wish to linger over Hamlet's soliloquy, I think it fair to raise the question as to what Hamlet is saying in the lines I have quoted. Clearly he expresses a conflict, a conviction that we dread some hereafter more than the present, however insufferable, because we *know* the present while we do not know anything of that "undiscovered country." Here Hamlet is very explicit: we rather bear the "ills we have/Than fly to others that we *know* not of" (italics mine)—hence "conscience [knowing, that is, consciousness] does make cowards of us all." Despite the definition of conscience as consciousness in the *OED,* this very line from *Hamlet* is nevertheless given as an example of conscience meaning "consciousness of right or wrong," which in effect defines conscience as a state of being conscious. Although the critics have begun to turn away from the strict moralistic interpretation, taking Hamlet to mean conscience-consciousness, the issue remains open; yet nowhere can I find a better point of departure for maintaining the "once-and-future" identity of conscience and consciousness than in this speech spoken on a London stage sometime on the razor's edge between the end of the sixteenth century and the beginning of the seventeenth century.

Clearly, then, both words referred to a state of human awareness, awareness brought into focus, awareness of a fallen self, of guilt and remorse—words which if not identical with conscience are certainly close relations.

The Historical and Philosophical Foreground

If conscience-consciousness constitutes a major dialectic, probed and refined in the course of the last three centuries, we would certainly not expect to find the accompanying debate confined to etymology. Conscience-consciousness is often a central issue in the developing philosophical landscape beginning with

Spinoza, Leibniz, Locke (born the same year as Spinoza), and, beyond Locke, in all the major philosophers whom Locke inspired, whether as disciples or opponents. To examine so broad a spectrum requires some mention of Hume, the French *philosophes,* Rousseau, Kant, Fichte, Hegel, Schopenhauer, and Nietzsche. No major analysis of so many figures and their interlocking relationships can be attempted here, but one way of limiting the field is to set some questions around which the conscience-consciousness problem can be accommodated.

First, I should think, we must ask to what extent conscience, when considered as synonymous with virtue, was thought to be an innate quality in man and how this, in turn, influenced the view toward the nature and expression of conscience. As for consciousness, we must ask, How was knowledge conceived? Was it a value innate, acquired, or intrinsic? Indeed, was it a value at all? Or was knowledge (for which consciousness was a necessary precondition) a process which tended, by its very nature, to be damaging and dangerous? The eighteenth century (and no less the nineteenth in its own fashion) provides us with major examples of self-conscious moralism, a moralism, moreover, to which, in varying degrees, the individual is held accountable. Such questions lead to the major conceptions of duty which so preoccupied Hume, Rousseau, Kant, to name only a very few of the major philosophers. It was through the discussions of duty that, eventually, Conscience was to be filtered and distilled. Definitions of duty invariably led to definitions of Conscience and vice versa. How does Man know, and how does this relate, *if* it does, to a perception of "reality"? Here was another major question among philosophers emanating from rationalists, skeptics, empiricists, and idealists, spanning better than two centuries. In summary, then, it will certainly help to illuminate any discussion of conscience-consciousness to ask: What in man is innate? What in knowledge is value (if anything)? What is the nature of duty? and *how* do we know, particularly in the sphere of moral questions?

In that sphere of moral questions Spinoza spoke of the good in evil, Leibniz of man's essential "philanthropy." Spinoza linked "conscience" to the supremacy of reason which always keeps us on the straight path, provided we use reason properly. What he called "our good Conscience" teaches us what is virtue because conscience is incapable of error.[11] For Leibniz it was not the cognitive power that separated men from animals but moral consciousness, a state of being "subject to remorse of Conscience, and to feel these *laniatus et ictus,* these tortures and torments," of what came to be known as a bad conscience. Man's "natural instincts," he insisted, "tend toward what is right and decent."[12] Such benign views of human nature survive, as will be clear, throughout the eighteenth century, though not without change, indeed even serious challenge. Certainly Locke, whose *Essay Concerning Human Understanding* still belongs chronologically to the seventeenth century (1690), agreed that, by and large, man's social instincts were "good." But Locke did *not* agree with Leibniziens that man's natural instincts, whether for good or evil, were innate. Locke's empiricism was based on a realistic appraisal of how men behaved, and on that basis, he confessed, he saw no ready inclination in men "to do as one would be done to." Yet he thought it equally mistaken to abandon the principle itself and conjectured that "perhaps *conscience* will be urged as checking us for . . . breaches" of the principle, acting as a kind of dam which binds us to "internal obligation," thus preserving a principle not innate but acquired.[13]

Locke felt that men come to know moral principles as they come to know anything else and that their becoming convinced of their moral obligations was a matter of practicality, background, milieu, and education. Conscience was, in effect, an expression of "our own opinion or judgment of the moral rectitude or pravity of our actions," an individual not a universal judge. When pressed for a view of conscience as part of some given moral law, Locke told Thomas Burnett, "It is not conscience that *makes* the distinction of good and evil, conscience only judging of an action by *that which it takes to be* [eternal] rule of good and evil, acquits or condemns it." Conscience is a means of judging and measuring "the law of nature"; but it is not itself that law. The distinction is important: it is a little like saying that the thermometer judges and determines the illness but is in no way the illness itself. (A fine instance of this may be found in the section "Thermometer" of Mann's *Magic Mountain*.) If moral rules and principles were really innate, asks Locke, how could man transgress them so often "with confidence and serenity"—with impunity? By their very behavior men seem to contradict any idea that virtue, or Conscience, is innate. The *"power"* to distinguish good from evil, Locke protested, he did not deny as being innate; it was "moral ideas" or "moral rules" he did not allow as innate—"any *idea* or *connection of ideas*" on moral problems. Conscience could not, therefore, be a useful guide either to actions or some kind of revealed principle of eternity.[14]

At least in one important area Hume tended to agree with Locke: men act one way or another, not out of innate qualities— good or bad—but for reasons of self-interest. But Hume bestowed upon conscience far more power than Locke, raising it above reason which, at least in areas of moral behavior, Hume considered to be inoperative. "Actions," he argued, "may be laudable or blameable; but they cannot be reasonable or unreasonable"; and "moral distinctions" are not fathered by reason, which in such matters remains "wholly inactive, and can never be the source of so active a principle as conscience, or a sense of morals." The break with Spinoza and Leibniz was here completed. As for "obligation," Hume categorically denied that men can *will* it; we only *"feign* a new act of the mind," thereby pretending to be *"willing an obligation"* on the assumption that morality is based on such volition. But like reason, will has no power in the moral sphere.[15] Elsewhere, however, Hume concedes that *"reason* and *sentiment* concur in almost all moral determinations and conclusions"; yet this merely seems to suggest that man acts morally in such ways as the governing bodies of both thought and feeling can approve. Hume everywhere reasserts that any ethical system must be empirical, that self-interest more than any innate virtue guides men toward justice because society (on which men depend for survival) without justice cannot survive. (Theoretically that argument is irrefutable; history, however, has destroyed it with relentless eagerness.) Therefore, virtue equals an approved action, vice a disapproved one. Hume also recognized something that became obvious to his disciples: "Inward peace of mind, consciousness of integrity, a satisfactory review of our own conduct . . . [are] very requisite to happiness." All "moral speculations," necessarily, it would appear, have as their aim "to teach us our duty," to show us the "beauty of virtue" or the "deformity of vice," not to frighten us by threat (as Church or State might do) but to make the virtuous so attractive that it will seem the only sensible and agreeable course to follow.[16] Such general optimism, however reasonably based, appeared to become even less acceptable to later times than the notion of innate virtue, for although both positions clearly underestimated the nature of evil, Hume's empiricism, his conviction that common sense would dictate a virtuous course, seemed more vulnerable to instant contradiction. If men acted solely in accordance with self-interest, it still remained to inquire whether the nature of such self-interest was unequivocally defensible. Kant attempted to clear up this problem in a number of ways, and his place as an intermediate step to modern conceptions of moral principles was indispensable. Kant's contribution was, however, as Ernst Cassirer and others have shown, a direct consequence of the influence of Rousseau, for it was Rousseau who broke openly with the lingering rationalism of the Encyclopedists.

By and large the Encyclopedists rejected the earlier Cartesian rationalists—"Cartesians, Melebranchistes and Leibniziens"—but on the central issue of innate goodness, la belle âme, they looked, surprisingly perhaps, to Locke. In their zeal to make strict divisions, the Cartesians and their followers distinguished between those perceptions the soul felt and those of which it had a knowledge. Locke, however, insisted that "the soul has no perception whatever of which it has no knowledge"; perception and consciousness (knowledge) was therefore to be considered identical. So at least runs the interpretation of M. de M. le Chevalier de Jaucourt, the contributer of the entry "Conscience" to the Encyclopédie.[17] Implicit in this position, the identity of perception and consciousness, is the assumption that such consciousness (knowledge) is necessarily a value; and that particular equation—knowledge = value—became one of the strongest arguments of German Idealism. Condillac, says the entry in the Encyclopédie, was correct in assigning to consciousness the function of imparting to the soul whatever perceptions it ultimately knows.

Conscience is "an act of the understanding," which decides what is good or bad, judges omission and commission, and endows us, when we deserve it, with "cruel remorse." As Kant was to develop it in subtle detail, conscience in the Enlightenment is, according to de Jaucourt, an "interior tribunal which judges us." Indeed conscience is a judgment each man renders on his own conduct, his actions, by holding such actions up against the conceptions he has of the law. A man then decides whether his action conforms to or transgresses that law. Yet the *Encyclopédie* entry stresses that we judge as "*compared with the ideas* which [we have] of the law, and not the law itself," since only that law which we know can rule our actions and we do not, presumably, know all the law. That leaves a man with a very generous margin for error. Nevertheless de Jaucourt cautions that such generosity does not imply an invitation to relativistic morality—each man acting according to what he knows of the law. A commitment of one's conscience must first be tested to see whether one has the enlightenment to make judgments in the first place; and further one must discover whether what is to be judged, as proper or not, has already been generally accepted and judged by custom and practice. (One may commit error simply by being ignorant that such an act has been judged as error.) True to its reputation of insisting on the sacredness of freedom in thought, the *Encyclopédie* article insists that if one man thinks another's judgment of conscience is in error, he must try to correct it by peaceful means of persuasion. In short, freedom to act according to one's conscience is deemed essential. Recalling the discussion of etymology, we might conclude this view of the *Encyclopédie* by stating its initial definition of conscience as the feminine noun used in Philosophy, Logic, and Metaphysics: "The opinion of the feeling which we have within ourselves about that which we do; that which the English express by the word *consciousness,* which one can only put in French by periphrase."[18]

Rousseau, once he touched on the problem of conscience, gave it a full airing in *Emile,* and his excursus on conscience in that pedagogical "novel" has been considered one possible source for Kant's treatment of duty.[19] A distinction was needed between duty and reason, which both Locke and Hume had tended to regard either as synonymous or at least compatible. In seventeenth-century novels, some psychologists of the heart, such as for example Mme de la Fayette, described the conflict between reason and duty in graceful detail. In her famous *Princesse de Clèves* (published in 1677 and written, it is thought, with the help of La Rochefoucauld), Mme de la Fayette raises the question of the sometimes conflicting demands of duty and reason, and leaves us, I think, with some ambiguous conclusions. The Princess is married but is in love with another whom she scrupulously avoids, thus remaining chaste in deed—but not in thought. When she is widowed she is free to marry her true love, but she renounces the man on grounds of duty, blaming both the lover and herself for her husband's death. In fact, her own passion, while never consummated, constituted a case of surrogate adultery; while she never quite admits this, it is clearly that knowledge and its attendant guilt which prevent her from enjoying the available fruit. She does concede that she is sacrificing a great deal "*à un devoir*" (for duty) which exists only in her mind. Reason and duty, she contemplates sadly, at times appear to indicate opposing choices; while duty may compel one's conscience to forego, reason counsels that forebearance is not necessary or even justified. Mme de la Fayette allows duty to triumph (as Henry James was to do on a grand scale), but not without considerably attenuating that triumph. Feeling ("passion") is stronger than reason; Conscience defies what may appear both unreasonable and unjustified.

The development of duty as a concept beyond the maxims of La Rochefoucauld, the imperatives of the Encylopedists, and the *Humanitätsideal* of Kant and Schiller offers sufficient material for a separate study. Yet it is irresistible to compare, if only for a brief space, Mme de la Fayette's tidy and severe treatment of duty with Stendhal's, nearly two centuries later for, in a certain sense, the string had now run out. Julien Sorel, that quixotic and disturbing young man of *Le Rouge et le Noir,* is a devotée of what Stendhal repeatedly calls in his novel duty—*devoir.* Yet duty has by now ceased to be some moral code, whether towards Church or State; it has also ceased to be a personal dedication to keep faith with one's own values. What is it? It is difficult to say, really. For Julien *devoir* is not, as some may think, merely the prescribed patterns of behavior as social conventions dictate for a successful parvenu: that is only half the truth. The other half of *devoir* is best illustrated towards the end of the novel.

That ancestor of Strindberg's Julie, Mathilde, aristocratic daughter of a marquis, has permitted herself the pleasure of being degraded by an upstart. In now transferring the master-servant relationship to give Julien the power of master, she abdicates her prescribed role. She addresses an eight-page letter to her father confessing her transgression but defending herself, now that she is with child, on the ground that the act was conceived in duty—his (Julien's) right, and her duty. Julien, having read this letter while waiting to be called into the chambers of the marquis, asks himself: How should he behave? This is characteristic of him. But, he adds, not only where lies my duty but where lies my interest— *"mon devoir . . . mon intérêt?"* The conflict is *not* between duty and *inclination* but between duty and *interest*. Clearly duty itself has become divided in Julien's mind; his sense of duty is not necessarily what is right vis-à-vis his benefactor, even in the light of prudent and self-protective action but, beyond that, whether such a duty truly coincides with his interest. To do what is conventionally prudent, therefore, no longer is necessarily consistent with what is correct for one's ultimate interest. Interest as a conception has become almost a thing-in-itself: it has no moral or psychological relationships and no self-serving function; it stands aloof outside the self. It is precisely this stark view of "interest," which abandons inclination—or the capacity to feel—which in the end defeats Julien. Such interest subverts duty and is humanized only when it becomes truly self-interest, *amour de soi* not *amour-propre*. In Julien's case this comes too late. One of the grotesque discoveries of his brief life (and it is surely a parabolic life of the nineteenth century) is his realization how mistakenly he has conceived of duty, how *devoir* has undone rather than made him. Having at last secured Mathilde, in a false state of euphoric triumph, he decides to abandon all caution. At that moment, in a state of confusion and loss, he nevertheless realizes that duty as he has used it never served the self towards outer gain at all. His cynicism at such a discovery is not unwarranted; he sees his experience as the special mark of his age, and that age as leading to chaos: *"Il faut renoncer à toute prudence. Ce siècle est fait pour tout confondre! nous marchons vers le chaos."* As we shall see, he is right.

Paul Hazard has traced the decline of reason in the realm of metaphysics by linking this eventual demise of reason to the trends of empiricism and skepticism preceding Kant. The limits of human knowledge, of "understanding," immediately created frontiers which, like all frontiers, erected obstacles beyond which one might not travel. The realm of knowledge, thus enclosed, was at least definable, and an earlier overoptimism, the *sapere aude* (dare to know), shibboleth of the Leibniziens, became tempered. Reason was to become increasingly viewed not as innate but as established authority, the first significant move against standard rationalism for the empiricists and the skeptics. Knowledge, too, no longer was conceived of as innate nor, it was argued, did we have the capacity to know all, regardless of how much we might dare: the data of the senses were becoming identified as the chief sources of knowledge.[20] "Consciousness," wrote Locke, "is the perception of what passes in a man's own mind ... No man's knowledge here can go beyond his experience."[21]

Even Rousseau was careful in ascribing moral impulses as innate: a clean slate is neither virtuous nor evil. Reason, as we shall see, becomes the mediating faculty in man's recognition of what may be innate: if a man's soul is the photographic negative, reason is the agent that develops it. Cassirer pointedly stresses Rousseau's assessment of man as a creature bent on self-preservation, distinguishing, however, between self-love (*amour de soi*) and selfish love (*amour-propre*), the latter being chiefly the product of society and its corrupting institutions. Yet Rousseau holds *men* responsible for their sins (which Irving Babbitt conveniently forgot in *Rousseau and Romanticism*): sin is "closely bound to the consciousness of the subject of the action," and is nontransferable.[22] The same holds true for moral redemption: both sin and redemption are the individual's burden, neither society's nor God's. "O Man! seek no further for the author of evil; thou art he": this sentence is quoted from *Emile* (composed 1757-1760, published

1762). Nevertheless man's first obligation (duty) is towards himself, and this despite the threat of being called selfish, a sentiment Nietzsche was to echo later in far more strident tones.

To guide such self-interest (*amour-propre*), man must listen to his soul, not his passions; and the voice of the soul (Fichte would say precisely the same thing) was for Rousseau man's conscience. Such a voice was completely reliable: conscience never deceives, "she is the true guide of man," and to obey conscience is to obey nature herself: when man heeds nature he will "find a joy to the answer of a good conscience." The identity of nature and conscience seals an affinity which reason or passion could never approach. Conscience is neither of mind nor of body, it is of soul—*die schöne Seele, la belle âme:* "Conscience! Conscience! Divine instinct, immortal and celestial voice, certain guide . . . infallible judge of good and evil, which renders man in the likeness of God; it is in you that the excellence of [man's] nature and the morality of his actions reside; without you I can find nothing which elevates me above the beasts."[23] What God has given man is not conscience but a universe in which, by aid of will, he may exercise the judgment, for good or evil, which the voice of conscience provides.

However, Rousseau negotiated the relation of reason to conscience more subtly than any of his predecessors. In his lengthy discussion of child psychology in *Emile,* he argues that "reason alone teaches us to *know* good and evil" (italics mine); but man does have an innate sense of right and wrong. Conscience is the gauge that eventually alerts us to love good and despise evil; and although conscience is "independent" of reason it cannot develop without reason because, acting like a beam, reason directs us as we learn to acquire the use of its power. Without reason, without consciousness of good and evil, the child commits acts in either direction: it has no moral direction. It is the express function of reason, then, to cultivate the innate sense of justice (or to curb injustice if that predominates). This view influenced not only Kant but all of German Idealism, especially that of Schiller. For reason Schiller substituted a broad conception of education (*Erziehung*), the subtitle of *Emile.* The education of man would be achieved by giving man (as Rousseau suggested for the child) not a right to rule over others but a genuine liberty that placed responsibility on the individual. Under the control of aesthetic discipline, the play instinct (*Spieltrieb*) would provide freedom for the individual man. But individual man would be held accountable in preventing liberty from degenerating into anarchy.

As all subsequent philosophers have discovered, not always with sanguine acceptance, in giving us freedom Kant placed us in bondage to the demands of exercising it. Conscience was a "marvelous faculty" capable of practically infallible "judicial sentences." A guilty man might try to excuse some improper act, placing blame on "natural necessity," thereby proclaiming his innocence. But "advocate" and "accuser," the terms are Kant's, are an uneven match, for the accuser will not permit a man to plead innocent "when he is conscious that at the time when he [the man on trial] committed the wrong he was in his senses, i.e., he was in possession of his freedom."[24] Our concern with our "dear self" *(amour-propre)* stands in the way of "the stern command of duty," and causes Kant to voice some very pessimistic views about his fellow men. Actions are deceptive; it is not to them we should look but to the inner principles, which unfortunately are often intangible, always invisible. Still, actions are visible barometers; they must, however, proceed from a sense of duty to have any "moral worth"; and it is not the "purpose" but "the maxim by which [an action] is determined" that endows that action with value. Duty itself is "the necessity of an action done from respect for the law." Kant was not interested so much in the results of behavior (few theoreticians are) as in the process and the source. The assumption of an autonomous will places the burden on individual responsibility to fulfill "duty," which Kant defines as the "objective necessity of an action from obligation." Or, less abstrusely said, duty is an individual's proper choice of fulfilling a moral action from the advantage both of a free will and a practical reason, which at times appear to be inseparable.[25]

Cassirer emphasizes that for Kant, as for Rousseau, the question is not the *is* but the *ought;* but this in no way precludes a realistic appraisal of what *is* and *ought* are. It was the distinction that needed to be kept clear. As Yeats said, clearly under the influence of Kant, when the Soul speaks to the Self ("A Dialogue of Self and Soul"):

> ... For intellect no longer knows
> *Is* from the *Ought,* or *Knower* from the *Known,*

and that condition can be dangerous unless we remain lucid about sequence and priority. The action we do and the action we ought to do may at times be the same; when it is not we should know it. Kant (as Cassirer shows) credited Rousseau "the ethical philosopher with having discerned the 'real man' beneath ... all the masks" men have worn throughout history. So Kant, taking Rousseau further along certain paths, comes to rest finally at an "ethical rigorism": it disregarded Schopenhauer's pessimism while it upheld his concept of renunciation; it recognized value not in pleasure but in the performance of duty: "Duty's title to respect has nothing to do with happiness. It has its own peculiar law and its own peculiar tribunal."[26] But lest we think that Kant's harsh judgment is a direct parallel to the Puritan admonition to stick to duty for its own sake, we must keep in mind Kant's major emphasis. For Kant the ultimate reward of performing one's duty lay not primarily in the beneficial result for society or, for that matter, for Heaven; it lay, rather, in the exercise of a free spirit: "The consciousness of a free submission of the will to the law, combined with an inevitable constraint imposed only by our own reason on all inclinations, is respect for the law. The law which commands and inspires this respect is ... the moral law ... The action which is objectively practical according to this law ... is called duty."[27] Kafka, after his own fashion, would take up the spirit of these thoughts in *The Trial,* and later we will examine Kafka's extraordinary encounter with "law," "duty," and "conscience."

After publishing both Critiques, *Pure Reason* in 1781 and *Practical Reason* in 1790, Kant returned once more to the conscience-problem in 1797 with the publication of *The Metaphysical Principles of Virtue.* Here conscience is regarded, unequivocally, as an innate quality; the notion that it is one's duty to acquire a conscience Kant pronounces as absurd: "it would be like having a duty to recognize duties." Also Kant is now prepared to make a definitive separation and distinction between duty or obligation and conscience. When man takes up the mirror of practical reason and beholds its reflections he may therein judge "acquittal" or "condemnation" of the duty reflected. Conscience is wholly the province of the subject, and to speak of a man without conscience is really to say that such a man fails "to heed [conscience's] dictates." A man may err; a conscience never.[28]

Moreover guilt or innocence are a matter of consciousness, of having acted according to conscience, in short, of having listened to its voice in the process of performing one's duty. Again conscience (as innate) is the judge who oversees what and how we act. In itself the exercise of conscience—conscientiousness—cannot be a duty else we would require "a second conscience to be aware of the act of the first"; but it *is* a duty to heed one's conscience in order to fathom one's "moral self-knowledge." We tend to forget Kant's increasing awareness of what he demanded because we are distracted by the rigidity of the categories themselves, but Kant was fully conscious of the awesome road ahead: "only descent into the hell of self-knowledge prepares the way for godliness."[29]

Kant always viewed such descents into hell in the shape of trial and judgment. His definitions of conscience repeatedly fall back on the analogy of the court, with an insistence that it is awareness that counts. "The consciousness of an internal court of justice within man," he writes, "('before which his thoughts either accuse or excuse one another') is *conscience.*" Kant also came as close as he could to decreeing such a conscience as an autonomous Eumenides: when we try to escape our conscience we fail because conscience "follows . . . like a shadow." Whatever pleasures we might devise to avoid our conscience there is always the inevitable awakening, the "awful voice." Even in his "utmost depravity," though a man may fall so low that he no longer obeys his conscience, "he cannot avoid hearing its voice."[30] From Faust to Poe to Camus that point appears to be stressed with increasing assertiveness. To be conscious of such power in the voice of conscience is to be responsible, to be "accountable," ultimately, "to God for one's deeds." Such thoughts are categorical as well as imperative.

After Kant, German Idealism tended in most aspects to elevate knowledge to a variety of values while moving steadily away from the relation of perception to knowledge itself. What in Kant were categories became in Fichte transcendental relations and in Hegel (towards whom everything seemed for a time to be moving) transcendental absolutes. But in Fichte at least conscience remained a function of consciousness, the latter making us aware of the former; and conscience remained a judge (*Richter*). One of Fichte's most lucid works, *The Vocation of Man,* is divided into three sections: Doubt, Knowledge, Faith. It is a thinly disguised philosophical version of Dante, who had set the sequence for the future. What Fichte says here about both conscience and consciousness is of considerable importance because, like Rousseau's *Confessions, The Vocation of Man* traces the *process* of inner struggle much as a syllogism with its three parts might once have traced the process of an argument. The "Doubt" section grapples with the nature of freedom, nature, and self-consciousness. In the discourse on Knowledge, Fichte proposes the possibility that our consciousness of things is really *"a consciousness . . . of a consciousness of things"*—one of those tortured paradoxical phrases common to idealists or potential solipsists. Central to the argument, however, is the conclusion that knowledge can be only self-knowledge; yet in this discovery, that all emanates from within, outer nature, on which we had seemed dependent, disappears; and lest we are content with a void faith can be our only solace. The vocation (*Bestimmung*) of man is finally not knowledge but action. Our actions in turn are governed by conscience, "the root of all truth," the inner voice of the soul, which commands absolute obedience: "Through the edict of conscience alone, truth and reality are introduced into [one's] conceptions." Action does not follow knowledge, it precedes it: "we know because we are called upon to act." And it is "the voice of conscience" (the measure of our duty) which marks off the limits of our freedom, governs our moral actions, and judges our transgressions.[31]

Fichte brings us full circle, back to Spinoza, in insisting that conscience distinguishes us from beasts, that conscience is an innate judge who rules over an all-encompassing territory (*das Gebiet des Gewissens umfasst alles*).[32] If conscience does govern over so wide a province, then any question of man's freedom is contingent on how we dispose of our charge. Fichte tried to convince himself that obedience to conscience would propitiate the dread of freedom and that faith might guide men towards right action. Kierkegaard was skeptical. Despair, he felt, was a state measurable precisely in proportion to consciousness. "With every increase in the degree of consciousness, and in proportion to that increase," Kierkegaard discovered that "the intensity of despair increases: the more consciousness, the more intense the despair." That eventually became Freud's conclusion, too, though the value of consciousness and despair were to be quite differently assessed. But on the following note we may conclude this brief survey, namely that despair, an equivalent, in some way, to conscience, deepens (and darkens) as men become conscious—not as Fichte thought merely of being conscious but of being conscious of a self hopelessly involved in guilt. Such guilt need not be specified, it is mortality: "Despair is potentiated in proportion to consciousness of self,"[33] and that self was for Kierkegaard inescapably committed to consciousness. The confident *sapere aude* had transformed itself from challenge to question; inwardness became a clear liability. After all, what was innate could be far more painful than what was not. For what was now innate was no longer Spinoza's "philanthropic" impulse but Kierkegaard's daemon—or demon.

The Three Trees: Good, Evil, and Knowledge

What is glibly called existential guilt is a reaction against certain nineteenth-century efforts to divide conscience from consciousness; but the provenance of such existential guilt (which seems too often offered to us as a discovery of our own time) can be found in the Bible, not especially in the New Testament and the concept of Original Sin but in Genesis. Surely the guilt and shame which overcome Adam and Eve was not in itself sexual—sexuality is the visual manifestation of an encompassing awareness. The awareness of mortality (sin and death) is basically an awareness, of consciousness, of conscience. Adam and Eve, as Genesis describes them, are overcome by a sudden shift in perception, a new dimension of eyesight; they saw what after all had always been there, their own and each other's nakedness. But now it was the cause of shame. Only Satan, the nonhuman principle, can be conscious without conscience, for he is an admitted transvaluator of values without himself possessing any values, not even those he transvaluates. In *Paradise Lost,* Milton has him say:

> Farewell Remorse: all Good to me is lost;
> Evil be thou my Good . . . (IV, 109-110)

> . . . all good to me becomes
> Bane . . . (IX, 122-123)

Christianity teaches that knowledge is a kind of self-awareness, and the chief meaning of the Fall is that such a state must bring some ill. Milton's Satan disputes this equation (knowledge equals evil) with characteristically unsophisticated, if not unintelligent, logic, seeing in Evil far more the old Morality Play character than a consequence of awareness and knowledge:

> . . . Knowledge forbidd'n?
> Suspicious, reasonless. Why should thir Lord
> Envy them that? Can it be sin to know,
> Can it be death? and do they only stand
> By Ignorance, is that thir happy state,
> The proof of thir obedience and thir faith? (IV, 515-520)

All the questions are rhetorical; the basis of Christianity lies in the recognition that knowledge (consciousness) leads to a state of sin (though, of course, not exclusively to that state); that a state of sin is the conscience revealed to our parents in the Garden of Eden, at least as a Puritan saw the meaning of the Fall:

> Those Leaves
> They gather'd broad as *Amazonian* Targe,
> And with what skill they had, together sew'd,
> To gird thir waist, vain covering if to hide

> Thir guilt and dreaded shame; O how unlike
> To that first naked Glory . . . (IX, 1110-1114)

Paradoxically, nakedness, once the symbol of innocence, shall henceforth become a symbol of guilt. "To strip oneself naked," as has the expression "to let one's hair down," has come to mean not merely undressing but revealing the hidden. The stripteaser arouses not only (if even primarily?) the sexual appetite but the "guilty conscience"; she reenacts the awareness of Adam seeing Eve naked in the postlapsarian state. The renewed emphasis on nudity in the arts, especially in drama and film, is in part no doubt the *expression* of guilt, not its removal. However, the guilt is expressed as truth and therefore unabashedly. What the new nudity seems to be trying to say is, "Look at us, we *are* Adam and Eve; we *have* fallen, and no amount of fig leaves can change that!" We are being reminded, certainly, brought back to that painful instant before the fig leaves covered us up. And, in effect, we are being asked to acknowledge the Fall, its guilt, its exile, before revelling in its felicitousness. Historians may see the nudity in the arts of the sixties as far more grim than funny, though no doubt it is, in all its ironic sense, a "put-on" as well.

Keats was not alone in struggling with this dilemma of guilt and fallen man; but with his realism he often submitted to the inevitable and overriding power of thought. When he has fears that he may cease to be and he comes finally to the last abyss, he submits to the danger by confronting it:

> . . . then on the shore
> Of the wide world I stand alone, and think
> Till love and fame to nothingness do sink.

Thought does not subvert shame and guilt; indeed, as we have said, it tends if anything to heighten them. But thought compels us to confront ourselves. In his struggle with the "immortal" nightingale and its thought-lessness, Keats again sees clearly:

> Here, where men sit and hear each other groan,
> Where palsy shakes a few, sad, last gray hairs,
> Where youth grows pale, and spectre-thin, and dies.

> Where but to think is to be full of sorrow
> And leaden-eyed despairs . . .

In an interesting essay Geoffrey Hartman reminds us that in many Romantics "thought as a disease is an open well as a submerged metaphor," and that the Romantics were well aware how "every increase in consciousness is accompanied by an increase in self-consciousness, and that analysis can easily become a passion, one that 'murders to dissect.' " Hartman argues that for the Romantics the solution lay in converting knowledge into "energy" and imagination, in, say, Blake or Wordsworth. It is also true, as he says, that "the Romantic poets do not exalt consciousness *per se*" and that they looked upon it as a "death-in-life, as the product of a division in the self."[34] (All of this may incidentally account for the rather consistently bad reception in England not only of *Werther,* the epitome of self-conscious analysis, but of German literature and Idealistic philosophy in general.) Still, however much the English of the nineteenth century, beginning with the Romantics, feared thought as a "disease" (Hamlet, after all, had feared that long ago), they were no more successful than their contemporaries in America or on the continent in evading introspection. It may well be argued that they were more keenly aware of its dangers and that they did indeed fight it off—with wit, with evasiveness, with an ever-deepening immersion in reality, with Tennyson's Lady of Shalott floating downstream as the principal exemplum. But no one could avoid Consciousness: the time was ripe and it would bear fruit, in England too, sooner and later.

An admirer of Keats, and especially of the "Ode to a Nightingale," F. Scott Fitzgerald has John, the hero of that absurd fable "The Diamond as Big as the Ritz," express a sentiment hardly original: "His was a great sin who first invented consciousness." Hemingway wrote much about the relative value of to think or not to think; and surely one of his best-known endings is the ironic and sad dialogue with which he concludes "The Killers," when young Nick Adams says,

"I can't stand to think about him [the doomed victim] waiting in the room and knowing he's going to get it. It's too damned awful."

To which the wiser and older George replies,

"Well . . . you better not think about it."

In *Cain* Byron seems to protest: after all the Greeks had cultivated knowledge without sin. Knowledge was virtue. Adam laments:

Oh, God! why dids't thou plant the tree of knowledge? (I, i, 32)

And Cain replies:

> And wherefore pluck'd ye not the tree of life?
> Ye might have then defied him (I, i, 33-34),

words blasphemous in Adam's ears. But Cain persists:

> Why not?
> The snake spoke *truth*; it *was* the tree of knowledge;
> It *was* the tree of life; knowledge is good,
> And life is good; and how can both be evil? (I, i, 35-38)

That is without doubt one of the most perplexing and tormenting questions which nineteenth-century writers ask, over and over. Nearly all the major writers of the century, on the continent, in England, in America, faced (even if they phrased it differently) the dilemma of the trees—the Tree of Life, the Tree of Good and Evil, or Knowledge, and the Tree of Death. Were they one tree? Were they three trees? Did they support one another, or did they lead, sequentially, to Sin and Death? Do three or four trees make a forest which might prevent us from seeing the trees?

The Possibilities of Consciousness

Drug-taking for consciousness expansion, or for other reasons, is, as we know, not a new phenonemon; Coleridge, De Quincey, and Baudelaire (among others) have left us terrifying, memorable accounts of just what drugs did or did not achieve—at least for their minds. In these cases the feeling seems to be that far from mind-expanding, drugs were mind-constricting, focusing the mind mercilessly upon some phantasmagoric vision so that little remained of the vision except the terror that accompanied it. (The vision I speak of is, of course, opposite to the vision of abstinence, which relies on the renunciation of any stimulant, even food.) Baudelaire found himself slowly reduced to physical and creative impotence by hashish (though obviously this was but one cause); and, like De Quincey (whom he had read), though admitting the temporary elevation of stimulants, he advised against their use. In his *Journal Intime* (particularly in the section called *"Mon coeur mis à nu"*) he writes, at the end of his life, endless warnings and resolutions under such headings as "Hygiene, Conduct, Method." One of the more painful of these final confessional entries in his resolution to *will* his conduct: "To pray every morning to God . . . to work all day long, or *as long,* at any rate, *as my strength allows me*; . . . to offer, every evening, a further prayer . . . to obey the strictest principles of sobriety, the first being the abstinence from all stimulants whatsoever [. . . *obéir aux principes de la plus stricte sobriété, dont le premier est la suppression de tous les excitants, quels qu'ils soient.*] "

De Quincey's visions of Asiatic dissolution (Yeats's "vague Asiatic immensities" of "The Statues" had their ancestors) brought him not only terror but a hollowness of consciousness, the awareness of so much that it was, in the end, nothing,[35] "the abyss of divine enjoyment." De Quincey readily admitted that opium "brightened and intensified the consciousness," but he shrewdly added that, unlike the drunkard, the careful opium-eater can rid himself of conscience. Such a man "feels that the diviner part of his nature is paramount; that is, the moral affections are in a state of cloudless serenity." But this state of "cloudless serenity" could not last; the more he sought to prolong it, the less he could retain it in the intervals without drugs. He paid dearly: "I paid a heavy price in distant years, when the human face tyrannized over my dreams and the perplexities of my steps in London came back and haunted my sleep with the feeling of perplexities, moral or intellectual, that brought confusion to the reason or anguish and remorse to the conscience." The conscience he felt was not, of course, mere remorse for taking opium but "the oppression of inexpiable guilt." To the tyranny of the "human face" and "inexpiable guilt" we shall return from time to time, for De Quincey's experience was not unique.[36]

The faith that the august imagination could conquer life animated, at one time or another, Goethe and Wordsworth, Schiller and Hugo, Shelley and Novalis, Coleridge and Hölderlin. But such faith collapsed when imagination entered hitherto closed doors. Biographers tell of several times when Goethe had to struggle against total breakdowns because he saw too much of himself, or his "daemon." (The motif of the *Doppelgänger* records that struggle throughout the nineteenth century.) And in later life Goethe complained that life was being ignored in the very process of being pursued. In time, the imagination became an agent not of wider perception but of narrowing containment: it died in a vacuum, undernourished, starved by a surrogate existence denying the life it was intended to conquer. Consciousness, focused upon one passion, became obsessive and exclusive rather than expansive, unique and narrow rather than eclectic. Goethe's *Wahlvewandtschaften* (*Elective Affinities*) might be an early, and classic, example of such obsessional "consciousness," a subtler elaboration of *Werther.*

"Know thyself" was a fine Greek maxim: but the Romantics were unable to become good Hellenists, not really through any fault on their part but simply because Hellenism was a nonnegotiable culture. One could no more rekindle its flames in the urbanized and industrialized Europe of the nineteenth century than one could in the Renaissance, a period already suffused with a Hebraic-Christian ethic for fourteen centuries. Still, attempts to restore a Hellenic ethos were made frequently and in many countries; and I think much would be gained by interpreting the anti-Christian postures of the nineteenth century, whenever they involved the Greek way, more as attempts to fish out of the sea fragments of Greek gods rather than as cabals plotting a second crucifixion. Certainly not in Matthew Arnold, and not even in Nietzsche, was there anything to suggest *merely* a vendetta against Christianity. Nietzsche offered us a Dionysus because he felt

Christ had brought man to his knees; Arnold's Hellenism was offered as preferable to Hebraism (a term covering the whole of the Judaic-Christian tradition) because, in Arnold's view, culture had now to rid itself of excessive guilt, the sense of sin, so that once more it might *be* rather than *do,* "to see the object as it really is." Both dreams failed.

That Arnold wished to be in the avant-garde of those who were in every way abreast of the modern world and that he wished to be the interpreter of the world he lived in, and was dismayed with,—these are commonplaces. Turning to his inaugural lecture on the occasion of his being installed in the Chair of Poetry at Oxford ("On the Modern Element in Literature"), we read that "the culminating age in the life of ancient Greece I call, beyond question, a great epoch; the life of Athens in the fifth century before our era I call one of the highly developed, one of the marking, one of the modern periods in the life of the whole human race." Stylistically formal, the essay does not always make itself clear; but the word "adequate" is used in a sufficient number of contexts to justify its equation with modernity. Arnold felt a literature was "adequate" only when it properly interpreted its *Zeitgeist* (a word he liked).[37] Also the "critical power," which he later equates with the Hellenic "seeing the object as it really is," must be free, fearless. Both "adequacy" and the "critical power" Arnold finds in the Hellenic period of Greek culture. Modernity is not a progressive, time-measured, linear condition—what is new is hence modern—but a quality which, in Arnold's view, he found in the Greeks of Pericles' time but not, for example, in his own age. Like Nietzsche, Arnold abhorred the nihilism of his age: "Depression and *ennui*; these are the characteristics stamped on how many of the representative works of modern times!" Arnold spoke these words in the year 1857, the year of *Les Fleurs du Mal* and *Madame Bovary.* Would he have found either work "adequate" to its time, and hence, in his defined terms, "modern"? He remained silent on these works; it is doubtful he ever read them. But for his definition of modernity he turned always to Goethe, whom he considered foremost among those of his time in having surmounted its meanness to bask in the Light and partake of the

Honey which Hellenism was. Such a veneration for Goethe as a modern because he was a Hellenist persisted, at least in English, through Pater who, in his fine essay "Winckelmann" (*The Renaissance*), celebrated Goethe as the great cultural matchmaker who joined Greece and modernity in the marriage of Helen and Faust.[38]

What Henry Hatfield has called "aesthetic paganism"[39] was no less an ethical or moral paganism; and though Nietzsche still loomed in the distant future, Goethe was the inevitable magnet, the propagandist for what became later a more aggressive anti-Christian Hellenism. As for other writers, so for Goethe, the over-riding strength of Greece lay in its *moral* beauty, its freedom from a remorseful *contemptus mundi*—indeed its joyful celebration of nature, its naïveté, as Schiller understood that term. Conversely, for modern Hellenists the overriding weakness of Christianity was its continual sense of renunciation, not disciplined renunciation of excess for the sake of balance but a denial of self for the sake of deity, in short a denial of life itself. Accompanied by guilt, this sense of renunciation destroyed for Goethe what he could not live without: freedom, however terrifying it might be.

At the dawn of the nineteenth century, the possibilities of consciousness were enormous; and so were the consequences. "Psychologically," wrote Coleridge in his *Notebooks*, "Consciousness is the problem, the solution of which cannot too variously be re-worded, too manifoldly be illustrated . . . Almost all is yet to be achieved." That might have been a Coleridgean exaggeration were the century and a half following to prove him wrong. In fact time has proven him more right than he might have anticipated. Consciousness has indeed been what he called it, "the narrow *Neck* of the bottle"; and through that neck, in or out, the passage was to bruise multitudes. "Whither Consciousness?" Coleridge asked, and answered, as if he knew it only too well, into the world of doubt and uncertainties, for "the lowest depth that the light of our Consciousness can visit" still fell far short, still remained "at an unknown distance from the Ground." Perhaps it was also a ground which, as in dreams, we had rather not reach.[40]

Still, Coleridge was much tormented by the prick of conscience, by guilt, by remorse, which became the title of one of his plays.

And Coleridge read Kant, and though he quarreled with that mercilessly strict master, he remained nevertheless a good pupil—most of the time.[41] However his conjunction of conscience and consciousness, he made not so much a Kantian as a Christian *in extremis,* the fell of dark upon him, grim and dreadful: "Few are so obdurate, few have sufficient strength of character, to be able to draw forth an evil tendency or immoral practice into distinct *consciousness,* without bringing it in the same moment before an awaking *conscience.* But for this very reason it becomes a duty of conscience to form the mind to a habit of distinct consciousness. Such a habit was in fact more remorseless than opium. Frail man, frail Christian, Coleridge observed sadly, who walks among "snares" and "pitfalls," asking God not to tempt him and yet positioning himself "on the very edge of [temptation] " because he failed to "kindle the torch"—the light, the conscience itself, which might prevent disaster (*I.S.,* p. 35).

If, Coleridge contended, "the Head be the light of the Heart," then "the Heart is the Life of the Head," another way of insisting that if intellect illuminates feeling, feeling makes that possible by generating intellect, therefore conscience and reason, which Coleridge often equated, were dependent on each other. Indeed, "Consciousness itself . . . of which all reasoning is the varied modification, is but the Reflex of Conscience."[42] Holding court, conscience, is in a commanding position: once we become conscious we are either obeying any reflex or, in turn, alerting conscience of what it is the mind has discovered.[43] This reciprocity between consciousness and conscience becomes the illustrative thesis of what Kant came to call the "judicial conscience dramas"[44] of modern man. As Coleridge lamented, man had lost the luxury he enjoyed in some golden age when "conscience acted in Man with the ease and uniformity of Instinct"; modern man must take his bruising trip through the neck of the bottle (*F.* p. 7). In E. T. A. Hoffmann's tale "The Golden Pot," the aspiring poet Anselmus does in fact find himself locked in a bottle at the end of the story as evil and good carry on a grand mock-epic battle. Only his final profession of faith in the power of poetry permits Anselmus the opportunity to exit from the bottle; but through its neck he is transported to Atlantis where, as in the Golden Age, there is no conscious conscience. Hoffmann, left behind, is disconsolate, for he must remain locked in the bottle, content with the quotidian world with the rest of us, staring (presumably) up to the forbidding and narrow neck, "the contracting orifice or *outlet* into Consciousness" (*I.S.*, p. 31).

"Why, suffering is the sole origin of consciousness," says Dostoevsky's Underground Man. "Though I did lay it down at the beginning that consciousness is the greatest misfortune for man," he continues, "Yet I know man prizes it and would not give it up for any satisfaction."[45] Though he is being "spiteful," he speaks truly; man seems unwilling to give up consciousness despite the miseries its possibilities propose to him. But the truth is he could not really give up consciousness even if he so desired. Whether this reluctance to part with his greatest source of pain implies a yearning for the limits which conscience imposes upon consciousness is a question. Certainly consciousness entails many risks and exacts a heavy price; as many neo-Hellenists discovered as proponents of consciousness, much to their anguish, a guiltless consciousness might become, practically speaking, a contradiction in terms. The doggedness with which conscience clung to consciousness, despite the availability of two words in German and English, exasperated Schopenhauer. He insisted on separating Kant's moral imperatives from "consciousness"; our consciousness, he argued, is by and large not "self-consciousness" but "the consciousness of other things"; stressing such an outward rather than an inward direction, he hoped to forestall the impending fixation on self-consciousness which he saw enveloping his century.[46] In this he failed; and the possibilities of consciousness remained pointed inward, though the outward urge was there as well. It was a dilemma, and Goethe's *Faust* and Byron's *Manfred* illustrated it, while proposing very different maneuvers.

II. The Price of Consciousness: Goethe's *Faust* and Byron's *Manfred*

> *... Consciousness is conflict.*
> —W. B. Yeats

> *What exile from himself can flee?*
> *To zones, though more and more remote,*
> *Still, still pursues, where-e'er I be,*
> *This blight of life—the demon Thought.*
> —Byron, "To Inez"

The Conscience of Manfred

Most discussions about *Faust* and *Manfred* have concentrated on how much Byron might have borrowed from Goethe, what Goethe said about Byron, and how Byron responded. These questions have been the subject of a recent book and one may say it has pretty well resolved them.[1] My interest in these works is not at all concerned with influence: rather I aim to focus on the remarkable differences between Byron and Goethe, differences which the very young Nietzsche, in an early essay on Byron, discussed with accuracy and sensitivity: "The chief charm in Byron's poetry consists in the consciousness that in it we encounter [Lord Byron's] own world of feeling and thought, not Goethe's quiet, gold-clear conception of poetry, but the stormstress of a fiery spirit, a Vulcan." Admiring the "Hebrew Melodies," Nietzsche comes to praise the dramas, especially *Manfred* (fragments of which he even translated). Though he saw its weakness as theater, he called *Manfred* the "monologue of a dying man raging in the midst of the deepest questions and problems," a play "shaken by the terrifying grandeur of this spirit-governed superman" (that is, Manfred). Despite the ready admission that Byron fails as the creator of character in the conventional dramatic sense, the young Nietzsche (perhaps already thinking of Zarathustra?) sees in Manfred as hero an awesome spectacle; in his "gloomy features, his disdainful resignation, his superhuman despair" he conjures up a man who in "every respect transgresses the boundaries of the ordinary." In short he sees the familiar Romantic Prometheus-Cain figure: defiant, proud, lonely, "above" humble humanity. Nietzsche was a philosopher, and it is noteworthy that he appreciated the *Ideenfülle,* the richness of ideas, in *Manfred*; indeed, he felt it a supreme achievement that such a wealth of ideas should be able to overcome the shortcomings of the work.[2]

What is this "richness of ideas" in *Manfred* and how does it differ from that in *Faust*? It is easy to update Manfred and make of him an existential hero, a Romantic version of Camus's Meursault. After all there are striking resemblances: crime, defiance, a faith not in God but in Self, and an indifferent universe. In the early version of Act II, Manfred's treatment of the Abbot was very rough indeed, as rough as Meursault's treatment of the prison priest. All this makes for a very tempting comparison and one not altogether without foundation, but there are real differences between Manfred and a hero like Meursault. Guilt: the hero of Camus's novella does not feel any guilt in the ordinary sense, for Camus has tried to create, in the late Nietzschean sense, a character without conscience. But Manfred is a Romantic and, within the purview of that term, modern enough; but he is far from an authentic existentialist, being an exemplum, rather, of the Romantic paradox: the more consciousness the more awareness, the more conscience, for it is consciousness of Self that reveals to Manfred his "crime" and occasions his guilt. That Manfred's crime in the "all nameless-hour" most probably refers to Byron's incest with Augusta (Manfred's incestuous relationship with Astarte) in no way diminishes the point, the *Ideenfülle* of the play.[3] Manfred tells us very early the orthodox position he represents in lines which Nietzsche quoted and called "immortal":[4]

> Sorrow is knowledge: they who know the most
> Must mourn the deepest o'er the fatal truth,
> The Tree of Knowledge is not that of Life (I, i, 9-12)

(a view Byron challenged in *Cain*). What Manfred asks of the Spirits they emphatically are unable to give: "Forgetfulness"—

Of that which is within me . . . (I, i, 138)

.　　.　　.　　.　　.

Oblivion, self-oblivion　. . . (I, i, 144)

Slowly Manfred realizes the speciousness of such a wish, for for-getfulness in itself is a mere justification of whatever cause lies behind the wish itself. As he stands prepared to plunge down the precipice at the beginning of the play, something within him checks his impulse toward self-destruction:

> . . . wherefore do I pause?
> I feel the impulse—yet I do not plunge;
> I see the peril—yet do not recede . . .
> There is a power upon me which withholds,
> And makes it my fatality to live,—
> If it be life to wear within myself
> This barrenness of spirit, and to be
> My own soul's sepulchre, for I have ceased
> To justify my deeds unto myself—
> The last infirmity of evil. (I, ii, 19-29)

This decision to bear the consequences of his deeds is not made in the spirit of repentance but rather in the spirit of defiance; yet it is a decision to confront one's conscience, to pay the ultimate price of the opposite of forgetfulness—consciousness. Manfred's struggle to remain condemned to live or to justify his past deeds, whatever they may be, hangs in the balance, and the Chamois hunter who saves him is a clumsy device for deciding that issue in the inevit-able direction of life. Manfred's pain is deep and abiding:

> I tell thee, man! I have lived many years,
> Many long years, but they are nothing now
> To those which I must number: ages—ages—
> Space and eternity—and consciousness . . . (II, i, 44-47)

Not merely life but consciousness, and also *memory*, Manfred must now endure; he must face interminably the "gulf of [his] unfathom'd thought" and "live—and live for ever."

His defiance is very specific: he refuses to bow to the Spirits, to traffic with the Devil, to allow himself requital for his sufferings, not for a day, not for twenty-four years. Herein lies the fundamental difference between him and Faust. No wonder young Nietzsche admired so steadfast a human will, pitted against God's emissary and equally against Satan's:

> Back to thy hell!
> Thou hast no power upon me, *that* I feel;
> Thou never shalt possess me, *that* I know;
> What I have done is done; I bear within
> A torture which could nothing gain from thine:
> The mind which is immortal makes itself
> Requital for its good or evil thoughts ... (III, iv, 124-130)

Whether Nietzsche fully appreciated Manfred's claim that he was his "own destroyer" and would be his "own hereafter" remains a question, for this is expiation through the burden of the kind of guilt he was to call pernicious. True, Byron's conscience produced what Lady Byron accurately described as "Remorse without repentance," but remorse nevertheless. Indeed the remorse itself becomes the agent of defiance: without it, Manfred would have had an ineffective weaponry at best. Condemned to live with his memory, his consciousness of guilt, and acceptance of his burden is a price Manfred is prepared to pay for the freedom of will that permits such acceptance. Out of the necessity to suffer consciously, Byron creates the defiant triumph of mastering one's own conscience. That is why he can say to the Abbot, finally, "Old man! 'tis not so difficult to die." Manfred had envied the Chamois hunter his "health, and nights of sleep," his "toils," dangerous "yet guiltless"; lacking the guiltlessness of innocence, Manfred creates with guilt—in fact, *through* guilt—a not unenviable freedom.

Like Byron's "Turkish Tales" heroes, Manfred comes to the play already burdened with a "Scorch'd" soul; the problem becomes not how to save it but how to make its presence less painful. When he invites the Witch of the Alps—the "Earth Spirit" in this play—Manfred tells her in dignified cadences of his self-conscious egotism, his superiority, his singularity, a condition that hinders rather than helps his cause:

> My joy was in the Wilderness,—to breathe
> The difficult air of the iced mountain's top,
> Where the birds dare not build, nor insect's wing
> Flit o'er the herbless granite . . . (II, ii, 64-67)

Knowledge begat "thirst of knowledge"; power fathered the desire for increase of it "until—"—until, in some way, he transgressed. Self-realization, so favorite a phrase in describing the problems of heroes in countless works in the last century and a half, does not really apply appropriately to Manfred. If anything, he has already squandered his opportunity for any such self-realization before the play begins. However, it is legitimate to speak of Manfred's having to come to terms with that failure. It may be argued that Manfred's inability to resolve his dilemma is the result of an insufficient imagination rather than the cruelty of *la condition humaine.*

Such an approach (which also puts Byron in his place) is certainly valid in assessing the failure of that anomalous quester, Childe Harold, who unintentionally becomes his own antihero. But no amount of imagination can help Manfred; on the contrary, the more imagination (consciousness, memory, awareness) he has, the worse his plight. His very powers have made him a "stranger" to the ordinary. What he asks of the Witch is merely to look upon Beauty and to confess his despair. Beyond that he seeks at this point nothing for himself, having already patronizingly dismissed the uncooperative spirits who failed to give him simple oblivion. Now the Witch has her turn; she disgustedly dismisses Manfred because he foregoes the grand things she has to offer, were he only to seek them. Not only that but, she says with contempt, it is for a mortal—"A being of the race thou dost despise"—that he begs:

> . . . thou dost forego
> The gifts of our great knowledge, and shrink'st back
> To recreant mortality—Away! (II, ii, 123-125)

Manfred answers that he lives in his despair "for ever"; but when the Witch offers help on condition that he obey her commands, Manfred dismisses her with the same arrogance that characterized his dismissal of the earlier Spirits. The soliloquy that follows is typical of Byron's manner: he stumbles, not unerringly, into infusing a single line with a platitude and a startling idea:

> We are fools of time and terror . . . (II, ii, 164)

The platitude is clear; but to be a fool of terror? What is meant? Does terror make us fools because we are helpless? If that were all that was intended it would be merely another platitude. I think Byron means something else: terror reigns over us and we do not even mean to flee it, for we remain "fools" not out of helplessness but because mortality, even more than suicide, binds us closer to embracing terror. In terror we can feel aliveness:

> . . . we live [therefore],
> Loathing our life, and dreading still to die. (II, ii, 165-166)

Aspects of Hamlet's dilemma are surely in such thoughts; in ways not always explicit, Byron must often have thought of Hamlet, more than of Faust: in both, certainly, the dilemma of existence without resolution is a major theme, but like Hamlet in the first four acts, Manfred has accepted only the inevitability of death, not yet of life. Nietzsche justly saw a richness of ideas in such probings of existence, for they were fundamental to any progression beyond the values he rejected. If a man is guilty and wishes death but dreads the loss of mortality how does he live? The answer, strangely enough, comes for Manfred from one of the Spirits invoked to produce Astarte. When one Spirit comments with condescension on Manfred's mortality—"This is to be a mortal," that is, to be "convulsed" when confronting cosmic matters, another Spirit explains:

> Yet, see, he mastereth himself, and makes
> His torture tributary to his will.

> Had he been one of us, he would have made
> An awful spirit. (II, iv, 159-162)

To anticipate *Lord Jim,* Manfred is nevertheless not one of *them;* he is totally *"one of us."* This may reveal certain limits of mortal abilities, but it underlines the intensity of humanness. Not only has he now learnt that "knowledge is not happiness," but also that the very knowledge of this truth intensifies the truth itself. Still Manfred clings to life and to defiance. When the Spirits of Death come to fetch him he still denies their power—he will die when *he* chooses not when they command. And they mock him:

> Can it be that thou
> Art thus in love with life? the very life
> Which made thee wretched! (III, iv, 107-109)

Manfred vigorously denies that it is life he seeks to salvage; now he wants only the *freedom* to choose with no intervention from Heaven or Hell. He is not yet prepared to be swept up like a beetle with a broom, or to be knifed by two gentlemen in black, "like a dog!" On the other hand he has not yet understood Kant's warning that "conscience is the internal judge of all free actions."[5] One may reject accountability to gods and demons; can one reject it to oneself?

Manfred is not existential, but it is a far more modern work than *Faust.* To be more modern implies nothing, necessarily, of value or merit. Goethe's modernity, so wonderfully celebrated in the "Winckelmann" essay already referred to, was a contingent modernity: wedding past and present, Helena and Faust, Pagan and Christian, Classic and Romantic. Few can quarrel with this; on literary merit alone, *Manfred* pales beside the titanism of *Faust,* and a comparison would not even be fair. But *Manfred* speaks more intimately to us than *Faust,* in part because Goethe's dramatic-epic poem is perhaps the last major work in western literature to engage self-consciously supernatural metaphors, to manipulate Fate, to create abstractions in the tradition of humanistic dualisms. Like Manfred, Faust too is in despair, wishes death, and flaunts himself against an inferior world: but in winning the day Goethe gives him infernal and divine aid both, and that makes for an entirely different spirit. For without these interventions Faust cannot be said to *will* anything; Manfred ultimately wills everything.

The Consciousness of Faust

In order to proceed to the adventures of what has traditionally been called the "large world," Faust must first be purged of all pity and remorse for a personal deed which he can no longer afford to remember. While he was no sentimentalist, Goethe was not being pitiless, but he must make Faust so; the murder, however unintended, of Baucis and Philemon shows this at its clearest. That of course comes at the very end of the play. And yet we are not allowed to forget that the great overcoming at the start of Part II, so similar to Zarathustra's overcoming, yet so different, is effected by Spirits on a mesmerized Faust, not really by Faust himself. Here lies the distance between Faust and Manfred; though Nietzsche would agree, as he suggested in *Ecce Homo,* that "a prick of conscience" is not worthy of great esteem, he could not have approved the manner in which that prick of conscience is removed from Faust.

Recall: this man has just abandoned a doomed Gretchen; directly and indirectly he has not merely murdered her but her child (and his), her mother, and her brother. In short he has wiped out the family and any chance of future heirs. He has also murdered love, compassion, trust, loyalty. As Thomas Mann reminds us, it is Faust, not Mephistopheles, who utters the great curse against Life.[6] That he feels these things deeply is attested to by the efforts of Mephisto to counteract such feelings. So Part II opens with a restless Faust, lying "in a charming region," on a flowery meadow, trying to sleep. Above him hover lonely spirits, led by Ariel, who succeed in being potent tranquilizers. Ariel's chief command is clear: *"Entfernt des Vorwurfs glühend bittre Pfeile"* (Remove the red-hot bitter arrows of remorse); this done, Faust awakens "renewed," facing the sun guiltlessly and feeling more powerful than ever. Blinded by the pain of radiance from the sun, he turns to the cataract and its ceaseless onrushing *streben,* wherein he realizes the nature and the meaning of man. Yet the Hegelian justification of *streben* is implicit in the refracted images of the cataract and the rainbow, splitting, fragmenting, "mirroring human strife," thrusting forward at the expense of the things that stand in the way. The Hegelian justification is explicit: "so mighty a [world historical] figure must trample down many an innocent flower, crush to pieces many things in its path." Faust, then, is cleansed: "*Sein Inneres reinigt von erlebtem Graus!*" says Ariel, rendered literally: cleanse his inner self of experienced horror, that is, of experience. Once this has been accomplished Faust moves onward, bathed "in Lethe's dew" and free, in the conventional sense, not in Manfred's, whose freedom is dependent not on forgetting but on remembering.

Yet all is not so simple: to say that Goethe's Faust is a sort of Hegelian hero purged of conscience so that he may allow full and free play to his consciousness is not the whole story. To the very end Goethe seems to be ambivalent, and such ambivalence was bound to engender the kind of critical debate Goethe decided not to endure; he placed under seal the last act of *Faust,* not to be opened until after its author's death. A strong objection came from Friedrich Theodor Vischer; but it is Georg Lukács' objection to Vischer which is of interest. According to Lukács, Vischer erred, proceeding "in Kantian fashion" to apply criteria of "purely individual morality to transitions and stages of evolution which, from the standpoint of the species, must necessarily transcend this level." "Necessarily" means, of course, according to Hegel's version of evolution, which Lukács, in order to get to Marx, must first accept. So Lukács is dismayed that Vischer objected to that opening scene of Part II. After all, he argues, Ariel and his helpers are amoral nature and they are needed, if Faust is to move on, to help him "get over the Gretchen tragedy." Vischer's expectation that Faust show some signs of remorse is unfair, says Lukács, because the whole Gretchen episode culminates in the "tragic contradictions only at the stage of the 'joy of life', of the 'little world'; [Vischer] overlooks the fact that the evolution of the species necessarily [Hegel] requires precisely the transcendence of *this world in its entirety.*" In the end "the destiny of the species" is, "necessarily," a greater aim than the destiny of an individual: "such progress is necessary." The argument, taken to its inevitable conclusions, runs something like this: Faust genuinely loves Gretchen but there is in this love (as the great Gatsby said) nothing "personal." In short, just as Faust's love is at its highest pitch he (and his love) soar beyond the seamstress's little world, and so the "most spiritualized stage of Faust's love becomes fateful for the destiny of Gretchen." Lukács' conclusion that "Faust flees Gretchen in order to save her" leaves us much to ponder: Is the corollary true? Would his staying have damned her, assuming her further incorruptibility? Lukács is a careful critic who seldom destroys the integrity of the text; he admits what is obvious, that in the dungeon scene Gretchen "senses the end of [Faust's] love." If that much is conceded the rest appears a little odd; for if Gretchen does indeed see that the personal love has somehow transcended her she does not allow it to diminish her sense of spiritual outrage:

> Kiss me!
> Else I will kiss you! (she embraces Faust)
> O woe! Your lips are cold,
> Are mute.
> Where has your love been left? (Part I, "Dungeon")

Only after Gretchen feels this with the certainty of grief (which Goethe treats with special sensitivity) that woman bereft of love can show is she able to say, "Heinrich! I shudder to look at you!" Faust's continued insistence that he loves her and wants to save her are belied by his last-minute flight from the dungeon—"in order to save her"? Gretchen is saved by her own refusal to join Faust; it is she who must renounce Faust in order to save herself. As for Faust, granted the necessity of fleeing the "little world," he saves only himself.[7]

Erich Heller objects to Faust's salvation, not only because Goethe avoids tragedy but because he has boxed himself into an insoluble problem: resolution of the "morality of knowledge."

Goethe was incapable, according to Heller, of separating "the aspiration of [man's] mind from the destiny of his soul": the "problem of knowledge" could not, and was not, detached from "the totality" of what constitutes a man's self. The trap is inherent when Goethe stipulates in the Faust-Mephisto wager, preceded by the God-Mephisto wager—that Faust is damned both if he ceases to strive or if, in the process of striving, "he overstepped the elusive measure of his humanity," an overstepping never defined.

Clearly Goethe was not, even without knowing it, "on the side of the devil"; when he did side with Mephisto he did so consciously and often ironically. Nevertheless it is true that Faust is never defined as "Human Being," remaining, therefore, unjustifiably exempt from the judgment of his peers. Throughout *Faust* Heller sees Goethe's imagination "fascinated" but also "enthralled and terrified" by the *possibility* of "man's mind rising above the reality of his being and destroying it in such dark transcendence" as Hegel might have defended (or a disciple, like Lukács).[8] Disembodied, Knowledge becomes an infectious disease; Lukács rightly sees it so in Adrian Leverkühn, Mann's Faust, but not yet in Faust.[9] Still it is Faust himself who lends credibility to Goethe's fears (as Heller defines them) when he says, after arriving at his Kantian wisdom,

> The earthly sphere I know well enough.
> The view beyond resists being seen.
> A fool is he who blinks his eyes in that direction,
> Trying to create his like above the clouds. (Part II, Act V, "Midnight")

Faust's disease of disembodied knowledge is shadowed forth in his blindness, a disease which is progressive and terminal, progressing towards finality long before Anxiety breathes into his eyes. First the Earth Spirit appalls him; later he gazes at the waterfall to avoid the glare of the sun; and Helen vanishes from his sight, leaving only her garment as a means of return from her realm just as the growing key had been a means of entering it. Now even the sky, the clouds, the "beyond" are not for human sight. In all speculative realms, Cassirer cautions, "the problem of nature and the problem of knowledge are very closely connected with . . . one another." A man cannot turn his mind (thought) toward an external world "without reverting it to itself."[10] Certainly such a conclusion seems exemplified in Faust's dilemma: as he attempts to penetrate nature—Earth Spirit, sun, waterfall, the "clouds" beyond—he recoils always upon himself. His famous lament is special pleading, that he is the one who flees (*Bin ich der Flüchtling nicht?*), *that he is the homeless one (Der Unbehauste)*, inhuman and without aim or rest, like the waterfall plummeting from rock to rock into some abyss (*Abgrund*). This pleading contains not only some of the finest poetry of *Faust* but some of its most revealing truths. Faust sees that his homelessness is the divider between nature and knowledge, which Cassirer correctly saw as an unworkable divider at best. Faust, so long as he is human, cannot survive such surgery. Between these two worlds of Nature and Knowledge, Faust sees himself for the moment as the waterfall he had admired as the symbol of life and energy on which the refracted sunrays played and revealed to him the beauty of *streben*. That vision, however, as we have mentioned, appears In Part II, following the removal of those arrows of remorse. The vision of *himself* as the waterfall comes in the midst of his realization that he is betraying and destroying what he loves, before Ariel's intervention, when he still had the capacity to *feel* guilt, not merely to mouthe it.

Consider the Midnight Scene, Faust's penultimate, when the four gray women-spirits enter: Want (*Mangel*), Guilt (*Schuld*), Need (*Not*), and Anxiety (*Sorge*). Guilt, Need, and Want fail to move Faust; only Anxiety slips through the keyhole and gains entry. *Sorge* (which in addition to anxiety may be translated as sorrow, care, grief) is chosen to be the agent which blinds Faust. Why should not Guilt be successful? Or Want, or Need? Because apparently Goethe interprets Anxiety as the ubiquitous agent of Life, superseding all others, even Guilt. Anxiety is, then, the price Man pays for striving—indeed for being alive at all; and Anxiety alone has the power (and the privilege?) to accompany Man unto his last. Faust is visibly shaken by Anxiety: he no longer wishes any sorcery, any mechanistic interferences from the "other" world. But Anxiety explains her omniscience—"*Ewig ängstlicher*

Geselle" (eternally anxious companion). Fear itself, Anxiety, is the one force Faust has never encountered or challenged. Here Faust renounces his own law of infinite striving and espouses the wisdom of *"Beschränkung,"* of limitation: Man should pursue what he can reasonably be expected to conquer. But such humility cannot save Faust now; Anxiety berates his ambitions, asserts the blindness of Man as an inevitable condition, breathes upon him the breath of blindness apparently leaving him to die in final darkness (ignorance?), as Goethe, on his own deathbed seemed most to fear when he reportedly cried out *"Mehr Licht!"*

Faust survives long enough for one more short conversation with Mephisto, and Goethe's reluctance to let Faust die at the moment of blindness seems worth a second look. Blinded, Faust feels an inner illumination, and what seemed a defeat has become, at least temporarily, a triumph. For one more act of his life Faust is determined to make a beginning: he will reclaim the swamp land to make way for a land reform plan, envisioning millions of "free" men on a green and fruitful earth. It is a properly constructive vision, a positive note at the end of a questionable life; yet it also sounds distinctly plebeian and diminishes the authentic moment when Anxiety blinds Faust. Inner light appears to give Faust undreamed of outer accomplishments, and this stands in contradiction to the tragic implications of acknowledging Man's limitation when an ubiquitous Anxiety breathes blindness and declares Man blind in his ceaseless struggles. Goethe seems especially concerned to leave Faust one final positive dream, but one wonders whether Mephisto is not nearer the mark in his own comment on this:

> He was not satisfied by pleasure, no piece of luck
>   was enough;
> So he reeled forward pursuing changing forms;
> The last, the worst, the empty moment,
> The poor man wants to hold fast.
> He who withstood me so mightily,
> Is conquered by Time; the old one lies here in the sand,
> The clock has stopped—(Part II, Act V, "Large Forecourt of the Palace")

So Faust manages to assuage not only Guilt, Need, and Want but, it would seem, Anxiety as well. His "freedom," specious as it has seemed to many readers of *Faust,* is Goethe's insistence that Deed and even Dream of Deed are stronger than any Negative Forces. Inner light can still project a future, and "insight" does not render Faust susceptible to remorse, guilt, conscience; he transcends them all, not with defiance now but with good works.

Many admirers of Goethe have faulted him on the ending of *Faust,* and no single explanation will ever satisfy all the objections that have been raised.[11] Indeed, the future promises only further instances of those who will take exception. Most of the objections do not concern themselves with Faust's shaky salvation but question rather his consistency of character. With a work that preoccupied him a lifetime, Goethe ought perhaps not to be held accountable for strict consistency, but the work stands and so is vulnerable. There can be little doubt that he created a guiltless, conscienceless creature whose dreams of progress at the close of his life are perhaps intended to justify, in some measure, the tempestuous and bloodstained life he has led. But, unlike Manfred, Faust seeks salvation, and gets it, in the *process* of striving; Manfred, finally reconciled to guilt, seeks no salvation. He pays the price of consciousness, not in death but in life, not in blindness turned to inner vision, but in mental anguish, in suffering. Faust's Consciousness, ever-widening from the small to the large world, is essentially an abstraction, an impersonal awareness. Deprived of conscience for the sake of consciousness, for the sake of being receptive to total experience, *Faust* traces the progress of man unfettered by guilt, justified ultimately by God's magnanimous dictum that he who strives may be saved. Quite to the contrary, *Manfred* traces the heaviness of the burden which guilt imposes, and Byron saw no way of striking a bargain: conciousness means conscience. The only "victory" lies in the acceptance of both. So, at the end of his life, Nietzsche commented: "I must be profoundly related to Byron's *Manfred:* of all the dark abysses in this work I found the counterparts in my own soul—at the age of thirteen I was ripe for this book. Words fail me, I have only a look, for those who dare utter the name of *Faust* in the presence of *Manfred.* The Germans are *incapable* of conceiving anything sublime!"[12]

Extravagant praise? Exaggerated language? Perhaps; but I am not so sure that even in *Ecce Homo,* admittedly written in the shadow of approaching madness, Nietzsche was not being consistent with his youthful admiration which I have already quoted. To be sure, his relationship to Goethe was ambivalent, precarious, but the identification he feels with *Manfred,* the sublimity of that work, these are quite compatible with Nietzsche's philosophy. In fact Manfred does not go far enough, but he does go in a direction very different from that which Faust takes. Nietzsche's outrage stems not only from his feeling that *Manfred* is "sublimer" than *Faust,* but that the two works should not be compared as in any way attempting to portray the same problem or the same solution. Nietzsche's perception was perfectly accurate. *Manfred* is not a pale carbon copy of *Faust,* and in no way should or can it be measured as a parallel work. As conceded long ago, similarities of names, incidents, and even language can be found, and we have Byron's own word that he knew of *Faust.* But the fact is that although the two works *begin* in somewhat similar fashion, individuals embittered by life, satiated with knowledge, superior to common man, and so forth—their reasons as well as their courses of actions are very different. While Faust submits to outside agents, divine and diabolic, Manfred abjures all intervention; while Faust's aim is to saturate his consciousness with experience and then to have it conveniently absolved of guilt (it is part of the bargain), Manfred's whole effort after the initial realization that he is his own destroyer is devoted to sustaining his consciousness uncensored, that is, identical with his conscience. Faust, then, is not really allowed to pay the price of consciousness. Manfred's triumph is to seek that payment in the fullness of the terror it will cost him. Goethe himself, it should be recorded, did not quite understand this difference between his great work and *Manfred,* Byron's "monologue of a dying man raging within the deepest questions and problems," very much a precursor of something like Tolstoy's *Ivan Ilyitch* or Unamuno's *Abel Sanchez.*

Faust struggled with the rewards of consciousness; Manfred with its torments. But both engaged in battles still reducible to abstract dualities: crime and punishment, transgression and retribution, the human pitted against the infernal and divine—that last in the shape of the familiar Dantesque triangular architecture. During the half-century between the publication of *Werther* (1774) and the death of Byron (1824), almost every poet was obliged to confront the same question: What price consciousness? And if consciousness was knowledge, or at least its objectification, why and how did we lose it? What is the function of conscience in a man bereft of all other values? Characteristically Blake created his own parable to express this problem, and, though differently configured, it paints a sequence of events similarly felt by others:

> 'Tis Contemplation teacheth knowledge truly how
> to know, and Reinstates him on his throne, once lost;
> how lost, I'll tell . . . I'll shew how Conscience Came
> from heaven. But O, who listens to his Voice. 'Twas
> Conscience who brought Melancholy down, Conscience was
> sent, a Guard to Reason, Reason once fairer than the
> light, till foul'd in Knowledge's dark Prison house.
> For knowledge drove sweet Innocence away, and Reason
> would have follow'd, but fate suffer'd not; then down
> came Conscience with his lovely band.[13]

That phrase describing Reason "foul'd in Knowledge's dark Prison house" bears the singular initials of Blake; but the conception that knowledge can contract rather than expand subtly expresses the urgency of the crisis when others too discovered this phenomenon. Goethe and Wordsworth, as we shall see in the chapter following, anatomized the problem: Goethe explored how we get into the prison, Wordsworth how—short of suicide—we might break out of it. Emily Dickinson was surely right when she wrote in "One Need Not Be a Chamber," that there were safer rendezvous than "interior confronting," that she preferred to run the risks with anything outside to the terror of "unarm'd, one's a'self encounter," that there is an Assasin hid in our Apartment"—a "superior spectre." She too knew the mind when its self-awareness could turn it into a prison, frightful and fatal.

Not introspection itself was dangerous but the expectations measured against the find. If one metaphor can usefully describe that dilemma it might be the metaphor of the treasure hunt. Clues deliberately mislead; the paths deceive, as in fairy tales; indeed the journey, never forward but always inward, is into a darkening world. Expectations of an infinite inner space were rarely met; the exceptions are possible only when there is a complete severance from the world to which the ego, the "I," clings. The use of the first person in Romantic literature has often been used to prove the egotism of the Romantics, but that is shallow and even misleading reasoning. The use of the Romantic "I" far from being a symptom of egotism was a symptom of fear—a fear that the "I" might disappear into any one of the strata in the multicolored spectrum which urged the Romantic soul to transcend itself: God, Nature, Infinity, and certainly not least the ocean of consciousness itself, where the "I" might (and sometimes did) drown. Ishmael survives Ahab not because he is less egotistical (he is more) but because he protects his ego whenever it threatens to transcend its identity. To learn about whales is also to fill the mind—to keep it from contracting with self-absorption, to keep it from collapsing into its own void. To fill the mind is activity. Ahab loses himself to the whale because the whale is all he can think about; were he truly to think more of *himself* he might have saved himself. To say "I" is not to assert oneself *over* something but vis-à-vis something. And so Wordsworth will increasingly use "we" for "I" in *The Prelude* as he feels safer with himself, as he conquers, in his own fashion, the terrible spectres from which Faust was in the end "saved" and from which Manfred saved himself by sheer assertion.[14]

Of all the Romantic poets, certainly in France, Germany, and England, Coleridge is among the most complex. No simplistic answers could keep pace with an inquiring spirit which he could not, even if he wished, temper. So it is both surprising and charming to find in Coleridge a brief poem which so simply and starkly places the problem before us:

> What is life?
> Resembles life what once was deem'd of light,
> Too ample in itself for human sight?
> An absolute self—an element ungrounded—
> All that we see, all colours of all shade
> By encroach of darkness made?—

Is very life by consciousness unbounded?
And all the thoughts, pains, joys of mortal breath,
A war-embrace of wrestling life and death? (c.1805)

That was written about 1805, when Wordsworth, long since spiritually and poetically alienated from his friend, had finished the first version of *The Prelude*. But Coleridge always felt himself to be part of the problem, the question; Wordsworth, in the end, was convinced he was part of the solution.

III. The Risks of Consciousness: Goethe's *Werther* and Wordsworth's *The Prelude*

To be conscious is an illness.
—Dostoevsky's Underground Man

*... The mind is educed, drawn forth, or developed, in exact propor-
tion as the consciousness is extended.*

—Coleridge

Werther's Distempered Idyl

Werther has by now been subjected to all manner of interpretations, and all but the most conventional readers agree that
Goethe's novel is more than the story of a disappointed and un-
consummated love. Georg Lukács, in his 1936 essay, suggests that
in Goethe's presentation of Werther's passionate love, he was able
to confront us with the "insoluble contradiction between personality development and bourgeois society." Werther, therefore, is
viewed as the victim of two forces between which he is crushed:
his spontaneous, passionate, sensitive nature and the rational, con-
servative, restrictive bourgeois culture, represented not only by
Lotte and her husband Albert, but by Werther's family, by the
Court, by Werner (the recipient of Werther's letters)—indeed by
nearly all the novel's participants save those equally outside society, the passion-torn murderer of the widow (Werther's "might-
be" *Doppelgänger*) and the madman. Lukács's version of the
novel has gained favor among many readers for it crystallizes
divergent views, allowing such disciplines as sociology, cultural
history, psychoanalysis, and even biography to have their say without completely distorting the original intent of the novel which
was at least in the first instance the stark anatomy of unrequited
love.[1]

Where Lukács's interpretation might be faulted is in its notion of an irreconcilable contradiction between individual and society, a view still too close to the oversimplified version of the Romantic Rebel, the Byronic Hero, the "isolato." I think the conflict Lukács cites is central to Goethe's purpose, but I do not believe that is is imposed upon Werther solely by the clash of impulse with restraint—whether one applies, with Lukács, the Marxist dialectic or, with Freud, the psychoanalytic. Both versions are too deterministic, for Werther *creates* the better portion of his conflict, creates it purposefully and almost always consciously. He permits himself the freedom of consciousness and its risks, only to discover that he really cannot be master of himself in the world, inner or outer, which he has in effect made. The Beauty becomes the Beast. Thomas Mann called Werther a "master of pain, of merciless introspection, self-observation, and dismemberment [*Selbstzergliederung*]." And, to underscore Werther's willful course, he reminds us to observe how much "his life, his person, his individuality are his prison," and how, therefore, his "death-wish appropriates" the love-story, which Mann sees essentially as a "screen" for the inner psychological drama of the novella.[2]

To claim that Werther creates his world is necessarily to invite the question of further amplifications. What is meant is this: Werther is a sophisticated, "sentimental" man, sentimental in the sense Schiller used that word in his extremely important essay *Über Naive und Sentimentalische Dichtung* (1795). Werther's feeling toward Nature is "like the feeling of an invalid for health," one of Schiller's definitions of sentimental. Here is Schiller's own analysis of *Werther:* "It is interesting to note with what fortunate instinct everything that nourishes the sentimental character is concentrated in *Werther*: fanatically unhappy love, sensitivity to nature, feeling for religion, a spirit of philosophical contemplation; finally, so that nothing shall be forgotten, the gloomy, formless, melancholic Ossianic world. If one takes account with how little recommendation, even in how hostile a manner actuality is contrasted with it, and how everything external unites to drive the tortured youth back into his world of ideals, then one sees no possibility how such a character could have saved himself from such a cycle."

True. Werther has trapped himself, but Schiller puts his finger on the pulse of the novel when he detects the *hostility* in Werther's contrast of actuality with ideal. Just prior to the passage I have quoted, Schiller tried to account for Werther's curious misanthropy: "A personality [such as Werther] who embraces the ideal with burning feeling and abandons actuality in order to contend with insubstantial infinitude, who seeks continuously outside himself for that which he continuously destroys within himself, to whom only his dreams are the real, his experience perennial limitations, who in the end sees his own existence only a limitation, and, as is reasonable, tears this down in order to penetrate to the true reality—this [illustrates the] dangerous extremes of the sentimental personality."[3]

This description of Werther merits attention. One who "abandons actuality" does so consciously unless otherwise incapacitated, which Werther is not; and one who does so consciously is not in any sense naïve; yet to seek outside what one destroys inside is at best an unconscious act, which, psychologically, has, nevertheless, motivation. Precisely what Schiller means remains in doubt, but it seems logical that Werther destroys a sense of order, a sense of arrangement not foreign to an intellect such as his. Werther's is a deliberate *Verwandlung* (metamorphosis) from the perspective of rationally (not rationalism) to irrationality. To put it differently, Werther creates for himself an idyl, and it is when that idyl no longer can bear up under its own weakness, when the details of the idyl dissolve into a cold pastoral, that Werther gives in—and methodically, and rationally, and with full consciousness shoots himself. The view that "Werther's outstanding characteristic is a thorough lack of willpower, whose immediate consequence is a disinclination for action," is—like a similar view of Hamlet— still widely held but, I think, very much mistaken.[4] I would not hesitate to call Werther a willful man; indeed it is a quality, related to his stubbornness and frequent distemper, which shows itself from beginning to end. Werther is a victim, not of fate alone or merely of society but far more of himself, a victim of his own willful idyl-creation. (That such idyl-creation has causative roots in the times is not in dispute: of course it has.)

Why, one may ask, does Werther create an idyl? Is it really simply a means of turning his back on "reality"—another view of Werther that has endured? Or is he truly attempting to reverse the terms, that is, to turn his back on an unacceptable world, yes, but to create a fictive world more real than the one he abandons? Or is it primarily an experiment, the working out of a process which sets the question: What happens when a man tries to undo one reality to replace it with another, it being understood, of course, that for that man each reality is equally real though not necessarily equally valid? Probably all these questions should be answered in the affirmative, but the last perhaps best suits the particular view of *Werther* I have so far suggested.

Lotte and Werther's involvement with her become agents, not causes, and it is not a disillusionment with the world so much as a disillusionment with himself, with his inability to shape that world, as only the artist can, which drives Werther to despair. His is the first recorded instance in fiction, placed in a modern context, of a long progeny: men who attempt to make of life a work of art. Unlike some of his successors in fiction, Werther does not really confuse art with life; he merely wishes to make the latter conform to some conception of the former.

Werther is an artist quite incidentally, a sketcher (like Goethe). Very early in the novel he reports with an almost ludicrous self-importance that his work has suffered, and he decides that art *cannot* better nature, and that in nature he has now found complete harmony. It proves to be a fatal, but decisive, reading of the truth. Werther's progression is testimony to his self-deception. When he first arrives in Wahlheim, he disapproves of the town, but he finds the country surrounding it full of the beauties of nature (May 4, 1771).[5] By May 10, he complains, half-heartedly, that his "art is suffering" because he has become so completely charmed by the bucolically inspired peace of soul that artificiality repels him; and by May 13, he abjures books, his heart full to the brim with the simple things surrounding him. One exception he does make, Homer, and from this Greek he will take inspiration for that special Hellenic Romanticism, the spirit which Pater sometimes referred to as *Heiterkeit* (serenity). It is a spirit eventually displaced (rather than replaced) by the melancholy and passion of Ossian.

For a time Werther enjoys his consciously constructed idyl, his self-conscious dream (the true dreamer never knows he is really dreaming), much as a child might muse over a sand castle: "That the life of man is but a dream has been felt by many a man before me, and this feeling attends me constantly, too . . . I turn back upon myself and find a world! But again, more in imagination and obscure desire than in actuality and living power" (May 22). His self-deception, though far from being clear to him at this point, comes when he asserts that knowledge, or at least awareness, is conducive to happiness: "He who recognizes in his humility, what it all amounts to . . . such a person is serene and *creates his world out of himself* and is even happy to be a human being" (May 22. My italics). He appears to contradict himself a little later in a somewhat different context and form when he speaks of his faith in God making us "happiest when He allows us to stumble about in a pleasant illusion" (July 6).

My point so far has been twofold: one, to state that Werther is building an idyl (not a "dream") in the hopes of surviving in its pleasure and two, that this "creation" runs counter to the thing it is: no man, except the genuine artist, can hope to create an idyl. Werther's self-consciousness is self-condemning. Confirmation for asserting Werther's conscious strategy and willful manipulation is often implied by Werther himself; in one instance it is stated clearly: "I am astonished to note how deliberately I have walked into the whole situation step by step. How clearly I have always seen my situation" (August 8). While this refers specifically to the "situation" of the triangle, husband, wife, and intrusive supplicant, the observation is no less true for the situation as a whole. Of course, Werther's deliberative progress is not a well-planned strategy; he knows, however, the course he is taking, whether always at the precise moment of taking it or just prior to it is of no consequence. Increasingly the sexual frustration, real enough, is accompanied by a rising anger in his whole being at the failure which he sees beginning to unfold. His self-consciousness, a cultivated prescience, makes him prideful and breeds contempt and disdain. "Consciousness," complained Nietzsche, "is . . . thoroughly tyrannized over—and not least by the pride in it! It is thought that here is *the quintessence* of man." So Werther too seems to feel, and his grave disappointment is largely the consequence of discovering the weakness of relying on such a "ludicrous overevaluation and misconception of consciousness."[6] In saying this I am somewhat shifting the focus from Werther the victim to Werther the victimizer of himself. There is a difference.

What Werther sees happening is a reflection of transitoriness, indeed of his own changes. Yet the acknowledgment of a kinetic life brings fears of instability; movement disturbs the kind of fixed, framed stasis which any idyl attempts to convey. On August 18 Werther writes in anguish, "Can you say 'this is,' when everything is transitory, when everything rolls by with the speed of a tempest . . . is swept along, alas, engulfed by the current and shattered on the rocks? There is not a moment that does not consume you . . . not a moment in which you are not a destroyer, and necessarily so; the most innocent stroll costs the lives of a thousand poor little worms." Such a discovery did not disturb the Goethe of *Faust,* Part II (or Hegel) but the young Goethe, as young Werther, was not yet reconciled to the impossibility of holding down Time itself in an effort to preserve some illusion worthy of having been created in the first place. *Werther* seems sometimes to have been written to prove to himself the hopelessness of such a wish.

The paradox that such a creation of idyl requires the exercise of much will is not lost on Werther; in fact the perennial struggle inherent in the motion of creating a stasis ultimately exhausts him. The energy spent on creating a feast for one's soul is ceaseless until he finally complains that his "active powers have atrophied into an uneasy indolence" (August 22) that both imagination and his feeling for nature have been spent, that his inadequacy threatens the very will to live on, to act. Ennui, the *maladie du siècle,* the Coleridgean emasculation of will and imagination—all are prefigured here and analyzed by the patient who recognizes each new symtom with uncanny precision. His single act of will at this point of his malady is his decision to change scenery, in short his departure for the Court. It becomes very quickly a disastrous decision.

What makes it disastrous is not merely his encounter with a shabby aristocracy, humilating as that is, but his indecisive break with his idyl. The time interval between leaving Wahlheim and returning to it is only five months, and this is devastating to the idyl which Werther still seems somehow hopeful of recapturing when he returns. But the return marks the reversal of the novel's scenario. His decision to leave the Court is made on March 24; his actual departure takes place on May 6, but he first returns home, visits the Prince, toys with the idea of joining the army, and feels himself to be "a wanderer, a pilgrim on earth" (Book II, June 16). Always he is drawing nearer to a return to Lotte—and to the idyl, which is no longer recognizable: "When I walk out of the town gate, on the road which I traveled the first time to fetch Lotte for the dance; how different it was then. Everything, everything has passed by. No trace of that former world, not a throb of the emotion I felt then" (Book II, August 21).

All has changed: The woman who sat under the linden trees has lost a son, and the husband expected back with an inheritance has returned empty-handed. For trying to violate the widow he passionately desired, the peasant boy has been dismissed from his post. Even the chestnut trees, under which he and Lotte sat and played out their strange minuet, their charade of love, even these have been rather symbolically cut down.[7] Werther is East of Eden, and his reaction to the chopped-down trees is at the very least an overreaction: "Cut down! I could go mad, I could murder the dog who struck the first blow at them" (September 15). (How differently Chekhov's epigone-Werthers would react a century later!)

Despite all this, Werther, in one of the most ironic gestures of the novel, is determined to make appearances conform again, wherever possible, to his original experience. His blue coat and his yellow vest and trousers have worn out, but he has a second suit made: "But it doesn't produce quite the same effect" (September 6). Indeed not.

By October 12, Ossian displaces Homer; Werther's world is now no longer idyl nor the process of creating one; it is the inevitable descent down the other side of the mountain into a valley that looks more and more like an abyss: "Oh, this void," he writes on October 19, "this dreadful void which I feel here in my bosom!" By November 3, he feels that "the fault [*Schuld*: guilt] is all mine," and each succeeding episode confirms the disaster, first of having left Wahlheim and second, after having left, of returning to it. Highly suggestive of the Werther situation, and refractively rendered, is the episode with the madmen. After seeing the lunatic, Werther asks the mother, "What time was that he talks about so fondly, when he was so happy, so well off?" "The silly boy," she replies, ". . . he means the time when he was out of his mind; he's always praising that; that's the time he was in the madhouse, when he knew nothing about his condition [*von sich*: himself]." And, significantly, Werther writes: "This struck me like a thunderclap" (November 30). Why should he be so surprised? Not because he doubts the implications of the incident; the incident, however, suddenly confirms what he already suspects.

Happiness is to know nothing at all about oneself; misery to know too much. Standard psychoanalytic theory notwithstanding, this idea is as old as the tragedies of Sophocles. Overawareness, in certain individuals, leads to paralysis. Besides, the analyst wishes his patient to become aware only when necessity makes the "illness" a mask for self-orientation and prevents knowledge of certain particular psychic experiences. Werther's case is quite different; his oversensitized consciousness is simply unable to balance the ambiguities and contradictions of the human predicament. He is of all men least endowed with "negative capability" (and hence no artist at all). Even more, self-consciousness destroys illusions necessary for carrying out the deliberative process of creating, and maintaining, the idyl. Werther (echoing Hamlet) admits the dilemma himself: "What is man, that vaunted demigod? Do not his powers fail him precisely where he needs them most? And when he soars in joy or sinks in suffering, is he not arrested in both, brought back to dull cold consciousness [*kalten Bewusstsein*] just at the very moment when he yearns to lose himself in the plenitude of the infinite?" (December 6). How like Keats's realization in the "Ode on a Grecian Urn":

> O Attic shape! Fair attitude! with brede
> Of marble men and maidens overwrought,
> With forest branches and the trodden weed;
> Thou, silent form, dost tease us out of thought
> As doth eternity: Cold Pastoral!

"Cold consciousness" and "Cold Pastoral" are very close, as are eternity and infinity. As Poe so vividly described so often, something mesmerizes us toward limitless vistas, "till human voices wake us and we drown," until the barrenness of consciousness makes us stand at the edge of an abyss, until thought "saves" us from one fall only to plunge us into another. In the face of "cold consciousness" Werther must adopt a kind of existential faith-after-death (hardly a religious faith in immortality): "No, Lotte, no—How Can I pass away? How can you pass away? For we *exist!*" (p. 89). This conviction of existence does not save Werther's life (though it saved Goethe's), but it renders his suicide more purposeful than that of Kleist, for whom the naked discovery of existence was the last blow to the illusion of certainty. Existence is something Werther feels he can assert, anticipating Kant; for the shifting temporal winds have destroyed his manipulative attempt to create, preserve, and be master of his idyl. As an artist he might have succeeded; as a man (and really an *artiste manqué*) he was doomed to failure from the start.

I have spoken almost exclusively of Werther's consciousness, the risks he takes with it, and the failure to marshall and expedite the consequences of such consciousness. It is, I have argued, in the deliberately created aura of "total awareness" that Werther sets out to build his idyl; because the disappointment of that failure is experienced with the same total consciousness as was its creation, Werther steps to the edge of an abyss. In the act of suicide he enters it, defying ultimate meaninglessness with the certainty of existence beyond death, or, to put it differently, with the refusal to accept death as finality. Since this belief is not anchored in any deep religious conviction nor supported by any metaphysical faith, it must be supposed that Werther remains (almost childishly) stubborn about the limits of mortality. Existence is really another way of claiming consciousness.

What of Werther's conscience, not, of course, his scruples about Lotte and Albert, but his guilt as a human being, his consciousness—being so total—of its corollary? This kind of conscience defies precise definition, but it lies at the root of that guilt which Nietzsche sought to explain, and then to banish, in the *Genealogy of Morals.* On Sunday, May 29, in the year before his death, Goethe is reported to have told Eckermann a story about a youth who could not forgive himself a small mistake: " 'I did not like to see this,' he said, 'because it points to a too refined [*zarten*] conscience, which values the individual moral self so high that it can never forgive it. Such a conscience makes hypochondriacs if it is not balanced by some great deed.' "[8]

The qualification is very important; even a refined conscience may survive, if it is balanced by some great deed. In Werther such balance is wanting; he becomes a hypochondriac or, as Goethe might say today, a neurotic, because once embarked on his disastrous course the little mistake grows in dimension until all of life becomes viewed as folly and error. Molière's misanthrope, already dangerously balanced between tragedy and comedy, has become once more a serious, if not tragic, figure. Werther cannot forgive— neither life nor himself. The twinge of conscience he feels for his transgressions against a married woman and her patient husband is inconsequential; what becomes unforgivable for Werther is his awareness of *failure.* To create so much requires sensitivity; to fail at so much is evidence that one has taken enormous risks, and that one is prepared to pay the price in full, which Werther in his own fashion does. I speak not of his death but of his *Leiden,* his sufferings, which are precisely those of a man whose conscience cannot confront his consciousness when it reveals to him the process of accelerating the failure of achieving all goals. The disappointment of dreams is always traumatic; the inability to reconcile oneself to loss is, literally or methaphorically, suicidal. Freud, in analyzing the phenomenon of "Mourning and Melancholia," managed in large measure to describe Werther's "distemper." Those who complain as melancholics, he says, are really offering " 'plaints' in the

old sense"; and "everything derogatory that they say about themselves is at bottom said about someone else," so that these confessions cause no shame. In fact, such people are anything but
humble and submissive as would be normal for those who truly
think themselves worthless. "On the contrary," Freud argues,
"they make the greatest nuisance of themselves, and always seem
as though they felt slighted and had been treated with great injustice." Freud explains such behavior as a "constellation of revolt,—
which has . . . passed over into the crushed state of melancholia,"
perhaps the best definition of Werther's conscience we can offer.[9]
His mourning for a lost idyl is as powerful as it would be for a lost
person; besides, he objectifies such a loss in Lotte.

Wordsworth's Tempered Idyl

Where Werther fails to reach reconcilation, Wordsworth does,
and this alone justifies comparing his great autobiographical poem
with Goethe's novella. *The Prelude* is an "almost"-*Werther.* Wordsworth is an instance of Goethe's notion about an overly sensitized
conscience balanced by a great deed; he saves himself from failure
by the deed of the poem itself, in which he arrives at a kind of
acceptance Werther could never have entertained as acceptable. It
would be silly to argue here whether in fact Wordsworth really did
achieve what I have claimed for him: the point is he thought he
did and, in *The Prelude,* he sets out to illustrate the curve of an
experience (this curve is symbolically presented, in capsule form,
during the episode of crossing the Alps) that begins with expectation, centers on failure and doubt, and consummates in faith and
triumph. In telling his own tale, Wordsworth achieves a desired
intimacy which Werther's epistolary distance forecloses. Again the
exactness of the life as told in the art is not at issue; the first
person posture allows Wordsworth liberties of revelation denied to
Werther.

"Innumerable mistakes," wrote Nietzsche "originate out of consciousness, which, 'in spite of fate' . . . cause an animal or a man to

break down earlier than might be necessary." One of the misconceptions about consciousness, Nietzsche complains, is that men have tended to treat it as an accomplished state "accepted as the 'unity of the organism,' " so that no chance for growth and development, no option for maturation was open: "Because men believed that they already possessed consciousness, they gave themselves very little trouble to acquire it."[10] Like Freud, who learned from him, Nietzsche viewed consciousness, both on an individual and historical-mythic level, as a *process,* not a quality possessed but a quality to be earned. Although Nietzsche makes no mention of Wordsworth in his works, it would be curious to know how he would have responded on this one issue, for it would seem he and Wordsworth would have agreed, though perhaps from a very different point of view.

Throughout his works, especially in *The Prelude* and *The Excursion,* Wordsworth considers consciousness an unfolding process, a slowly moving sensitivity needle registering a kind of *correspondance,* not unlike Baudelaire's, on the mind: an awareness of self within the framework of memory responsive and responding to the dynamics of environment, in Wordsworth's case, nature. He writes of a "flowery ground [which] is conscious" ("The Haunted Tree," 30); of "conscious memory" (*Prelude,* I, 30); of "happy consciousness" dwelling in the "heart within the heart" (*Excursion,* IV, 627-628); of "awful consciousness," full of awe, at the approach of night (*Excursion,* IV, 1156-1160) and, most explicitly, of inner and outer consciousness, "inward consciousness" (*Prelude,* XI, 202), and "conscious nature" (*Excursion,* III, 111). On several occasions he uses the plural to make special points even at the risk of almost compromising his iambs:

> A tranquilising spirit presses now
> On my corporeal frame, so wide appears
> The vacancy between me and those days
> Which yet have such self-presence in my mind,
> That, musing on them, often do I seem
> Two consciousnesses, conscious of myself
> And of some other Being. (*Prelude,* II, 27-33)[11]

"Consciousnesses," an awkward word for poetry at best, is used again, in the same sense of plurality, creating an inner, spreading multiplicity of awareness, in "After Landing—the Valley of Dover, November 1820" (ll. 10-14):

> ... enrapt I gaze with strange delight,
> While consciousnesses, not to be disowned,
> Here only serve a feeling to invite
> That lifts the spirit to a calmer height,
> And makes this rural stillness more profound.

Rather consistently, then, for Wordsworth consciousness is a becoming aware, an awareness which grows and leads either to within or without but is always in a state of process. Consciousness affects and effects Man. Though its title was bestowed by Mary Wordsworth after the poet's death, *The Prelude* was referred to by Wordsworth himself as " 'the poem on the growth of my own mind' "; and this implies an epic attempt to render a *Bildungsroman,* to demonstrate the growth and maturation of a poet as man, and a man as poet—perhaps the first full-length portrait of the artist as young, and growing, man.

Unlike Werther's, Wordworth's self, whose biography he chronicles through fourteen long books of blank verse, does not succumb to the consciousness-process. Instead of being undone by consciousness he is (at least so he claims) made by it; the difference is not merely one of temperament (Wordsworth did not know nor care much for Goethe) but, I suppose, of philosophy. How successful *The Prelude* is in finally convincing us of success is, as I have already suggested, a matter of dispute; from all accounts of Wordsworth's life, despite periods of turbulence, it would seem that he became a tranquil if not a happy being—perhaps even an overtranquilized one. His early childhood provides him with some of the most convincing poetry of *The Prelude* as it recounts the escapades of a young, sensitive, imaginative boy whose sense of right and wrong, though conventional, is always being tested. In time the young lad discovers not only the picturesqueness of Nature but its "soul":

> Thus were my sympathies enlarged, and thus
> Daily the common range of visible things
> Grew dear to me . . . (*Prelude*, II, 175-177)

He becomes discerning; what others ignored become "gentle agitations" and "manifold distinctions" which he gleefully recorded. By "turning the mind in upon herself" he became not, as had Werther, a permanent victim of disillusionment and misjudgment of the will's destiny over events, but, instead, he "spread [his] thoughts" (*Prelude*, II, 295-300) to encompass and reach, by means of a Goethean *Steigerung*, a pinnacle:

> . . . enough
> Here to record that I was mounting now
> To such community with highest truth—
> A track pursuing, not untrod before,
> From strict analogies by thought supplied
> Or consciousnesses not to be subdued,
> To every natural form, rock, fruit or flower,
> Even the loose stones that cover the high-way,
> I gave a moral life: I saw them feel . . . (*Prelude*, III, 124-132)

Wordsworth, too, created his world but it correspondend with a genuine inner nature and was therefore not susceptible to the intellection of a Werther idyl doomed by events, not by its own source of feeling:

> I had a world about me—'twas my own;
> I made it, for it only lived to me,
> And to the God who sees into the heart. (*Prelude*, III, 144-146)

Nature for Werther was ultimately an unsuccessful symbol of artificiality as later it became a successful one for Baudelaire and his heirs; for Wordsworth nature was a way to man, with inherent and transcendent values. He seems to have lived out, and recorded, what Schiller could grapple with only theoretically in the 1795 *Briefe über die ästhetische Erziehung des Menschen* (*Letters on the Aesthetic Education of Man*). (Every careful reader of this important work has been struck by Schiller's varied and inconsistent use of the word "nature."[12]) The more abstruse forest of symbols in Baudelaire was in Wordsworth quite literally an immortal forest, "unapproachable by death," enduring, eternal, a solace from the "the blank abyss/ To look with bodily eyes, and be consoled" (*Prelude*, VI, 466-471). Knowledge is an end to be sought and to be desired; it brings not grief but options (much as Goethe conceived of knowledge in *Wilhelm Meister*, but not in *Werther*).

The struggles of *The Prelude*, and some of its dullest sections, occur with the onset of disillusionment at the turn of events in France after the Revolution. "I warred against myself" (*Prelude*, XII, 76); but out of that war emerged a renewed "sensitive being, a *creative* soul" (XII, 207). "Moderated" and "composed" Wordsworth turns once more to man for the proper study of mankind and also to secure finally the "knowledge that step by step might lead [him] on/ To wisdom . . ." (*Prelude*, XIII, 132-133), words added for the 1850 edition. Final Unity of Being, as Yeats, coming from a different entrance, was to call it, is achieved on top of Mount Snowdon where he finds

> . . . the emblem of a mind
> That feeds upon infinity, that broods
> Over the dark abyss . . . (*Prelude*, XIV, 70-73)

Of all virtues he finds the mind's self-knowledge the crowning experience,

> . . . the highest bliss
> That flesh can know is theirs—the consciousness
> Of Whom they are . . . (*Prelude*, XIV, 113-115)

The Prelude has moved Wordsworth inexorably from a dim awareness of self and nature to what he firmly believes to be a full consciousness, a self-awareness which the accumulated knowledge of man within nature had at last effected. But, throughout the poem, Wordsworth is sensitive to conscience, though he barely mentions the word itself. Whatever the naïveté of his early life, he assures us he never did, "in quest of right and wrong,/Tamper with conscience" (*Prelude*, XIV, 150-151). In a passage now included in *The Recluse*, published first in 1814 "as a kind of Prospectus of the design and scope of the whole Poem," this comprising the so-called "antechamber," *The Prelude, The Excursion,* and *The Recluse,* Wordsworth combines conscience and consciousness in a way that serves as a kind of coda for his view of the problem:

> On Man, on Nature, on Human Life,
> Musing in solitude, I oft perceive
> Fair trains of imagery before me rise . . .
> And I am conscious of affecting thoughts
> And dear remembrances, whose presence soothes . . .
> Of the individual Mind that keeps her own
> Inviolate retirement, subject there
> To Conscience only, and the law supreme
> Of that Intelligence which governs all—
> I sing:—'fit audience let me find though few!'
>   (Preface to the 1814 edition of *The Excursion*)

What rouses men to scorn or pity, to which they might otherwise be insensitive, are "the outward ministers/Of inward conscience" whose mission it is to thwart "evil purposes" and arouse "remorse" (*Excursion*, IV, 836-839). Indeed, our being "conscious that the Will is free" impels—the word is the poet's—us toward "the path/Of order and of good" (*Excursion*, IV, 1264-1270). Clearly, the consciousness of conscience is a single process of the mind and, again as in Schiller, the aesthetic awareness of self and nature leads inevitably to the ethical imperatives of both. In *The Excursion* Wordsworth insists that above all victory in life is "entire submission to the law/Of conscience—conscience reverenced and obeyed . . ." (IV, 224-225).

The reference to Milton's "fit audience . . . though few" is felicitous and not merely a genuflexion toward a great predecessor; it is a salutary reminder that The Great Poem (*The Prelude, The Excursion, The Recluse*) was to bear some resemblances to *Paradise Lost,* only, of course, it was to differ significantly. Milton has told the story of the Fall and, if one so interprets, that of the

resurrection of man too; of knowledge and its terrible consequences; Wordsworth was now prepared to tell us the story of a
man, himself, of a poet—not forgetting finally to link the Fall and
his Resurrection, the rebirth of a man to the rebirth of Man, nor
to ignore the individual experience leading to wisdom as being
merely emblematic of mankind.

The Prelude, often considered (even by Wordsworth) a typical
example of Romantic "egotism," is perhaps a desperate attempt to
fit a link into an existing chain. It is a poem about an individual
mind, but only as example of the rule; *Werther* was intended as no
such thing, being the tale of what at the time, at least, was the
exception. That the exception became the rule merely makes
Goethe, in this instance, a more prophetic poet, though he later
protested (too much?) that *Werther* was nothing more than an
example of a sickness not to be emulated.

Yet before we speak any further of differences, it is prudent
first to speak of likenesses, to show if possible how such initial
affinities led to ultimate divergence. Initially, both *Werther* and
The Prelude are examples of the "egotistical sublime." Both, too,
are in quest of the increasing certainty that there is some unity of
being, some *correspondance,* as it was later to be called, between
perception (consciousness) and knowledge (conscience), between
what a man felt and what he valued. One may put the last point
even more emphatically: what a man feels *must* be of value. Precarious in that sentiment, both for Goethe and for Wordsworth
was, of course, the obvious question: Is what a man feels controlled by whim, by disposition, by circumstance? And under what
possible moral optics are we obliged to place our perceptions—if
we are obliged?

Nearly every artist to whom the term "Romantic" even re-
motely applies was industriously engaged in the pursuit of con-
vergences, creating in the process always new versions of things
requiring harmony: Poets like Hölderlin, Gérard de Nerval, Blake
found little in the phenomenology of matter to comfort them; like
Hegel they turned to the phenomenology of mind, but found
there, unlike Hegel, no lasting unities, no transcendent absolutes.
Most likely that kind of certitude, mechanically unfolding from

thesis-antithesis, was not what they wanted anyway. They were searching for some miraculous metamorphosis, some arrested vision in which perhaps all phenomena, of mind and matter, fell away leaving only a soulscape of pure essence. Balzac provides his Louis Lambert, a Swedenborgian, with such an experience, but only at the expense of what the quotidian world calls sanity. Novalis's premature death, Hölderlin's madness, Nerval's suicide, Blake's frenzy—these are somber testimony to the fate awaiting such seekers. Kleist's suicide following his unfortunate misreading of Kant, which robbed him of certainty, is an exquisitely painful instance in the sorry history of those decades which, after Rousseau, seem to have no end. All these poets were heirs of Werther. Possibly Goethe's hostility towards Kleist had its roots at least partly in a vague sense of guilt at witnessing what his Werther had wrought, not among foolish dandies who threw themselves into the Thames, the Seine, or the Rhine, but among fine spirits, however unrealized. Richard Friedenthal has once again stressed how close Goethe himself was to psychic collapse during the period of *Werther*.[13] Goethe made some peace with his demon, but in correcting his position with the new doctrines of *Wilhelm Meister,* he succeeded only partially; he incurred the wrath of Novalis, among others, who (however unjustly) branded that book a betrayal of the artist.

If, as we have shown, conscience-consciousness was both etymologically and philosophically related to knowledge, especially "of oneself," then *Werther* and *The Prelude* begin with the aim of harvesting such knowledge as a value, *an sich,* in itself, a consciousness brimming in the receptive mind, perception of experience.

Yet I have called *Werther* an idyl. Can a man perceive anything in an idyllic state if it runs counter to his conceptions of blameless knowledge? I think not. And, therefore, an idyl, as I attempted to show it, runs counter to Werther's *perceptions*. He alone bestows values, and it is the terrible disparity between perception and value that destroys his quest for unity and harmony. After all the point is that Werther's "distemper" is a symptom of his frustration, his inability, finally, to unite perception and knowledge, for knowledge relentlessly contravenes whatever value he places—or forces—

upon his perceptions. In contrast Wordsworth's professed ability to transcend his childhood paradise and the adolescent's conception of nature as mere balm permits a vision of unity on the summit of Snowdon which, in terms of the poem, has been painfully and urgently earned. Such a level of consciousness as Snowdon offers is quite different from the "two consciousnesses" Wordsworth had felt within himself—like Faust's two souls—in Book II (see page 69).

Geoffrey Hartman has proposed that what Wordsworth called "imagination" was in effect consciousness, a *"consciousness of self raised to apocalyptic pitch,"* particularly in Book VI, which recounts the great event of crossing the Alps.[14] This argument, subtly developed over the length of a book, cannot be successfully abstracted, but its main thesis on the problem of consciousness emerges clearly. There are varieties of consciousness. Initially Wordsworth experiences the consciousness which arrests the "traveller-poet," transfixing him, creating a stasis separating man from nature, subject from object. This point had been made some years earlier by Schiller in *Naive and Sentimental Poetry,* though Wordsworth did not know of it. Feelings of "solitude," of "loss or separation," impinge on the poet's mind, creating genuine anxiety. In fact Hartman prefers to call such consciousness "self-consciousness" because the self stands stripped of any relationship to "other," always a very frightening cleavage. Wordsworth tried hard to avoid this "apocalyptic consciousness"; and Hartman views *The Prelude* as aiming to move gradually away from the *Angst* of self-consciousness towards the final vision from the summit of Snowdon, when self-consciousness transcends separation and therefore achieves harmony rather than anxiety. A "true consciousness of self," so the argument continues, is "born of betrayal . . . a crime essentially against nature" and yet a necessary function of the poet's growth. The crime against nature occurs in the unwitting severance from it when the shock of self-recognition is at its most acute level, that is, "apocalyptic." It is not easy to say how Wordsworth atones for this crime. A crime against the natural is a crime against the divine, and how is it possible, in Wordsworth's terms, for an "autonomous self" to make moral judgments? Between the apocalyptic self-consciousness of Book VI and the harmonious self-conscious in Book XIV, there is indeed a transition, what Hartman identifies as the crisis of the poem (Books X-XIII), in which Wordsworth was "tempted to divorce head from heart, himself from nature," tempted to become trapped in the "I" of the poem, the "I" so necessary to the telling of the crisis, the "I" which would have cancelled the very writing of *The Prelude* and which "expresses a consciousness of nature." However, this self-consciousness, moving from dissociation to harmony, was successful precisely because the separated self became in time infused with value, whether religious or other is of no consequence in this context. Apocalypse freezes the self, empties it from a too facile relation it has taken for granted (see "Tintern Abbey"); the growth of the poet is not the process of leaping from separation across the abyss to the enfolding arms of a maternal nature but is, rather, how to make the self substantial and free to stand in relation to "other"—a freedom earned. Wordsworth does not lose himself in nature; nor, if it comes to that, does he find himself in nature: he becomes a self which harmonizes with an external world *only* because it has learned how to harmonize with itself, how to adjudicate the disputes between head and heart, understanding and feeling, conscience and consciousness. For surely the atonement for the crime against nature is what engages Wordsworth's *conscience,* helping it to survive the self-consciousness which Hartman equates with apocalyptic imagination.

Wordsworth's "Ode to Duty" (1804) dates from the period of the first version of *The Prelude* (1805); it naturally belongs to this discussion. Opinions and interpretations of this poem have differed widely, as have attributions to sources and analogues, from Stoic or Christian to the German Idealists.[15] Though Hartman feels that duty "cannot be only conscience" (or "consciousness") but a "stricter guide than either," a MS variant of the Ode renders Wordsworth's description of duty more explicitly than the final version:

> O Power of Duty! sent from God
> To enforce on earth his high behest,
> And keep us faithful to the road
> Which conscience has pronounc'd the best;[16]

Conscience appears to be a larger and anterior power, but duty is clearly its representative. Although this stanza was cancelled, the fifth stanza, as it remains, reads:

> Through no disturbance of my soul,
> Or strong compunction in me wrought,
> I supplicate for thy [Duty's] control.

"Compunction" surely means, in its original sense, "Pricking or stinging of the conscience or heart; uneasiness of mind consequent on wrongdoing; remorse, contrition."[17] It depends on how one interprets Wordsworth's use of words like conscience and duty (their appearance, by the way, is most frequent in *The Excursion*), but in the Ode, the "Duty" Wordsworth invokes seems very close indeed to the duty of Kant, despite the fact that he probably knew nothing of that philosopher.

It is *not,* Wordsworth argues in the Ode, through remorse or prick of conscience that he has called upon duty, "But in the quietness of thought," because he feels a burden of freedom: "Me this unchartered freedom tires," making him "long for a repose," unchanging. This specific attempt to define the problem helps us because it eliminates a certain amount of speculation. For Wordsworth conscience was never merely remorse or guilt: it was also the burden of freedom itself: "I feel the weight of chance desires." As in Fichte, duty in that sense *is* conscience, the "Voice of God!" Wordsworth calls it. Precisely because Wordsworth asks for limitation in the atmosphere of quietude rather than perturbation, he invokes a guide for *directing* energy (which he saw as well as did Shelley or Blake), surely not one for *suppressing* it. It is a Goethean *Beschränkung* (restraint) he seeks, not passivity. As for all the Romantics, the energy of imagination was for Wordsworth a real threat; it is, then, that very energy, and the many unnamed and unnumbered paths it may travel, which constitutes the burden. That energy, in its demonic thrust, is freedom itself. Concern with our "dual self," we recall Kant warning, blocks "the stern command of duty," and it is in part that excess of *amour-propre* of which Wordsworth now desires to rid himself in order that he may become, in Milton's phrase, "lowly wise," prepared now to attain the "confidence of reason" and the "spirit of self-sacrifice." Duty, or conscience, was a value which consciousness (perception) might shape or destroy. If man is frivolous and narcissistic in his perceptions, he cannot at the same time heed duty; but if he channels his freedom selectively, by heeding the voice of duty or conscience, the perceptions, of senses or of mind, need in no way be a burden:

> . . . by the storms of circumstance unshaken,
> And subject neither to eclipse nor wane,
> Duty exists . . . (*Excursion*, IV, 71-73)

Wordsworth's plea for duty's guidance, despite all the implications of repose and self-restraint in that plea, in one sense constitutes his poetic "rage for order." It may also very well be a warning that the freedom of harmony with nature is not enough without the discipline of conscience; that the lure of harmony reveals a treacherous landscape of possibilities potentially as dangerous as the anxieties of a severed self-consciousness, of separation from nature and God.

Wordsworth calls duty a "stern lawgiver," and Kant could only agree: "Duty is the necessity of an action done from respect for the law."[18] All actions take on value only if they proceed from duty. What, then, is duty? It is certainly no longer what Hume had thought: "No action can be requir'd of us as our duty, unless there be implanted in human nature some actuating passion or motive, capable of producing the action." Such a motive cannot itself be a "sense of duty," because that sense of duty "supposes an antecedent obligation." This is in keeping with Hume's general conclusion that justice as a virtue is artificial, largely dependent on *amour-propre*. Hume does not consider duty as law or innate virtue, although actions consonant with duty, when actuated by "inner passion or motive," may express themselves as the fulfillment of an obligation—an obligation antecedent to duty.[19]

Kant expressed himself very differently: "Duty! Thou sublime and mighty name that dost embrace nothing charming and insinuating and requirest submission and yet seekest not to move at all . . . but only holdest forth a law . . . before which all inclinations are dumb."[20] So it is exactly through moral autonomy, aided by obedience to moral action impelled by moral value, that man bestows law upon himself. This becomes the process, the moment of intersection between consciousness (perception) and conscience (value). Like Kant, at least in this respect, Wordsworth saw duty as law; and in obedience to that law rested the fate of those hostages of freedom itself—anxiety, terror, doubt:

> 'O blest seclusion when the mind admits
> *The law of duty;* and can therefore move
> Through each vicissitude of loss and gain,
> Linked in entire complacense with her choice . . .
> (*Excursion,* IV, 1035-1038. Italics mine)

It is such an imperative that makes Wordsworth ultimately (not on first glance certainly) a modern self-conscious moralist, a "friend of the modern mind," as Willard Sperry wrote nearly forty years ago.[21] Wordsworth's modernity, however, is considerably attenuated, foreshortened by his inability to individualize and humanize his imperatives, an ability his friend Coleridge possessed in excess when suffering could not be transformed into poetry.

Like Baudelaire's *Journal Intime* and *Mon coeur mis à nu,* Coleridge's *Notebooks* are a compendious testimony of self-accusation and guilt, full to the brim with disappointment in himself, resolutions to become disciplined, the whole frail apparatus hanging, it seems, on the thinnest threads of sanity—"I humbly thank God, that I have for some time past been more attentive to the regulation of my thoughts."[22] As usual Wordsworth was more certain of himself (he desperately needed to be) than Coleridge who, enquiring beyond the limits of his spirit, was beginning to disintegrate, physically and mentally: "I am very, very, hopeless & heartless! I was about to say that I had written once wrote to W[ordsworth]. in consequence of his Ode to Duty & in that letter explained this as the effect of Selfinterest *selfness* in a mind incapable of gross Self-interest—decrease of Hope and Joy, the Soul in its round & round flight forming narrower cirlces, till at every Gyre its wings beat against the *personal Self*" (2531/f53). That slip of *Self-interest* crossed out and substituted by *Selfness* is certainly fortuitous because it tells us a little about Coleridge's anguished confusion between selfness and selfishness. He recognized and worried about the "egotistical sublime" more than Keats did, certainly more than Wordsworth, for he felt it deeply threatening within himself. So "Selfness" becomes a positive value only if it avoids "gross Self-interest" but, in more than one way presaging Yeats, if the body is bruised to pleasure soul, the *"personal Self"* becomes a Dantesque Hell in which the soul's wings, condemned to fly in ever narrowing gyres are literally in danger of being clipped.

Coleridge's fear of egotism was sometimes expressed in sexual-religious metaphors, the dread of being penetrated, overtaken, possessed. He must take heed not "to suffer any one form to pass into *me* and to become a usurping *Self* in the disguise of what the German Pathologists call a *fixed Idea.*" If successful, such penetration is "always a *Self*-love." It is especially dangerous because "the Conscience may be duped" by what Coleridge calls the "alterity and consequent distinct figurableness of the *form—*," that is the dissembling power of such self-love to be other than what it seems to be.[23]

For Coleridge, as for Dostoevsky's Underground Man about a half-century later, the acute problem was not merely *amour-propre* but the control of consciousness itself. Coleridge realized that "the mind is educed, drawn forth, or developed, in exact proportion as the consciousness is extended" (*I.S.*, p. 90); and he was even prepared to accept a humbling of the heart, a recognition that what "forces the mind inward" (and "remorse" was one possibility) places us in perspective "in proportion as it acquaints us with the thing we are, renders us docile," makes us accept the risks of knowledge (*I.S.*, p. 136). But he was never far from the dread of apocalyptic possibilities, always searching for any way that would soften the grim visages of conscience and duty: "And now, that I am alone, & utterly hopeless for myself—yet still *I love*—& more strongly than ever feel that Conscience, or the Duty of Love, is the Proof of continuing, as it is the Cause & Condition of existing, Consciousness" (3231/f15). As one reads the *Notebooks*, there can be little doubt that Coleridge's attitude is always defensive and preventive, staving off catastrophe. Often what he seems most certain about is also what he most fears. He felt that our life is a "Probation" and our obedience to Duty "for its own sake," in a state of human imperfection, was bound to be seen "in direct opposition to the *Wish*, the Inclination" (2556/f73ᵛ).

Of duty Coleridge had a good deal to say, much of it swatting at Kant much as a sick man might swat in frustration at the flies that continually torment him. He equated duty with the "hauntings of [his] conscience (2531/f52ᵛ); he sought to salvage something beyond Kant's rigorism. "How," he asked, "to make Duty add to Inclination" (3026/f34ᵛ); or, using Kant's own examples, he sought "The Coincidence of Duty & Inclination" (1705/l). And he thought only him happy "who in enjoyment *finds* his Duty" (2556/f75), which he seldom did. And of the mind's capacity to grow, Coleridge knew precisely the inevitable process and the equally inevitable risks: "Man must be *free*"; yet "Man must [also] *obey;* or wherefore has he a conscience?" This creates a "difficulty" but, at times, Coleridge glimpsed a solution: "for *their* service [freedom and obedience] is perfect freedom" (*I.S.*, p. 411). It was in some ways a rigorism equal to Kant's softened only by its inability to be an effective "solution." Such "freedom" which, I think, Coleridge wanted to rescue from the determinism of German Idealist "Necessity," was so dependent on obedience that the contingency made the freedom itself untenable. Of this more will be said in Chapter IV.

Like Schiller, Coleridge moves (or attempts to move) beyond Kant's insistence on moral objectivity towards an "outflowing activity of a truly moral being, i.e. a *schöne Seele.*" Actions, however, he considered suspect if they had what Kant had feared—a sense of self-serving in their altruism: "Does even the sense of Duty rest satisfied with mere *Actions,* in the vulgar sense, does it not demand, & therefore may produce, Sympathy itself as an Action/?—This I think very important/" (1705/o-p). Clearly Coleridge despaired of living up to the high standards which he above all believed he fell short of all his life, especially in the area of duty. "To perform Duties absolutely from the sense of Duty," he wrote, "is the *Ideal,* which perhaps no human Being ever can arrive at"; yet we must strive for the state in which "Duty and Pleasure are absolutely coincident" (2556/f74ᵛ)—yet another impossible "*Ideal.*" So while recognizing the sternness of duty and its demands, Coleridge yet pleaded, hoped for, the intervention of inclination, indeed hoped more than he insisted that these two apparent opposites were not irreconcilable. His faith in conscience he placed ultimately upon consciousness which, in turn, he felt was a necessary building ground for the self: "*From* what reasons do I believe a *continuous* <& ever continuable> *Consciousness*? From *Conscience*! Not for myself but for my conscience—i.e. my affections and duties toward others, I should have no Self—for Self is Definition" (3231/f14).

To define that self was to be Coleridge's *prise de conscience*; his inclinations were patently not absolutely coincident with his duties. If Wordsworth fared better, *if* he did, perhaps it was because Wordsworth failed to see that such coincidence was ever in question. Yet he payed a price for that. His "*Law of Duty*," negotiating itself between "loss and gain," was one of those imperatives which remained in bondage to abstraction (for which Yeats, among others, never forgave him). To compensate for this Wordsworth wrote much about *humanizing* in his poetry; yet, in the end, he kept his distance from his poetry as his poetry so often tends to keep its distance from us.

A writer like Kafka also recognized laws and imperatives, and few writers have trafficked closer to rigorism and relentless self-demand. Yet I think that Kafka gave battle to his imperatives and pursued the rigorims that pursued him. Like Coleridge he attempted at least to humanize imperatives precisely in the process of confronting the individual with such laws and imperatives. Modernity has read its Kant with more care and experience than Coleridge and, in so doing, possibly has wrecked at least some of Kant's intentions simply by candidly emphasizing them. When one believes, as Kant did, that a man's integrity of action must be based on morality as well as legality, on sentiment as well as obligation, then obligation and legality may indeed become, as they do in Kafka, autonomous monsters (the same as those who ravaged Coleridge and De Quincey in their dreams).[24]

Wordsworth's conception of nature is, of course, too complex a

subject for brief review. But if we agree with Hartman that, funda-
mentally, Wordsworth dissociated himself from nature in the process of creating his self, then we see at once how essential was the
difference between such dichotomizing and Coleridge's belief in
wholeness. In *Werther* Goethe to some extent demonstrates the
case of his own theory of the archetype of nature by setting it in
opposition to an artificial one: Werther's idyl. A man who rages
against the dislocation of nature (for example, the chopped-down
chestnut trees) is in fact a rational positivist whose greatest error is
to expect nature to conform to dreams without permitting those
dreams free play, reciprocity of nature and the imagination that
shapes it. Werther's archetype is wholly self-made and, as Yeats so
often said, in that direction no man can successfully travel towards
Unity of Being.

Like Goethe, Coleridge was an archetypal communicant with
nature, even anticipating in one remarkable passage the more schematic articulation of Baudelaire's *correspondances*. (Coleridge's
reading of Swedenborg antedated 1800.[25]) Significantly, Coleridge's vision of man's walk through the forest of symbols (which
in concept may well have owed something to Schiller's *"Spazier-
gang"*) is pessimistic and characteristically paradoxical. The search
for correspondence, he feels, leads away from, rather than towards, what it aims to discover, the light before casting the
shadow behind. Man is lost, as in a Dantesque wood; he is "disturbed" and "restless" as he "sallies forth into nature," like
Quixote, ". . . to discover the originals of the forms presented to
him in his intellect." Man is seen hanging "Narcissus-like" over the
"shadows" of what appear to be correspondences, but such delight
turns out to be illusion when "finding nowhere a representative of
that free agency which yet is a *fact* of immediate consciousness
sanctioned and made fearfully significant by prophetic *conscience,*
he learns at last that what he *seeks* he has *left behind,* and but
lengthens the distance as he prolongs the search" (*F.*, I, 509).
Such is the dilemma in which Schiller had placed the modern
(sentimental) poet, leaving him three alternatives: to measure the
distance with yearning and a sense of loss (elegy); to measure the
distance juxtaposing it to reality (satire); or to refuse to recognize

that the distance exists (idyl). Wordsworth, essentially, was an elegist; Coleridge, incapable of satire, was equally unable to write idyl by ignoring the distance which insistently stared up at him. His vast epic conceptions of poems about the universe remained no more than conceptions; imaginative paralysis was the result, not the cause, of writing poems of dejection, poems fathered by his "prophetic conscience," his consciousness of the "distance" ever lengthening, the search always prolonged.

The difference between *Werther* and *The Prelude* can now be more clearly stated from the perspectives in which I have examined them. Werther is a young man who intellectually constructs a love for nature as part of the creation of an idyl; lacking inventiveness he produces something different: the process of deliberately creating an idyl gradually sets in motion the counter-process of recognizing the failure of the whole venture. Hence the more conscious Werther becomes, the more distraught, and the more conscience stings at his illusions (not delusions). Wordsworth, on the other hand, feeds on consciousness; it leads him not only to knowledge and wisdom but to a kind of monastic obedience to conscience, that minister who points the way to the steep and narrow path. Consciousness for Werther, as for Dostoevsky's Underground Man, is ultimately a mirror reflecting horror, disgust, realities inconsistent with *la belle âme, die schöne Seele*;[26] but consciousness for Wordsworth, allowing for the struggles attendant on any initiation into the disputed realm of "appearance" and "reality," is a mirror reflecting Truth, Beauty, Goodness. Indeed Wordsworth would claim—he does so implicitly—that conscience without consciousness is unthinkable, while Werther cries out, in effect, that consciousness without conscience is impossible (alas!), and that once consciousness has given birth to conscience, the latter brutally proceeds to disfigure and to destroy the former. It was inevitable that some would continue their quest to have the best of both worlds, that some would divide and seek to conquer—either with conscience or with consciousness. Few, however, after Wordsworth will find it possible to recover from consciousness, and many will explore in greater detail the process of a defeated will, though paying tribute to its continued tenaciousness. Few after Wordsworth will be able to write—and to believe that

> . . . knowledge is delight; and such delight
> Breeds love . . . (*Excursion*, IV, 346-347)

For Wordsworth "the shock of awful consciousness" was analogous to the shock of a beatific vision—momentarily blinding but, full of awe, a permanent gift of wisdom. Knowledge, love, and awful consciousness—these were sufficient to dissuade Wordsworth from idyl-making:

> Dismissing therefore, all Arcadian dreams,
> All golden fancies of the golden Age . . .,
> (*Recluse*, 625-626)

Wordsworth sought compensation in certainties. For him the "one sufficient hope" was the abundance, the riches of the sentient world which, he was certain, would never be exhausted. But he wrote these lines in 1800 and never published them in his lifetime.

IV. Some Versions of Consciousness and Egotism: Hegel, Dostoevsky's Underground Man, and *Peer Gynt*

But conscience is this deepest inward solitude with one self where everything external and every restriction has disappeared—this complete withdrawal into oneself.

—Hegel

Therefore when it is said that this man has no conscience, this means he does not heed its dictates.

—Kant

Preliminary Note

Perhaps no philosopher is more treacherous, and yet more fascinating, than Hegel; professionals and amateurs approach him at their peril. Hegel's challenges infuriate some of us today as they did in his day; his terminology continues to confound even the patient reader; his dialectics, often covering a venomous polemic, makes many of us sway with vertigo on edges of precipices. But for all that in Hegel there remains the "fascination of what's difficult"; it would have been impossible to omit him from my argument. Hegel paid a good deal of attention to consciousness, self-consciousness, and conscience, primarily in *The Phenomenology of Mind* (1807) and in *The Philosophy of Right* (1820). Though his influence among poets was often negative (initial embrace was often followed by revulsion and disavowal), few in the nineteenth century escaped Hegel's extended, almost brooding, presence. I now want to appraise Hegel's influential history in Russia as a means of interpreting, in the light of our present interest in conscience-consciousness, Dostoevsky's Underground Man. Whether Hegel's *Phenomenology* came into Dostoevsky's hands directly no one seems to have bothered to ask. But, indirectly, and in some cases directly, Hegel was no stranger to Dostoevsky. Hegelians and anti-Hegelians (sometimes embodied in the same men) abounded in Russia from the 1830's on, and, in the appropriate places, that will be documented, both in the text and the notes.

What occurred to me as both important and revealing was Hegel's conception of conscience in general and, in particular, his theory of the evolving self-consciousness. That self-consciousness Hegel traces from the master-slave status to the condition of the Stoic and later the Skeptic, culminating in the "unhappy consciousness" of the paradoxical split personality. This discussion occupies a long section of *The Phenomenology*. In addition, in a subsequent section of the same work, Hegel launches a frontal attack on "the beautiful soul" which seemed of further help in explaining and accounting for the behavior of the Underground Man. Not only the preface but most of *The Phenomenology* is an attack both on Romanticism and on Nihilism; to put it differently, Hegel indicts Romantic idealism as inevitably headed for the disastrous negation of solipsism, a denial of life, action, duty, an evasion of commitment and obligation (which, after all, was the opposite of what Kant had intended).

The Underground Man seems to be almost an uncanny personification of some of the harshest critiques in *The Phenomenology*. And although I make no attempt to hang a fictional character on a philosophical (no less a Hegelian!) peg, a parallel reading of Hegel and Dostoevsky has illuminated the *Notes from the Underground* for me; if I can convey some of that light I will have considered the risks worthwhile.

Peer Gynt seemed to be a good counterweight to the Underground Man. Ibsen's poetical egotist is not pro-Hegelian as much as anti-Kantian: he is a man whose whole life is predicated on self-realization at the expense of duty, on the fulfillment of inclination—full speed ahead, imperatives be damned. Peer Gynt seems to solve some of the self-torturing and self-destructive questions which destroy the Underground Man. But as Hegel might say, not without some malice perhaps, he merely succeeds in delay: his struggle is a self-deceptive holding action, nothing better. Both Dostoevsky's hero and Peer Gynt are—as the title of this chapter suggests—exemplars, not merely examples, of the egotism of consciousness; and since that has been and will remain a central concern of this study, a close inspection of the phenomenon at this juncture seems appropriate.

The Underground Man and Hegel's "Unhappy Consciousness" and "The Beautiful Soul"

In 1854, several weeks after his release from four years of penal servitude at Omsk, Dostoevsky asked his brother for books. Among such requests as the Koran and books on history, economics, and the Church, he also singled out "Kant's *Critique de raison pure*" and "without fail Hegel, especially Hegel's history of philosophy." In a sentence that seems strangely incongruous in the midst of the Koran and the Church Fathers Dostoevsky added, apropos Hegel: "My whole future is bound up with this"—that is, getting hold of Hegel's *History of Philosophy*. Dostoevsky's interest in Hegel at this time was so intense he planned, but never wrote, a collaborative study of Hegel and Carus with Baron Alexander Vrangel.[1]

Hegel was, of course, not a new name in the Russia of the fifties; like Kant or Schiller, Hegel had been known among the Russian intelligentsia from the thirties onwards, especially among such important disciples as Mikhail Bakunin and Vissarion Belinski, both familiar to Dostoevsky. As I have already said, the precise nature of Dostoevsky's firsthand knowledge of Hegel remains uncertain; *The Phenomenology* had a limited first printing in 1807, but, in 1831, the year of Hegel's death, a second edition became available. Through Ludwig Feuerbach, who in turn influenced Belinski in the forties, Dostoevsky must have known a good deal about Hegelian philosophy. Assuming his brother obliged by sending the posthumously published *History of Philosophy* in 1854, one may conclude that Dostoevsky would have found there many things paralleled in *The Phenomenology*, Hegel's first book.[2]

Ten years after that letter requesting books by Kant and Hegel from his brother, Dostoevsky published the *Notes from the Underground*, a work that remains unresolved in part, I think, because it serves too many willing causes, from theological to psychiatric, from left to right, from sympathetic to hostile. In the following discussion I link Dostoevsky's Underground Man to Hegel's "unhappy consciousness" and his critique of "the beautiful soul," not as a mouthpiece for Hegelianism but to help us understand his dilemma—the burden of consciousness and its resultant egotism—in the light of these Hegelian ideas. If indeed Dostoevsky was familiar with these particular Hegelian analyses, his presentation of his hero affirms no Hegelian certainties: the Underground Man represents the problem, not the solution. Despite evidence adduced from other sources that indicate Dostoevsky's anti-Romanticism in the rendering of his hero's history, I very much doubt, for instance, that he would have agreed (or did agree if he knew of it) with Hegel's outright rejection of "the beautiful soul." The Underground Man is a striking instance of the problem; but Dostoevsky's yearning for Schillerism (as I will point out) was never quenched. He chided himself, and others, for false idealism, but all his major heroes, including the Underground Man, attempt to make out of their internal struggles an authentically "beautiful soul."

Most critics agree on one major fact: the Underground Man represents "freedom."[3] Whether such freedom is good or how it has been obtained or whether it has truly been attained are all issues that have elicited a great many divergent views. As in all such cases when a work elicits much debate, the text at times becomes a little lost behind the positions of the critics themselves. I will attempt to avoid adding to that problem: I offer no reading which excludes necessarily any others.

"I, for instance, have a great deal of *amour-propre*,"[4] the Underground Man tells us; and while he makes no fine distinctions between *amour-propre* and *amour de soi,* he clearly means to convey a kind of self-love which he expects us to condemn as egotism. At first such an admission seems to be contrary to anything we have so far seen, for our hero has exposed us to the image of a masochist whose self-hatred far exceeds his self-love. Yet the somewhat swaggering sentence about his *"amour-propre"* comes nearly at the very start of his confession. So he is throughout—a "paradoxalist." In Part II his egotism becomes much clearer for there he illus-

trates, in retrospect, what sort of life has brought him underground, the position from which he begins Part I. That division has
provided us with some convenient historical explanations of the
Notes, especially the revealing and perhaps corrective essay by
Joseph Frank. That interpretation, to oversimplify it, argues that
Part I is a parody of the Nihilism of the sixties; Part II is a parody
of the Romanticism of the forties. That Dostoevsky lived through
both periods and indeed was critical of them both is certain;
whether he did so by means of parody is a different and harder
question to answer. The *Notes* are *not* uncharacteristic Dostoevsky; and although many works, especially the shorter ones, are
ironic parodies, there appears to be too much shared suffering
with the Underground Man to assign the *Notes* a place of objectivity as severe as Frank seems to imply.[5]

The first pages make clear that our hero's main preoccupation is
consciousness—indeed the "unhappy consciousness" of Hegel; and
his *amour-propre* is a function of that consciousness and an ironic
description of a symptom of rebellion against his "beautiful soul,"
which he has not been able to excise. "To be conscious," says the
Underground Man, "is an illness," and he defines this explicitly as
a condition *beyond* "ordinary human consciousness," already
more than enough for the average "cultivated man of our unhappy
nineteenth century": the Underground Man suffers the condition of an "unhappy consciousness."[6] It is this diseased consciousness (Poe had already examined it in detail)[7] which occasions that
peculiar perversity in his behavior. Whenever thoughts of the
"good and beautiful"—a phrase attributed to both Kant and Schiller—seem at their most promising, they are driven away by their
opposite impulses, the desire to defile, a perverse urge to commit
actions "when I was most conscious that they ought not to be
committed." (This precisely parallels what Hesse's Steppenwolf
complains of, when he laments the fact that the man is always
sabotaged by the wolf, and vice versa.) The "paradoxalist" presents us with what appears to be a psychogenic dilemma: "The
more conscious I was of goodness and of all that was 'lofty and
beautiful', the more deeply I sank into my mire and the more
ready I was to sink in it altogether." Such contradictory impulses,

which he objectifies in Part II in his account of his earlier life, have been the chief defining principles of his alleged "freedom": the ability to subvert goodness and decency with base inclinations or, put differently, to convert "good" inclinations into their opposites, to make pure energy express itself in demonic (not daimonic), destructive actions. What has been slighted in many discussions of the Underground Man's freedom is its extreme contingency, its frailty accentuated by a continual feeling of remorse—of conscience.

After periodic immersions in a life of depravity, the Underground Man always "felt sick afterwards," and this sickness was accompanied by "remorse" which he unsuccessfully sought to banish (from his "consciousness"). He concedes that his baseness was not all "shameful" but possessed in its very nature impulses of the "good and the beautiful"—in "the Manfred style," he says rather pointedly, for Schillerism and Byronism were linked in the Russian awareness, as indeed they should be. His perpetual vacillation between the pitiful "romantic" full of noble impulses and the ruthless skeptic full of cruelty is not mere pathology but a genuinely objectified philosophic war between the ethical man's faculties of high dreams and low achievements. Such a man's cruelty is, by his own admission, a form of revenge, not only against himself and the failure of his own ideals but against ideals themselves. Nietzsche was to call this *ressentiment*. Even after addressing himself passionately to Liza as the embodiment of "the beautiful soul" and then regretting his outburst ("yet it was not merely sport") he cannot quite admit total deception. "Something was not dead within me, in the depths of my heart and conscience it would not die, and it showed itself in acute depression." The Underground Man plays games with himself, making gestures towards the "good and the beautiful" that he knows he will never complete—in Camus's words, describing his descendant-hero of *The Fall*, "Fortunately!" But there is no reason to doubt his confession. After cruelly abandoning his previous "beautiful soul" and ripping the prostitute Liza from any moorings he had established for her, he felt those pains of conscience that are a constant counterpart to his consciousness: "So I dreamed as I sat at home that evening, almost dead with the pain in my soul. Never have I endured such suffering and remorse, yet could there have been the faintest doubt when I ran out of my lodging that I should turn back halfway?" Such *bonum interruptum* is symptomatic of a condition in which the acute consciousness of conscience gets the upper hand, awareness being the very agent preventing redemptive gestures while promoting a pleasurable punitive suffering and hence protecting "the beautiful soul" from further exposure to disenchantment.

The Underground Man's remorse, his "guilty conscience," is clearly more than an ordinary sense of guilt for committing cruel deeds. If he is to be believed at all, say only half the time, in his youth he seems to have been more sinned against than sinning, whether from a fundamental flaw in his character or by the rank-conscious society that had thwarted other finer spirits, ever since Rousseau and Goethe had made out of personal confession a kind of new art. His conscience is an unresolved feeling, a compass needle poised to go either way: towards the "good and the beautiful," the inclination towards "duty" and obedience to his "better self"; or towards negation, the inclination to obey inertia, the will that annihilates itself by consuming its own power. This problem of action and passivity controlled by conscience was a particular concern in Hegel. It was not his imposing system but his certainty that generally speaking tended to frighten away poets, who were, like the Underground Man, more skeptical. But as I have already indicated, Hegel's influence in Russia was considerable; and the Underground Man is certainly a fit figure who in a number of ways combines, alternately, Hegel's certitude and Dostoevsky's doubt.

In Chapter VII I will have more to say about Schopenhauer's fundamental hostility towards viewing conscience as an a priori objectification, whether a Kantian imperative or, even worse, a Hegelian Idea. "It lies in the nature of the case," argued Schopenhauer, "that conscience speaks only *afterward*; and thus conscience is said to *pronounce judgment*." Schopenhauer's "is said" forewarns us of his distrust. "Conscience," he continues, "can speak *beforehand* only in a figurative, not in a literal sense, and thus indirectly," because on reflection men recall from sins past the "future disapproval" of deeds as yet only thought, not done. Thus far, he concludes, and one might stress *thus far,* goes the "ethical fact of consciousness," or, more syntactically: ethical consciousness is contingent upon a mnemonic response to deeds future based on the (negative) experience of deeds past.[8]

Dead when Schopenhauer wrote these words, Hegel was his senior and his adversary when he delivered himself of quite a different notion about conscience in *The Phenomenology of Mind:* "Conscience (*Gewissen*) is spirit sure and certain (*gewiss*) of itself." Hegel, indeed, may have been the source for Schopenhauer's conjunction of conscience with certitude, though Hegel does not use the word *"gewiss."*[9] So far, then, Hegel's position is in agreement with Schopenhauer's and later Freud's, namely, conscience is certain of itself. Hegel repeats this fact more than any other. But for Hegel conscience is not only a priori but a posteriori (after a complicated process), an idea, an infallible oracle. Conscience is itself really nothing in the realm of action until it is caught up in the dialectics of good and evil, action and passivity, duty and neglect of duty. Conscience *is* many things, but in the world of things in itself it *does* nothing: it is the unifying agent of moral individuality. Conscience is "moral self-consciousness" finding the proper "content" to fill the voids of duty, right, and will, hence endowing "moral self-consciousness" with a "definite existence." Conscience is God breathing life into man's moral awareness, exacting the price of absolute obedience and obedience to its absolute existence. In fact, says Hegel, "The actual reality of conscience . . . is one which is a self . . . conscious of itself, the spiritual element of being recognized." That phrase "the spiritual element" is not the decisive issue (though it is one of several); what Hegel insists is that conscience alone makes self which in turn objectifies duty in action: "For the essence of the act, duty, consists in the conviction conscience has about it." The "is"-ness of action is contingent upon conscience's unerring self-assurance: there is nothing relative about that aspect of Hegel's formulation. To make the chain of command quite clear Hegel charts it very specifically. By itself conscience is "detached" from all "content"; it has the power to absolve itself from any specificity—duty, for example. In its "majesty," like an absolute monarch, conscience has "absolute self-sufficiency"; this power determines its "absolute conformity" to what is required: duty. In Hegel's hierarchical declension, such knowledge creates "selfhood" which, through the filtration of an "immanent principle and essence," becomes "pure self-identity." That self-identity finally resides in "consciousness" itself. The process is abstruse and complex. To make it clearer we may turn it around, beginning at the lowest point of the scale. Consciousness houses self-identity; self-identity houses selfhood; selfhood houses knowledge of duty; knowledge of duty is the palace over which reigns the self-sufficient conscience. It should be obvious that between conscience, the highest on the scale, and consciousness, the lowest, Hegel has erected some crucial intermediaries, all of which the Underground Man encounters during his ordeal, his duel between the two parts of his self.

But this is an incomplete account. The reality of action, Hegel insists, is indeed validated *only* by what Hegel calls "the language of conscience"; the "essential reality" is the certitude of conscience; but all action, all "doing," all duty must be *"expressed."* It is the *"conviction* that the act is a duty" that alone is able to make the act authentic. When consciousness is "convinced of its duty, and, being conscience, knows of itself what duty is," then an authentic moral act has been enacted. This is as close an identity of conscience and consciousness as Hegel allows himself, and is also, as we shall see, an explanation for the Underground Man's ethical failure. In the end we must consider all of Hegel's arguments about conscience parallel in effect to the ontological arguments about the existence of God: a priori conscience supersedes everything, "universal consciousness *and* the individual self" (italics mine): "When any one says . . . he is acting from conscience, he is saying what is true, for his conscience is the self which knows and wills. But it is essential he should *say* so, for this self has to be at the same time universal self . . . Conscience, then, in its majestic sublimity above any specific law and every content of duty, puts whatever content it pleases into its knowledge and willing. It is moral genius . . . which knows the inner voice of its immediate knowledge to be a voice divine." "To be a voice divine": that is the *operari* of Hegel's conception; that is part of what drove the poets away, for by 1807 too many, though by no means all, of them no longer felt conscience to be a "majestic sublimity" a *vox Dei,* but something rather different, neither majestic nor sublime but still potent, afflictive, and not altogether just.

That complaint Hegel sought to answer in *The Philosophy of Right.* Since "the nature of man is essentially universal," and since Hegel denies the existence of consciousness in any Wordsworthian "spots of time," the expression of duty is virtually a requirement that character exacts. Only through conscience can men express the "absolute claim" of their self-consciousness to sort out right from wrong, duty from dereliction, thus eliminating whatever it does not know "to be good."[10] Such absolute knowledge presupposes a capacity already placed in doubt by Kant: it is pure assertion. In *The Phenomenology,* Hegel even asserts that what he calls "true conscience" is disposed "to desire what is absolutely good," conscience being the "formal side" of whatever activity we ascribe to the will. Formal, abstract, majestically aloof, conscience presides over the mating of "rules and duties" with the "subjective consciousness" achieving a confluence in the "sphere of ethical observance." When a man expresses good, for example, his duty, he has attained freedom of ethical action. Good itself is abstract; subjectivity ultimately becomes "absolute certitude [*Gewissheit*] of itself" and thus the abstract becomes particular and "determines and judges"—"This," concludes Hegel, "is conscience." Needless to say, Hegel's complicated concept of freedom is so full of contingencies that few have been able to follow the thought that it is freedom at all. Dostoevsky, I suspect, was no exception. As with all absolutes one must at some point have faith in the *primum mobile* that is its support. In Hegel, at least with respect to conscience, one sometimes feels that it is not so much conscience that dictates as it is man (his "subjective consciousness") who obeys, simply because the majestic conscience allows no other course. Certainly the Underground Man's "perversity" may in part be his reluctance to obey an absolute imposed from outside himself.

Such certainty kept not only the Underground Man precariously balanced; for better or for worse, all manner of men generally had begun to accept conscience as a self-created, self-illuminated state of mind, adjudicating somewhere between individual inclinations and the demands of society. Moral imperatives as aloof as Hegel's conscience might exist, but no individual consciousness, however universalized, could *know* such imperatives as infallible guides towards action. Hegel's conception of conscience returns us to *Faust,* Part II, where remorse is removed and the process towards freedom and self-realization is generated by a force that governs Faust—even towards his salvation. Much as being governed by unerring guides would be more comforting than the ambiguities of choice, a different "freedom," few could countenance Hegel's "conscience" outside the theory of the State as a guide either for themselves or for their times. Schopenhauer, often offering Nothing, was more solace; and Nietzsche, promising his "overcoming," was at least a challenge. In both there was conflict (which Freud would plot out)—conflict, accompanied by terror; conflict now seemed not merely preferable but actual and inevitable. Any synthesis, however desirable, seemed forbiddingly remote. The Underground Man seems hopelessly trapped between Hegel's certainty, his absolute freedom, and the impulses questioning that certainty, either through the distant urges towards the "good and the beautiful" or the resultant inertia of overconsciousness, the parallel vice of the inactivity Hegel condemned in "the beautiful soul." In Hegelian terms, the Underground Man never attains the freedom of "Reason" and "Absolute Knowledge," but instead stops short at a point Hegel called the state of *"absolute Freiheit und der Schrecken,"* absolute freedom and dread.

What defines the motif of the *Notes* is precisely this problem of freedom and dread as it intertwines with the problem of conscience and consciousness. The Underground Man has been described both as a nihilist and an existential hero who discovers the absurdity of existence and rebels against the "good" because, in Nietzschean terms, "good" is not really "good" but evil dressed in societal garb purporting to represent a value-system of "morality" that is violated even in its conception. I think the Underground

Man comes closer to a state of Hegelian "skepticism," a condition Hegel was careful to link specifically with the "unhappy consciousness." The Underground Man himself admits that "all at once, *apropos* of nothing, there would come a phase of scepticism and indifference . . . [and] I would reproach myself with being *romantic.*" Hegel's "skepticism" occupies a particular position in this scheme.

The "freedom" of skepticism is, in Hegel, historically preceded by the "freedom" of Stoicism, that state in which the slave becomes self-reliant and hence independent of his master: "The consciousness that toils and serves . . . attains . . . direct apprehension of that independent being as its self." The slave becomes "free" the more he realizes his power by understanding his master's dependence on him. As a typical example of a Russian bureaucratic slave who cannot climb beyond certain limits, the Underground Man has already passed through the master-slave "freedom" and the freedom Hegel attributes to Stoicism, the condition in which the ability to think is the liberating force. Ready now for the next step, he stands on the brink of Hegelian "skepticism," the freedom to doubt, and this is a freedom of self-negation: "Scepticism is the realisation of that of which Stoicism is merely the notion, and is the actual experience of what freedom of thought is; it is in itself and essentially the negative, and must so exhibit itself . . . [In Skepticism] thought becomes thinking which wholly annihilates the being of the world with its manifold determinateness, and the negativity of free self-consciousness becomes aware of attaining . . . real negativity." Just as Stoicism found its expression and "freedom" in activity, so Skepticism finds it in "the negative attitude towards otherness, to desire and labour." The Underground Man identifies himself with those who, facing the "wall" ("reality" or "otherness"), "think and consequently do nothing." He correctly diagnoses his malady as ennui, as "the legitimate fruit of consciousness," an "inertia, that is, conscious sitting with-the-hands-folded," in fact a kind of "Oblomovism."[11] Through *activity* the stoic creates a free consciousness in the act of volition itself; the skeptic, on the other hand, finds acute self-consciousness the path towards another form of "freedom," a freedom that so separates, divides, and negates that Hegel himself recognized it as an illness leading eventually to the "unhappy consciousness." The very certitude (*Gewissheit*) of its own "freedom" negates the reality of all otherness: "the objective as such [is made] to disappear before the negations of Scepticism"; and an isolated self-consciousness finds itself severed, and frightfully alone. It is pure paradox in Hegel's view: the skeptic's conviction of his "freedom" makes him a stable figure in the midst of flux; yet that very stability becomes, in turn, the self-absorption that *excludes* the self from intercourse with flux, with life. (Whatever his hostilities towards Hegel, Kierkegaard was obviously much influenced by this reasoning.)

The Underground Man's self-diagnosis, "overacute consciousness," permits him to exempt himself, rather cleverly, from any moral obligations, since inertia keeps him from both commitment and action: "as the result of acute consciousness . . . one is not to blame for being a scoundrel." Indeed, he argues, the overly conscious man tends to think himself inferior, not superior, to ordinary men—like a "mouse" whose diminutive self-image engenders spite, visions of revenge, as well as romantic daydreams. Meanwhile one remains cut off, more and more a cornered "mouse," a self-consciousness with its inevitable inertia, saved only by *pain* (and the consciousness of it) which remains the sole source of reality to which the self can respond.

According to Hegel the "sceptical self-consciousness" is in constant self-contradiction: it "announces the nullity" of the senses but indulges in them; it "proclaims the nothingness of essential ethical principles, and [yet] makes those very truths the sinews of its own conduct"—as when, in Part II, the Underground Man as a youth visits the prostitute Liza. He pours out his Schillerism one day only to withdraw it, cruelly, the next, in the process contradicting all his original good motives. The "deeds" and "words" of such a self-consciousness "belie each other continually," Hegel says. With particular appropriateness for Dostoevsky's hero, he speaks of such a self-consciousness as a "doubled contradictory consciousness" which "keeps asunder the poles of this contradiction within itself" in a continuing series of episodes that string together "its purely negative process in general." The consciousness of its own "contradiction within itself" leads to the painful awareness of "being the double consciousness of itself . . . utterly self-confounding, self-perverting . . . , the consciousness of this contradiction within itself." What a better way to describe the psyche of the Underground Man? Like a child, says Hegel, such a consciousness is inevitably contradictory: if it sees A it will argue B, and vice versa. Why does such contradiction manifest itself especially and so intensely in the "sceptical consciousness"? "In Scepticism [such contradiction] realizes itself, negates the other side of determinate existence [hence its "freedom"], but, in so doing, really doubles itself, and is itself now a duality. In this way the duplication . . . is concentrated into one. Thus we have here that dualizing of self-consciousness within itself, which lies essentially in the notion of mind; but the unity of the two elements is not yet present. Hence the *Unhappy Consciousness*, the Alienated Soul* which is the consciousness of self as a divided nature, a doubled and merely contradictory being."

Is Dostoevsky's Underground Man a rendering of an Hegelian type of "unhappy consciousness"? He is certainly "divided and at variance with [himself] "; he explicitly reflects "the gazing of one self-consciousness into another," seeking somehow to "liberate itself from itself"—to break out of the deadlock of facing itself with an attendant isolation and severance from the world that certainly contribute to his unhappiness. After a particularly vicious attack on "systems" and an outcry for "independent choice," for freedom, the Underground Man stops short: "And choice, of course, the devil only knows what choice." Not even the Devil may know; he will be of no help to Ivan Karamzov. "Freedom" is desirable, even desired; yet once gained it brings not happiness but the contrary. "I confess I was rather frightened," the voice from the underground says, and he even doubts that there is such a thing as "freedom." Here he acts out Hegel's warning that the "unhappy

---

*"Alienated Soul" is not Hegel's phrase. The translator, obviously not content with "Unhappy Consciousness," adds the phrase to further explain Hegel's idea. In that he succeeds, and the phrase has a happy modern ring; but, to keep the record straight, Hegel did not use it.

consciousness," once *self-conscious* of its unhappiness, becomes immobilized; in bondage to its own so-called "freedom" it consumes it in the process of realizing it.

No; Dostoevsky must admit, with Hegel, that what precedes suffering is consciousness, nothing else: from it alone emanates all pain. So, too, Hegel maintained that "Consciousness of life . . . is merely pain and sorrow," a discovery "of its own nothingness." Any attempt of the single consciousness to transcend towards an immutable state is doomed: the particular consciousness merely reappears in the immutable consciousness. As in Schopenhauer, a particular will's transcendence through, say, suicide is useless. (For Hegel salvation lies in what he will call "Reason," a transcendence that universalizes self-consciousness by a series of further complex stages, discussion of which lies beyond our scope.) Certainly the Underground Man is a despairing man, but he never contemplates suicide nor sees death as a resolution to his paradoxical existence. For him (as for Dostoevsky) any resolution lies in keeping the process, the dialectic, alive. Although in the later novels Dostoevsky's "resolution" may lie in visions of a new Christianity, in the *Notes,* as we have them, it is still the ceaseless process of contradiction that sustains the hero, aimless in itself but therapeutic in its activity of exposing inertia—which of course is yet another paradox.

Mochulsky cites a notebook entry which Dostoevsky made on April 16, 1864: "On earth the law of personality binds us; the I stands in the way . . . After Christ's appearance, it became clear that the highest development of personality must attain to that point where man annihilates his own 'I,' surrenders it completely to all and everyone without division or reserve . . . And so, on earth man strives toward an ideal contrary to his nature."[13] When man fails to shed his "I" he is in a state of unavoidable "sin." How much of this conflict reflects Dostoevsky's version of the Russian East-West duality is not certain, but the issue is clear enough— man's egotism is not only conceded, it is postulated as inevitable. Nevertheless, like the Underground Man himself, man has a "beautiful soul"—which Hegel called "evil" because it negated life and which Dostoevsky makes the central metaphor of struggle throughout the *Notes.*

Schiller's influence in Russia was also considerable and it has recently been traced. Like that of his predecessors, Dostoevsky's Schillerism was largely centered on the conception of "the beautiful soul," a concept of Romanticism that Hegel, himself influenced by Schiller, singled out for attack in *The Phenomenology*. [14] By 1864, the date of the *Notes,* Dostoevsky's fiction was beginning to show signs of disenchantment with all forms of Schillerism although, like the Underground Man, he never fully rejected the "good and the beautiful" as potentially human *expressions* (despite the reign of the "I") of self. Still, most biographers and critics agree that Dostoevsky's attitudes towards Schillerism became critical after the events of penal servitude; although it is clear that he remained ambivalent, his receptivity to Hegel's indictment (if not his alternatives) appears likely.

All of Hegel depends on movement, whether we call it "dialectics" or by some other name. The spirit, individual and universal, is forever involved in a *process*; and such process always involves commitment towards realization, either of self or of an objective world made to correspond with the subjective perceiver. The Hegelian man moves forward, outward, inward, upward—but he *moves*. "The beautiful soul" is its antithesis: its "beauty" lies in declining any action, it lies in spiritual monasticism, in renunciation. Since, according to Hegel, "duty" can only fulfill itself in action—"moral action as action"—"the beautiful soul" which abjures all action cannot be moral. Indeed "the beautiful soul" becomes "evil" as it adopts inertia, thus sinking into self-absorption, self-indulgent abnegation. Withdrawn and static, "the beautiful soul" defines its evil by noncommitment: it is the epitome of the egotistical consciousness.

For Hegel conscience, consciousness, duty are all vacuums to be filled with actions. Conscience is also self-determining and will admit "no content as absolute for it, because it is absolute negativity of all that is definite." What this means for the Underground Man is that he can attain certitude only when he ceases to interpret his actions and attains not mere self-consciousness but "certainty of self" which alone can provide "the pure, direct, and immediate truth." Hence *mere* consciousness is only egotism, self-absorption, negativity, denial. To translate consciousness into duty it must first know "itself what duty is"—duty is action.

Much conjecture has enveloped Faust's famous outcry that two souls tear him apart; one wonders whether one of those souls—the soul that violently surges upward from the earth-bound—was not originally "*die schöne Seele*" that was neither earth- nor heaven-bound but bound (in Hegelian terms) for nowhere. Once loosened from inertia, Faust's greatest danger in fulfilling his end of the bargain with Mephisto, the soul now chooses transcendence. In any event, the Underground Man's soul is not yet arrived at that point; it is imprisoned in its chamber, space-bound and time-bound, condemned to self-contradiction. Now might such a soul once more attain "beauty" and yet act? Is this not Dostoevsky's major question in the *Notes*? I doubt that he accepted Hegel's version of "the beautiful soul" (if indeed he knew it in detail), for it denies that such "beauty" and action can ever meet. Hegel's attack is a terrible case of vengeance—against Kant, Schiller, Goethe, against enemies and teachers alike. A soul like the Underground Man's, Hegel would argue, is the result of "self-willed impotence to renounce a self which is pared away to the last point of abstraction." Like Schiller's "sentimental" poet, this soul's activity "consists of yearning" with a "feeling of emptiness," actionless, dead, merely reflective. One of the Underground Man's reasons for going underground is to "exercise" himself in "reflection." Set side by side, his analysis of his condition and Hegel's demolishing paragraph on "the beautiful soul" offer an astonishing relationship. First the Underground Man: "To begin to act, you know, you must first have your mind completely at ease and no trace of doubt left in it. Why, how am I, for example, to set my mind at rest? Where are the primary causes on which I am to build? Where are my foundations? Where am I to get them from? I exercise myself in reflection, and consequently with me every primary cause at once draws after itself another still more primary, and so on to infinity." In this instance infinity is the same as staying where you are, a mere metaphor for describing inaction. "I have," he says candidly, "been able neither to begin nor to finish anything."

Here is Hegel's indictment of "the beautiful soul": "The 'beautiful soul' . . . has no concrete reality; it subsists in the contradiction between its pure self and the necessity felt by this self to externalize itself and turn into something actual . . . Conscious of this contradiction . . . [it] is unhinged, disordered, and runs to madness, wastes itself in yearning, and pines away in consumption. Thereby it gives up . . . its stubborn insistence on its own isolated self-existence, but only to bring forth the soulless, spiritless unity of abstract being."

The harshness of this attack is surprising only in that it comes so early in the century (1807), for later, when "the beautiful soul" had made its transmigrations from solitude to lassitude, from asceticism to unwholesome aestheticism, from good intentions to high brutality,[15] Hegel's view becomes almost commonplace. Even on conscience the Hegelian position is stricter than Kant's: as a supreme and absolute entity, conscience can gain its meaning only through actions. Severed from vitality, it too becomes a lifeless and inert force, negative and contradictory to human inclinations. As a result men find ways of continually evading life and absolving themselves from moral acts, duty, obligation. It is the picture of an utterly egotistical being because it literally has no referents outside the intellectual ego.

Hegel goes even further; he calls this kind of consciousness (that is, "the beautiful soul") "evil" and hypocritical, particularly when judged by the "universal consciousness." However, even this "universal consciousness," in its early stages of development, in judging rather than acting, ends up in the same state of hypocrisy on which it set out to pass judgment.

So caught up, like the Underground Man, the individual is unable to make any compact with society: he remains isolated. Eventually Hegel foresees forgiveness for the "evil consciousness" through a transcendence about which Hegel theorized but which Dostoevsky actually hoped to achieve in the great novels that followed the *Notes*: "God appearing in the midst of those who know themselves in the form of pure knowledge," or absolute spirit. The Underground Man certainly never even approaches the condition which these words of Hegel imply; his existence remains that of a divided, tortured "beautiful soul," which is quite genuine, I think, as is his self-punishment that sabotages every "good" intention with an evil counter-thrust. Far more subtle than Poe's "perversity" (resembling more E. T. A. Hoffmann and Baudelaire), Dostoevsky's fictionalized condition in the *Notes* is, indeed, to remind ourselves of Frank's essay, an account of "idealism" and its fate. But the one additional step the *Notes* take is to incorporate something like the Hegelian view of conscience, self-consciousness, and "the beautiful soul" into its hero's dilemma. In all fairness, the Underground Man is never shown to be a Schillerian or Goethean exemplum of Pietism; but he is endowed with all the equipment of that acute consciousness which, by evading moral action, becomes egotism. "Well, anyway," says the Underground Man, "I know that I am a blackguard, a scoundrel, an egoist, a sluggard"; "They won't let me . . . I can't be good!" he cries out. "No, I was such an egoist, I was so lacking in respect for my fellow-creatures"; the gentlemen protests too much, but the protest is, paradoxically speaking, the only "truth" he has left. In the Underground Man Pietism has become brooding; selflessness—as Nietzsche was to scream—has become the worst kind of selfishness; the "beautiful" and the "good" have become negated and turned "evil." Like "the beautiful soul," the Underground Man ends up doing nothing, consuming the world to sustain himself, giving back to it nothing—not to Liza, not to the Universal Spirit, not to God, not even (to complete the paradox) to himself. He is the yearning "beautiful soul" turned into the "unhappy consciousness," the new spirit of negation whose fragile "freedom" consists primarily in the ability as well as the desire to deny it.

A contemporary of Dostoevsky who would have understood the *Notes* better than most was Baudelaire, who died three years after their publication. Baudelaire's understanding would be in part attributable to the underground life he lived. Even the most factual accounts of that life, and certainly the *Journal Intime* and the letters, confirm the picture of a haunted—one is tempted to say hunted—man. Complaining in a letter to his mother as late as 1860 about his "*conseil judiciaire,*" the humilation of a legal guardian appointed to apportion the one-time dandy small sums of money, Baudelaire betrays a central and tortured affliction of his life.[16] For that *conseil judiciaire* had its counterpart as a kind of judicial presence which Baudeliare invited by exercising his *"mal,"* just as he had earlier invited the imposition of the real legal guardian by acting the role of the injudicious profligate long after the pleasure of being a rake was expended. It appears Baudelaire had need—like the Underground Man—of self-revulsion and self-humiliation; he certainly worked hard at maintaining such feelings.

And despite the notorious record of his peripatetic existence in Paris, he conveys the distinct impression of a stationary creature, "frozen" as he says, by way of metaphor in "L'Irrémédiable," like a ship locked in polar ice. His was the voice out of hell ("De Profundis Clamavi") crying in the concluding line of that poem: *"La conscience dans la Mal!"* That consciousness of the act of evil was nevertheless pervaded by a brooding sense of guilt and remorse, emotions in which Baudelaire indulged incessantly because he created the freedom of *pur ennui,* a state of spatial and temporal scaling of dimensions remarkably suited for such purposes.

Jean-Paul Sartre's interpretation of Baudelaire (in some respects arguable) urges this case convincingly: the approach is single-minded but has the advantage of focus. Baudelaire, Sartre feels, quite accidentally really, stumbled upon the solitary nature of a consciousness which, though seemingly endless, was finite and collective, "at one and the same time *the* general consciousness and *his* consciousness."[17] Freedom, and the freedom of consciousness, Sartre insists, only served to make manifest for Baudelaire the "gratuitousness" of itself: "The great freedom which creates values emerges in the void and [Baudelaire] was frightened of it" (42, 51). Moreover, of Baudelaire's poems (which he rarely discusses in detail) Sartre writes that they are merely "substitutes for the creation of Good which he has renounced. They reveal the gratuitousness of conscience " (70). We may certainly object that this is an oversimplification, but it is of a kind that tends to make the point accurately if too vividly. Sartre's statement is not glib; if it overlooks Baudelaire's greatness as a poet, it amply compensates by revealing the state of mind that lies behind it.

"L'Irrémédiable" (first published in 1857) is a mature and characteristic poem. It is certainly more than a substitution for renounced good, but it is an admirable illustration of what Sartre calls the "gratuitousness of conscience," a poem which clearly enacts Baudelaire's experience of consciousness as a moral datum to its logical dénouement: moral stasis and a sudden awareness of its aridity and its mortal threat on the borders of the abyss itself— *"Au bord d'un gouffre . . ."*

What is irremediable is the poet's "fortune," his fate: the devil has imprisoned the poet's soul like some "perfect tableau." The ensuing dialogue of a heart with its mirror-image is predicated on the guilty recognition by Baudelaire of what Poe called the "imp of the perverse," the very knowledge of perversity creating, Baudelaire says with irony, a "unique" solace and glory. For the poet sees himself in many guises; one, like that of the Underground Man, is as an angel tempted by the love of deformity itself (*Qu'a tenté l'amour du difforme*) who then takes the ultimate delight in the final *"conscience dans la Mal!"*, the awareness of process and involvement in evil and perversity. Of course, Dostoevsky's hero goes far beyond Baudelaire, but both begin with the experience of the sensation rewarding the perverse desire of fouling one's own nest. The Underground Man's rationale is more advanced and far more scrupulously analyzed than Baudelaire's, whose defense of his own perversity rests the case merely by presenting it, by confessing it, for Dostoevsky merely a starting point.

Sartre is surely correct, if the poems, journals, and letters are authoritative evidence, when he describes Baudelaire as possessed of an ubiquitous sense of guilt and a bad conscience. In his letters, particularly in those addressed to his mother, we find repeated statements of involved and tortured feelings of guilt—guilt for dereliction of duty, guilt for having committed something or omitted something. He feels remorse for not having written or for feeling ill; he feels remorse or guilt and reproaches himself with obvious regularity, as if he were taking a prescribed dosage of medicine. Although he tells us that the furor over *Les Fleurs du Mal* has made him proud of having written a work which expresses the horror of evil, and that he feels no guilt at all—*"et je ne me sens pas du tout coupable"*—[18] he clearly felt constantly hovering over-head the avenging furies, whether he fashioned them or not. In one letter to Mme Aupick he confesses that he and she have ruined each other's lives; that neither can live without the other; that suicide is clearly the only way for *him* should she precede him in death. And if she should die he would feel a horrible sensation of absolute isolation—*"l'horrible sensation d'un isolement absolu."* True to his nature he predicates that fate, which was certainly a sincere projection, by saying that it is perfectly clear that his mother cannot live without him, that indeed he is the only reason for her existence: *"Après ma mort, tu ne vivras plus, c'est clair. Je suis le seul objet qui te fasse vivre."*[19] This combination of self-indulgence, of egotism, and horror of isolation is what Dostoevsky perfects in the Underground Man's psyche. Baudelaire wrote of what it might be like: *"l'horrible sensation d'un isolement absolu"*; Dostoevsky described it all.

Whether such a self-lacerating state of mind and soul was, as Sartre writes, fueled only "to pay tribute to Good" (82) is open to dispute, but its existence is everywhere manifest. Curiously the word Baudelaire preferred to express his feelings in the poetry was neither conscience nor guilt but *remords*—remorse. Remorse is a general term describing a feeling of regret for an act committed (or omitted), a word defining a condition somewhere between the far more abstract "guilt" and the bad conscience usually particular-izing a very specific act. My point is to approximate what Baud-elaire meant to tell us when he used the word *"remords,"* which occurs frequently in the poetry.

In the sonnet "Duellum" the conceit is that of two warriors in mortal combat, each representing the battle of life—lost youth, lost love, lost life. No one warrior wins; no one loses. Together they roll into the abyss, *"Ce gouffre, c'est l'enfer,"* where they are reunited with the friends that preceded them. Baudelaire has de-scribed this duel with such intensity, bestial imagery underlying the essential sexuality of the struggle, that he prepares with an adequacy almost sufficient for the final lines,

> *Roulons-y sans remords, amazone inhumaine*
> *Afin d'éterniser l'ardeur de notre haine!*

It is an invitation to continue the duel even in Hell, having now rendered the warriors inhuman, without remorse, in order to eternalize their passion turned to hate, love metamorphosed into its opposite. Baudelaire was always careful to establish this kind of transformation, as process; without remorse—"*sans remords*"— becomes acceptable *only* when the wrestling warriors, once in Hell, are on the verge of being "*inhumaine.*" After all as humans they would still have been incapable of acting without remorse.

"L'Irréparable" is the clearest expression of Baudelaire's poetic treatment of remorse as a personified quality with which he held close and sinister dialogues. The poem opens with a conventional analogy: remorse eats away at us like worms eating at corpses. Can we rid ourselves of remorse—"*l'implacable Remords?*" What stimulant is sufficiently strong to make men feel remorseless? he asks the beautiful sorceress, for he needs supranatural help. He sees himself a haunted man, dying and stalked by wolves and vultures ready for the kill and the devouring. The poem's dominant mode is interrogative; the questions are rhetorical. No, one cannot make a blackened sky light again because—as he answers—the light of Hope has been darkened by the Devil himself. Does the sorceress really know the true nature of Remorse, poised with deadly arrows aimed at the heart? Again, as in the irremediable fate of "L'Irrémédiable," a fatalism pervades. The irreparable sinks its teeth into our souls; it attacks the edifice at its very foundation. On the stage, the poet recalls having seen as a child some magic fairy clad in gold and gauze who purified evil, the *deus ex machina* of the innocent imagination. But the poet's heart is an abandoned stage; no gold and gauze fairy will come here. Waiting for redemption is in vain:

> *Mais mon coeur, que jamais ne visite l'extase,*
> *Est un théâtre où l'on attend*
> *Toujours, toujours en vain, l'Être aux ailes de gaze!*

I think one feels the impersonality of the poem (there was a time when such poetry was called insincere), the method of personifying remorse being used to define not so much the poet's immediate state of mind and soul but rather the condition of hopelessness as it defines and is defined by the ubiquitousness of remorse. What Baudelaire experiences is the sensation of remorse in a state of irreparableness rather than, say, the sensation of irreparableness which becomes a sufficient cause for remorse. The difference is not insignificant. Either we view man as hopeless awaiting the import of an awakening remorse, or we see him as filled with remorse awaiting the burden of hopelessness. In the latter condition, which Baudelaire most often chose to describe, the state of remorse is far more the consequence than the genesis of despair. This confirms Sartre's insistence that Baudelaire's remorse was a deliberate and ongoing creation: "He chose to have a conscience which was always tormented"(82). In the first quatrain of "Au Lecteur," the introductory poem to *Les Fleurs du Mal,* Baudelaire admits that as beggars sustain their lice so men feed their remorse (*"Et nous alimentons nos aimables remords, / Comme les mendiants nourrissent leur vermine"*).

Man, then, nourishes his remorse, creates conditions (such as despair) that make for the fertile soil in which remorse can flourish. In return he is able to maintain bitterness, hopelessness, even ironic detachment, and able to do so irremediably, irreparably, with a clear conscience that reverts to remorse as a residual evidence of suffering. This is precisely what the Underground Man perfects, self-consciously, so that at the end he uses his residual remorse far more devastatingly, and more subtly, then Baudelaire, permitting it to make him "free" to suffer in perpetuity without ever having to pay the price of redemption. Without such a preservation of *remords* Baudelaire's lament would appear almost sophomoric, and the Underground Man would truly sound like a man with an ailing liver. But like Hegel Baudelaire rejected the passivity of the beautiful soul and saw in its inertia a form of evil and hence desired always to defile "good." Ennui became a source of limitless energy for the *mal,* the perverse inversion of ascetic comtemplation through which the eremite attains not peace, only survival.

Peer Gynt: **Consciousness and Affirmative Egotism**

Three years after the publication of Dostoevsky's *Notes,* a Norwegian dramatist trying to make a name for himself settled in Italy and wrote what one may call the "comic" counterpart of those disturbing *Notes* from the East. Ibsen's *Peer Gynt,* like his *Brand* a year earlier, is also concerned with the egotism of consciousness (though *Brand* was more concerned with egotism of conscience, the other side of the problem). For those who think of Peer as a loveable Everyman, a caricature of Romanticism, or a parody of Faust, the connection with Dostoevsky's Underground Man will not sit well. But there are those who have seen in Peer more than a clown, an outrageously funny liar, who somehow misses what he really didn't want in the first place—hearth and home. Not that such a view is wrong; it simply does not go far enough. Peer is in fact all the things I have listed, but he is also Ibsen's most successful portrait of the egotist whose service to self—an *amour-propre* of gigantic proportions—makes him an heroic and tragic figure.
Peer's declaration of self is rightly regarded as one of the clues to the meaning of the play, and it occurs very early, in Act II, when Peer is about to join the Trolls, give up his humanness, and thereby also his self. Ibsen's genius here succeeds in having us cheer on our hero's decision not to surrender his human eyesight, symbol of reality, to retain his vision which allows distinctions between reality and fantasy, despite the fact that his decision is based on outspokenly selfish grounds. After all, he is "one of us"; and in retaining his humanness over Trolldom, he holds on to humanity, which though not implying "goodness" at least bares its frailty to which we are heir, and in Peer's case that is quite a bit. The Old Man of the Mountains is justifiably upset at humans:

> You human beings are always the same.
> You're always ready to admit an impulse,
> But won't accept the guilt for anything
> Unless you've actually done it in the flesh.[20]

Perhaps to this point Peer was willing enough: he had accepted a beast's tail, discarded his breeks, sworn that a cow is a beautiful girl. But when they want to take away forever his ability to be a conscious human being by slitting his eyes, he backs off, in spite of the reassuring and perfectly candid words of the Old Man: "Don't forget that sight is the source/Of the bitter and searing lye of tears" (Act II).[21] Whatever we call it, the Western preoccupation with consciousness as a virtue, the desperate holding on to individuality in the face of the dread and suffering it brings—Peer has it too. Like Keats he chooses to preserve his human senses to remain a man, to refuse to become a nightingale so as to return another day, *as a man,* to bathe in the pleasure that would otherwise be denied him. Presumably nightingales do not admire other nightingales—not in the manner men do, in any case. It is important to remember that Peer's decision comes after having heard— and in effect having accepted—the Troll code of life, an *amour-propre* even more total than man's:

> Out there, under the shining vault of heaven,
> Men tell each other: "Man, be thyself!"
> But in here, among us trolls, we say:
> "Troll, be thyself—*and thyself alone!*" (Act II)

"Thyself alone!" This phrase pursues Peer all his life (as he pursues its elusive meaning), though he seems never to recall where he first heard it:

> Being himself, and himself alone—!
> Himself and himself alone! Who said that? (Act IV)

Towards the end of his globe-trotting adventures, Peer begins to remember better what lies behind. Alternating between hectoring about his achievements and lamentably questioning his life, Peer reaches his inevitable encounter with finality: "I have always tried to be myself," he says, "modestly"; and actually he is being perfectly honest. But the "self" he has tried to be has no meaning, and despite Ibsen's caricature of German Idealism in the character of Begriffenfeldt (literally "field of concepts") Peer himself begins to voice a nihilistic conclusion:

> Now I have fathomed the riddle of my destiny . . .
> And know that I am myself, Peer Gynt, . . .
> I shall hold the whole of my past in my hands.
> I'll never more tread in the paths of the living.
> The present is worthless. Man has no faith nor courage.
> His soul is earthbound, his actions meaningless. (Act IV)

This Faustian despair comes towards the end of the play, not, as in *Faust,* at the start, and the difference should be noted. For Ibsen's Peer is indeed "earthbound"; his "energy"—in Blakean terms—is spent on pretense. He never succeeds in extending his "self" into the flux of life; he makes no contact with reality. So, for all his seemingly endless activity, those Faustian travels through the world, he has little to show in the end. Indeed Peer has suffered from inertia; his actions have gone nowhere. When, briefly, he is made "Emperor," he tells one of the cabinet ministers, "I'm a blank sheet of paper that no one will write on." (Act V)

Begriffenfeldt describes the condition of perfect selfhood as

> Each one shuts himself in the cask of self,
> Sinks to the bottom by self-fermentation,
> Seals himself in with the bung of self,
> And seasons in the well of self.
> No one here weeps for the woes of others.
> No one here listens to anyone else's ideas.
> We are ourselves, in thought and in deed,
> Ourselves to the very limit of life's springboard.
> So, if we are to have an Emperor,
> It's obvious that you [Peer] are just the man. (Act IV)

As Act IV concludes, Peer Gynt is crowned "Emperor of Self" in the deserts of Morocco or, as Ibsen might say, nowhere. Peer's cherished "freedom," for which he abandoned home, woman, everything, is now bound to the very self which so fervently strove for "freedom." Having come full circle, the freedom of the self now bites its own tail.

Bitter and disappointed, Peer turns towards home; wrecked at sea, he claims his life over another on the grounds of being as yet childless. But homecoming, even at such a price, presents him with only more bitter insights. The man who chose to live a narrow life and stay to till his land has at least produced something, but Peer—true to his self—is mummified:

> Forward or back, it's equally far.
> Outside or in, I'm still confined. (Act V)

Like the onion which he symbolically peels recounting what he has been, Peer discovers he is merely a series of layers with no heart. Like Faust, Peer is visited by spirits just before the play ends, and among them are the "deeds [he] left undone" (Act V). Ibsen is not ambiguous about his hero: he has been nothing, he has done nothing. To be a self in Peer's conception is no better than being a passive Hegelian "beautiful soul." Fate will bring Peer to the casting-ladle, and he is stunned to learn from the Button-Moulder that he has not *done* enough, "By the highest standards," to be considered a sinner. To be melted down! To be cast into the general "rubbish bin," the "great pool" (Act V), that is a hard fate for the Emperor of Self:

> To be melted, and to be Peer Gynt no more—
> It fills my soul with revulsion. (Act V)

The Button-Moulder tells Peer that he has never really been himself, that he is "waste," but Peer cannot comprehend that:

> I renounced my chances of love and power and glory
> Simply so that I could remain myself. (Act V)

But when, in the final moments of the play, The Old Man accuses Peer of having lived like a troll, Peer denies that too:

> ... A troll! An egoist!
> It's all absolute nonsense. I'm sure of it. (Act V)

But the Button-Moulder keeps in pursuit: "One question," asks Peer, "What does it mean: 'To be oneself'?" The answer is sharp:

> To be oneself is: to kill oneself.

Peer's version of selfhood is for Ibsen the same self-consuming and suicidal life as that Dostoevsky's Underground Man pursued by sitting holed up doing nothing. The Thin Person, one of the several symbolic figures whom Peer encounters at the end, gives the final explanation:

> There are two ways in which a man can be himself.
> A right way and a wrong way.
>   . . . Either one can produce
> A direct picture, or else what they call a negative.
> In the latter, light and dark are reversed;
> And the result, to the ordinary eye, is ugly.
> But the image of the original is there.
> All that's required is to develop it.
> Now if a human soul, in the course of its life,
> Has created one of those negative portraits,
> The plate is not destroyed. They send it to me.
>   . . . I develop it . . .
> Till the picture appears which the plate was intended to give.
> I mean, the one known as the positive.
> But when a soul like you has smudged himself out,
> Even sulphur and potash can achieve nothing. (Act V)

The "right way" to be oneself is to create the "positive" at once; but even the "negative" may be "developed," if it is not entirely ruined. Peer's negative—like the Underground Man's—is beyond "development." Ibsen's metaphor from the recently discovered principle of photography is a daring and accurate choice. When, finally, Peer confronts Solveig, the woman he gave up to be himself, and asks,

> Where was my self, my whole self, my true self?

she answers, perhaps a little too allegorically,

> In my faith, in my hope, and in my love. (Act V)

I do not think she (or Ibsen) means that one's true self is embodied in someone else's faith, hope, or love. Rather, Solveig seems to be saying that one's true self can be fulfilled only by sharing it, by extending it, by acting out what it is with another. Since it is clear that Peer has failed to do that, his self lies rather abstractly in Solveig's visions of what he *should* have been, not in what he was. And that is another way of saying what Peer himself says:

> . . . let the snow pile over me
> And let them write above: "Here lies no one."
>
> .   .   .   .   .
>
> I was a dead man long before I died! (Act V)

So even preservation of consciousness gives Peer nothing better than the tears the Old Troll had predicted. Yet had Peer a second chance, he would, one is quite certain, once again choose consciousness. The question Ibsen, like Dostoevsky, raises is not concerned with the attendant pain of consciousness (which both concede) but with the way in which a conscious self confronts the world outside itself—beyond, that is, the consciousness of the self's "freedom." By itself such "freedom" is only egotism, whether through inaction and inertia (the Underground Man) or action and aimlessness (Peer Gynt).

V. Consciousness and Will:
Poe and Mann

What *we should desire to do, the conscience alone will inform us; but*
how *and* when *we are to make the attempt, and to what extent it is in*
our power to accomplish it, are questions for the judgment.

—Coleridge

Despite the fact that Thomas Mann knew Poe very early, Poe and
Mann do not immediately seem either sufficiently congruous or
dissimilar for an instructive comparison. Leaving aside their relative literary merit, Poe—despite certain pretensions of having resolved his thoughts into a Philosophic System—seems remote
from the intellectual Mann, writer of myths and parables, symbol-
ist of the *Zeitgeist,* panoramic novelist. Yet Poe and Mann have a
great deal in common, not least of which is their enormous analytical concern with death, its relation to beauty, and the consciousness of a self continually experimenting with the mechanism of
motive and deed, deed and consequence. It is true that Mann,
especially in such a parabolic novel as *Doktor Faustus,* unveils the
entire allegory of conscience in the broadest context, cultural and
historical, while Poe seems riveted to a far more limited conception of conscience, interested primarily in plotting the graph of its
process. But both Poe and Mann were avid students of man's
nervous system and both devoted their artistic intelligence to re-
cording with extremely refined equipment the responses of the
particularly sensitive psyche to traumatizing experience. Both also
recorded the battle between individual will and cosmic will, and
although their conclusions differed their scenario was often similar. So Thomas Buddenbrook and Roderick Usher, Tonio Kröger
and the Man of the Crowd, Gustav von Aschenbach and any com-
posite Poe hero would no doubt understand one another. Health

117

and disease, the artist and the criminal, the horror of consciousness and the retribution of conscience, the chill of nerves caught
suddenly in the experience of assault or of being assaulted—all
these served both writers. Mann may be plotted, so to speak, on a
continuing line from E. T. A. Hoffmann and Poe—grotesquerie and
black humor, irony and philosophic quest, the anatomy of the
mind and the representation of process, particularly the process of
dissolution, of annihilation.[1]

Though the comparison holds for the works of both writers in
many incidentals, I will concentrate here on some of Poe's well-
known stories ("The Fall of the House of Usher," "Ligeia,"
"William Wilson," "The Pit and the Pendulum"), and Mann's *Buddenbrooks*. Pervading these stories and Mann's novel, in addition
to the theme of love-death-beauty, is a theme which E. H. Davidson, a Poe scholar, has himself linked to Mann (as well as to other
modern writers), a theme growing out of the "autobiographical
narrative of the accumulating richness of consciousness on the part
of a growing mind": *Pym, David Copperfield, Swann's Way, Buddenbrooks,* and *A Portrait of the Artist as a Young Man.* Davidson sees Poe "in some respects . . . the formulator of the
theme: . . . the chronicle of the consciousness of a hypersensitive
youth."[2] I would, however, insert a caveat: seeing Poe as a modern
psychologist primarily interested in *individual motivation* may be
a mistake. R. M. Adams recently cautioned (correctly, I think)
that "in the end we wrong Poe in taking him as a psychological
writer, for he is largely unconcerned with ruminative introspection, the careful analysis of his own or anyone's inner life."[3] In
short, Poe's preoccupation with conscience and consciousness is
not centered on any desire to explore the intricacies of an individual character; he seems rather more fascinated by general laws of
behavior from which, indeed, character must be purged for the
sake of process. Hence Roderick Usher, Ligeia, or the unnamed
protagonist of "The Pit and the Pendulum" are in themselves
hardly memorable people—no Stephen Dedalus, Swann, or Thomas
Buddenbrook, but humanized metaphors of the process. This
difference must be kept in mind, though it in no way precludes the ensuing comparisons; in fact the difference may in the

end help us to define something rather important in the evolution of certain particulars in the general development of the theme.

Will: The Struggle

At times, Poe measured the subtleties of the mind's processes better than anyone of his age, but he was not a subtle writer; his tales usually had a moral and he told it straight, which is why it makes him so eminently readable and also such an easy target of higher criticism. But Poe has recently been better treated, even overpraised, as happens whenever corrective trends get going.[4] Probably the truth remains between the extreme of seeing him as a theatrical hack, a popularizer for magazine and newspaper journalism, or a deep, philosophic mind, a genius to be placed side by side with Dostoevsky or Baudelaire. Although Poe's talents were special, within these limitations he could be a master. What he particularly mastered was the analysis of *process* and the analysis of motivation—or, at times, the lack of it, "analysing the imponderable forms of the nerves," as a sympathetic Arthur Symons wrote.[5] In these respects he created at least half a dozen masterpieces which contributed to a better understanding of human psychology. That Poe was obsessed with the nature of will, conscience, and consciousness is demonstrable in the best—and the best-known—of his work: "The Fall of the House of Usher," "William Wilson," "The Pit and the Pendulum," "The Tell-Tale Heart," "The Man of the Crowd," "Ligeia," *Pym.* The philosophic system of *Eureka,* as has been shown, underlies many of these tales but, as with, say, Yeats's *A Vision,* the art can be read without obligatory parallels to the intricacies of the philosophy. A story such as "Ligeia" is quite comprehensible even if independent of a philosophic system because it illustrates in fairly straightforward prose and action an instance of the difficulty of will, as the epigraph, purportedly from Joseph Glanvill, states: "And the will therein lieth, which dieth not. Who knoweth the mysteries of the will, with its vigor? For God is but a great will pervading all things by nature of its intentness. Man doth not yield himself to the angels, nor unto death utterly, save only through the weakness of his feeble will."[6]

So far as I know no one has been able to discover this passage in Glanvill (the same is true of some other Poe epigraphs); it is entirely possible that Poe wrote it himself. In any case the epigraph fits perfectly the thesis of the tale which, admittedly reductive, may be phrased as follows: will begets wish; wish begets dream (hallucination); dream begets consciousness; consciousness begets conscience. There is no contradiction in dream (or hallucination) begetting consciousness, for Poe's description of dreams, often resembling those of De Quincey (whose work he surely knew), are primarily concerned with the process of overacute awareness, clarity in madness. Consciousness in Poe is usually *not* the controlled and manipulative awareness of what psychologists might call an "ego-constructed world," but the fall into an unconscious, in that ordinary sense of leaving the quotidian, an unconsciousness, however, which then releases the kind of consciousness that Lear experienced—reason in madness.

As are almost all of Poe's stories (even the best), "Ligeia" is marred by claptrap and melodrama. The story itself, on a surface-plot level, is a gothic chill tour de force. The interest lies in the development of the abstractions: will, consciousness, and conscience. Ligeia, that *almost* perfect Amazon with the musical voice, "marble hand," beautiful like "the radiance of an opium-dream" with large eyes—"twin stars of Leda"—is, of course, interesting mainly because she possesses what Poe quotes Bacon as having described as " 'some *strangeness* in the proportion.' " This Poe inserts, *not* to play with the grotesquerie of Romanticism but to prepare us for the strange duality of this enigmatic lady: "she, the outwardly calm, the ever-placid Ligeia, was the most violently a prey to the tumultuous vultures of stern passion . . . fierce energy . . . wild words." In the end Ligeia embodies all the vital forces which do battle as eternal combatants, especially energy and quiescence, life and death. Here, then, will enters—for it is not really Ligeia's "immense" learning but her will, her always dominant role vis-à-vis the narrator's helplessness and passivity which so terrifies the imagination. Of course Ligeia is a symbol; she is, like

Pater's Mona Lisa, a symbol of the history she but briefly animates: "All the thoughts and experience of the world have etched and molded there"; Ligeia is a kinetic archetype, not only as old as the narrator's "memory" but as young as his next hallucination when she shall be reborn through another.

That much is the metaphysical side of the story. Put into current psychological terms, Ligeia is a construct, a reincarnation of some conscious desire to will herself—first into existence, then into "death," and then once more into a resurrection. Like Lady Lisa, Ligeia is the "embodiment of the old fancy, the symbol of the modern idea." Whether the other Lady, the fair-haired Rowena, really exists or is a hallucination of the man's increasingly exacerbated opium state we cannot know. But we do know that she exists in his mind, an opposite to that which is gone: color of hair, complexion, eyes, all are the opposite of Ligeia. Again whether the death of Rowena, assuming she exists, is murder ("I saw, or may have dreamed that I saw, fall within the goblet . . . three or four large drops of a brilliant and ruby colored fluid") or wish-fulfillment is not important. Ligeia *was* will: she dominated the narrator so utterly he had to rid himself of the tyranny upon which he was, nevertheless, entirely dependent. Of course he could not succeed. And though he hated Rowena (fabricated or real), the feared Ligeia returns: she will not surrender her hold over this man until she has presumably returned, metamorphosed from Rowena's dead body, to drive him mad. Or he wills that return because he needs the very thing that destroys him—not an uncommon predicament of a neurotic. Certainly the tale is never intended to be realistically plausible; Ligeia is will, cosmic, Schopenhauerian will. Against the individual will of a man she is far too powerful. She fills but does not fulfill his consciousness; she dominates it, until that consciousness is forced to surrender itself to her. In some stories Poe concluded that man cannot murder his conscience; in "Ligeia" he showed that, if will so wished, man cannot murder consciousness either, for the two become entwined, consciousness becoming, as it were, the receptive antechamber for a will prepared to dominate it—to the death. As

Schopenhauer explained: "although the individual consciousness does not survive death, yet that survives it which alone struggles against it—the will."[7]

An obvious way to approach "William Wilson" is as it traditionally has been, through the *Doppelgänger* motif, and it has yielded much of that story's rather obvious intent. But will plays an interesting role in the development of the story, as does the discovery that William Wilson, in killing his conscience, is killing himself. Readers sometimes forget that Wilson, the narrator, is dying as he retraces the events of the past, and that he is speaking of a life which has passed *after* the final incident of the "story" itself—the murder of conscience. "From me, in an instant," he tells us, "all virtue dropped bodily as a mantle . . . Death approaches"; he is aware of seeking pity and sympathy for himself from the readers of his tale, even of asking them to judge him as a victim of fate ("I would wish them to seek out for me . . . some little oasis of *fatality* amid a wilderness of error"). His childhood he describes as a nasty affair, subject to weak parents and therefore "left to the guidance of [his] own will," becoming "the master of [his] own actions." When his namesake, his double, arrives he becomes the only one to challenge the original William Wilson's "assertions," the only one to refuse "submission to [his] will." The "other" Wilson, with his "intolerable spirit of contradiction," becomes a test for the narrator's will; and the action of the story, if such it can be called, is in the main the defeat of William Wilson's adversary—his will prevailing—but the triumph is empty, death-filled. The "frequent officious interference with [his] will" annoys William Wilson, but he readily admits, true to the classic Freudian scenario, that his double was in all respects his moral superior: "His moral sense . . . was far keener than my own"; and had he "less frequently rejected the counsels" of his double he "might, to-day, have been a better and thus a happier man."

The struggle proceeds: William Wilson's will against his conscience. When one night he appears actually to "see" his double, William Wilson flees in horror; at this point will has severed itself from conscience and the "evil" self alone begins an increasingly dissolute life. Poe's handling of the double, because it attempts to be realistic, is often clumsy, but it is clear that William Wilson's conscience pursues him to the dénouement of the story when he confronts, after all, himself because "*I fled in vain. My evil destiny pursued me as if in exultation until,*" it conquered. During the final scene, when the identically masqueraded halves of William Wilson duel, the "better" half loses. But he warns: " '*You have conquered, and I yield. Yet, henceforward art thou also dead— dead to the World, to Heaven and to Hope! In me didst thou exist—and, in my death, see by this image, which is thine own, how utterly thou hast murdered thyself.*' " Now the epigraph, this time supposedly from Chamberlayne's "Pharronida," makes sense:

> What say of it? what say [of] CONSCIENCE grim,
> That spectre in my path?

The William Wilson without conscience lives on, but it is he who is dying without really living, he whose life after the fatal encounter with his conscience has become death-in-life.

"Now and then, alas, the conscience of man takes up a burden so heavy in horror that it can be thrown down only into the grave. And thus the essence of all crime is undivulged." So Poe introduces his "Man of the Crowd," the mysterious stranger whose conscience is so burdened that he escapes into the safety of crowds to escape the horror of loneliness in isolation, self-conscious, like the shadow of Hemingway's "A Clean Well-lighted Place." What nameless crimes this man committed we never know, nor can we guess, as with Manfred. It is clearly not a *specific* crime that haunts this wretch; it is, to begin with, the crime of death and birth, as Yeats wrote, the crimes of Adam and Cain, the crime of being alive that in "The Tell-Tale Heart" Poe (unwisely perhaps) embodies in an actual metaphor, as he does also in "The Black Cat," wherein the narrator readily concedes that rationalization only partially covers human experience: "Although I thus readily accounted to my reason, if not altogether to my conscience."

The protagonist in "The Imp of the Perverse" is undone (less subtly and far more swiftly than Dostoevsky's Raskolnikov) by his desire first to commit a crime and then to confess it. Why? Because the consciousness of evil, of crime, of transgression severed from a censorious conscience is unbearable: "I well, too well, understood that to *think,* in my situation, was to be lost." Thinking leads to awareness; awareness to confession. Only in "The Cask of Amontillado" does the hero transcend humanity to live with his crime—an Iago without intellect, for even Iago knows that he can survive in silence only by almost literally immobilizing his tongue.

If the preceding tales stress the nature of will and conscience, "The Pit and the Pendulum" explores the nature of will and consciousness. The entire story is an allegory of process, the process of consciousness (and the protection of unconsciousness) and, through that consciousness, the exercise of sheer will which in this instance struggles for mere survival and in the end succeeds only by introducing the gratuitous deus ex machina of friendly troops who come just in time to save the victim from the Inquisitorial tortures. It is tempting to play with this story in terms of symbols: abyss and time, unconscious and ego, bondage and freedom; all of these abstractions have symbolic roles clearly assigned to them in the working out of the process theme. But the basic symbols of the title itself dominate: the Pit one may see as surrender of consciousness (hence the pitched battle against it) and the Pendulum may be viewed as the will or that force which mobilizes the will (for example, Time) against capitulation. Even during his first swoon the protagonist cannot say that he has lost "all of consciousness." The first pages are almost a clinical account of "lapsing into life," of birth (comparable incidentally with that fine poem by Hart Crane, "The Broken Tower"): "Then the mere consciousness of existence, without thought—a condition which lasted long. Then, very suddenly, *thought,* and shuddering terror . . . Then a strong desire to lapse into insensibility."

So consciousness leads not only to thought but to memory, and memory often leads to the desire to forget, that is, to consciousness of what memory tells: the horror and the guilt. Finally it is thought which leads to survival but also to the terrible ordeal that readers experience with the hapless victim: the pendulum ever lowering, the gnawing rats, the dank, wet walls of the dungeon, the stench of the pit. Yet that very thought which saves cannot be had otherwise; without it death is certain; with it awareness and horror are certain, but life at least a possibility. These are the real alternatives of the story: annihilation versus thought, oblivion versus awareness. Every torture devised for the victim lures him to the actual or the metaphorical pit, and it is only through will, mobilized by thought, by consciousness, that the pit is avoided. What price is paid goes far beyond suffering—it is the terror of life placed here into the maximum metaphors of moving walls, razor-sharp pendulums, ravenous rats. The choice is for life (as in "Roderick Usher" it *had* to be for death, as we shall see), and life at any price or risk, life against the pit for "mere consciousness of existence, without thought," for thought only threatens.

From these few instances it is possible to draw some conclusions, not merely about Poe's meaning but about his focus, his preoccupation, some would say his obsession. Even those who read Poe for the first time quickly come to realize how he feared live incarceration, and whatever Freudian explanations there may be, one thing is certain: Poe fought against annihilation, unconsciousness, the abyss. Put another way, he fought desperately, if ambiguously, to preserve consciousness. It was not so much that conscience pushed him to maintain identity, but certainly conscience seems in some instances to triumph. Once again it is not easy to define what Poe conceived conscience to be, except that it was obviously more than remorse and guilt for wrongdoing. "Conscience," according to Schopenhauer, "is an acquaintance with our own unalterable character, which we make only through the medium of our deeds."[8] Poe, I think, would not have accepted this definition, because the question of "deeds" is peripheral to his conception of man. For Poe conscience seems more like the agent of suffering whom man must accept, whether he wishes to or not, along with consciousness, with life itself. Deeds are in themselves not important; the struggle to survive is. And in that struggle the desire for survival is aided by will—or at the very least will intercedes, though not always successfully. At times will succeeds only to lose ("William Wilson"); sometimes it literally saves man from certain annihilation ("The Pit and the Pendulum"); and sometimes it creates merely a hallucination, a self-deception, will succumbing to inevitable counterforces, the will of self against the will of "other" ("Ligeia"). By and large Poe's heroes exercise will to stay conscious, to avoid the pit, even in the certain knowledge that life (as against the pit) may mean the torments of conscience, that life may provide that mirror-image in which man sees himself condemned, guilty, not because of "deeds" but merely because he is. The analysis of man's struggle to stay conscious is most graphically explained in "The Pit and the Pendulum," but there is a detailed passage in "The Imp of the Perverse" that says it even better:

We stand upon the brink of a precipice. We peer into the abyss—we grow sick and dizzy. Our first impulse is to shrink from the danger. Unaccountably we remain. By slow degrees our sickness, and dizziness, and horror, become merged in a cloud of unnameable feeling. By gradations . . . this cloud assumes shape . . . [We think of] the idea of what would be our sensations during the sweeping precipitancy of a fall from such a height. And this fall—this rushing annihilation—for the very reason that it involves that one most ghastly and loathsome of all the most ghastly and loathsome images of death and suffering . . . , for this very cause do we now the most vividly desire it. And because our reason violently deters us from the brink, *therefore*, do we the most impetuously approach it. There is no passion in nature so demoniacally impatient, as that of him, who shuddering upon the edge of a precipice, thus meditates a plunge. To indulge for a moment, in any attempt at *thought*, is to be inevitably lost; for reflection but urges us to forbear, and *therefore* it is . . . that we *cannot*. If there be no friendly arm to check us, or if we fail in a sudden effort to prostrate ourselves backward from the abyss, we plunge, and are destroyed.

Such feelings are not uncommon for many ostensibly normal people: the urge to plunge, the fixation on the urge, the reverse results of such a fixation (that is, not salvation but an increase of the urge). What Poe underlines in his precise analysis is the process by which the consciousness of man, struggling for safety, rushes headlong towards annihilation. "To indulge . . . in any attempt at *thought,* is to be inevitably lost": thought would seem to lead to forbearance, but in reality the very forbearance thus mobilized induces only stronger resistance against it. We cannot resist, observes Poe: the more we think, the more we resist and the more likely we are to plunge. Why is this so? Because the more consciousness fills the mind, the more aware we become of our guilt, our conscience, our realization that self-destruction is tantamount to the oblivion that frees us from the thought responsible for initially making us aware that we *had* a conscience we desired to be freed from. Schopenhauer had put it in much the same way when he insisted that conscience is essentially a posteriori, the result of what has been: "*Before* the deed, conscience can speak at best *indirectly,* namely, by means of reflection, which holds before conscience the recollection of previous cases in which similar deeds subsequently met with its disapproval."[9] Such a view would, of course, find confirmation in Freud and the whole psychoanalytic machinery dealing with the dynamics of guilt in relation *not* to a specific deed (which Freud considered "remorse") but to awareness, the Freudian version of Original Sin, originating, according to Freud, in the classic Oedipal guilt common to all men: the patricide of ancient myth, the "eternal struggle between Eros and the instinct of destruction or death."[10]

Poe's world, then, is peopled by many victims of ineffectual will; and even when will succeeds it does so at its own expense, as I have already said: It annihilates rather than frees. Indeed, will is ultimately not freedom but bondage—bondage to universal guilt. A superfine consciousness destroys itself by producing an equally superfine conscience; the utmost exertion of will becomes a force of the utmost determinism—and, in Poe, all leads to decay and disintegration. No tale better illustrates this than the all too popular "The Fall of the House of Usher," and it is this story, with the others behind them as it were, which leads us most easily to Thomas Mann, who had the benefit of Schopenhauer, Nietzsche, and Freud—the first two as early as *Buddenbrooks* (1901).

Will: The Defeat

To put side by side one of Poe's stories, even one of the best, and Mann's large *Familienroman* may seem disproportionate. Yet despite the difference between their dates of publication (1839 and 1901) their scope, and even their literary merit, these two works have a kinship. They deal not only with a similar theme—

the fall of a "house," but Mann himself makes the link unmistakably clear. Friend and confidant of the last male Buddenbrook, the young Hanno, is Kai, Count Mölln. This imaginative, unkempt young boy, representing decay, especially that of the aristocracy, moves quickly and without fuss through some of the very last chapters of *Buddenbrooks,* scoring his points with precision and without any ambiguity. Unafraid to be different, Kai can resolve his problems with a nonchalance Hanno may never allow himself. Kai is uninhibited, Hanno lets himself go: There is a difference. For one thing Kai channels his imagination, without remorse or guilt, into a twilight world which ironically describes his own disintegration and decay. That directed energy, Mann suggests, might even save him. Hanno, on the other hand, submits to a kind of Dionysian *Übermut* (wantonness), manifesting itself in what for Mann was always a dangerous area: music. Hanno is the first important and detailed account by Mann of a type he would explore more fully in books like *Death in Venice* and *The Magic Mountain,* the artistically inclined sensibility which surrenders to death, not so unwillingly. The suspect and dangerous nature of music is made clear in *The Magic Mountain* and, of course, in *Doktor Faustus,* in which the hero is a composer who barters his soul in return for musical genius.

Poe's "The Fall of the House of Usher" is worked into the famous chapter describing a day in the life of Hanno Buddenbrook at school. Hanno is now the sole male survivor of the doomed family. Having no inclination towards the world of his father, indeed feeling intensely alienated from it, he finds no solace in the rigors of the schoolroom either. On a Monday morning, chilly and gray, he awakens to the predictable terror of not having done his homework. As procrastination and an unconscious defiance against authority conspire to prevent even a last-minute cram session early in the morning, a frightened Hanno approaches his day at school as if he were the candidate for an *auto-da-fé*: "I'm scared," Hanno said to Kai, who, however sympathetic a friend he is, does not listen for he is "deep in thought": "This Roderick Usher is the most remarkable character ever conceived," he said suddenly and abruptly. "I have read the whole lesson-hour. If I ever could write a tale like that!"[11] Kai has in fact been writing stories; Hanno has been passive, letting himself be overcome by music. Aside from improvisations which promised a facility bordering on original talent, Hanno has not been a truly creative student. For Kai the solution to countering a world he reviles is to *create* another, one far removed from the one destroying the legacy of the likes of Count Mölln: "He had lately completed a composition in the form of a fantastic fairy tale, a narrative of symbolic adventure, which went forward in the depths of the earth among glowing metals and mysterious fires, and at the same time in the souls of men: a tale in which the primeval forces of nature and of the soul were interchanged and mingled, transformed and refined—the whole conceived and written in a vein of extravagant and even sentimental symbolism, fervid with passion and longing." This might almost be a sequel to Poe's story, for which poor Hanno has no patience now: "He was not now in a frame of mind to think of Kai's work or of Edgar Allan Poe. He yawned . . . humming to himself a *motif* he had lately composed on the piano."

But in fact the Fall of the House of Buddenbrook, which Hanno completes, is more germane to Poe and Kai's story than is the music which Hanno, like Roderick Usher, is determined to manipulate as a screen against what is really happening. Of course, the Fall of the House of Count Mölln is equally involved, and I think that without developing the theme explicitly beyond this passing allusion to Poe, Mann sets before us the fortunes of three Houses: Usher, Mölln, and Buddenbrook. With Poe's story in the background, those of Hanno and Kai serve effectively as foils, for it is clearly no accident that Poe's tale should be mentioned at this juncture in the story, only a few fictional moments before the end of a long saga covering four generations, the complete collapse of the House of the Buddenbrooks.

One might conceivably visualize the three stories in a kind of *Steigerung* (gradation) sequence. Usher's house falls because consciousness is so totally vulnerable that, in typically Poesque terms, conscience necessarily drives Usher into attempts to subdue what consciousness has been making painfully clear (for example, the incarceration of Madeline is the attempt to repress what has become a revealed truth, that Usher must kill her to live, to stay alive). Kai's consciousness of the dark side of the world is a reverse way of battling the realities of his shabby life as a son of a dethroned aristocrat; he creates and invents goblins and myths in which hidden precious metals are found in the bowels of the earth (a German Romantic motif), a myth in which "primeval" nature and men's souls are "interchanged and mingled, transformed and refined." Kai's dirty fingernails become cleansed in some apocalyptic myth-world; it is escapism but creative, a denial of the real world with thumb-nosed gestures of artistic defiance. And what of Hanno? Hanno is paralyzed, observing the fall of his house without struggle, without real resistance because he knows, or feels, it is useless.

Repeatedly Mann stresses Hanno's passivity, his lack of "will," long before the famous description of the death scene. On the morning mentioned, Hanno decides to recede into oblivion after an earlier resolve to arise early to prepare the lessons untouched the night before. "And Hanno slept, his cheek pressed into the pillow, his lips closed, the eyelashes lying close upon his cheek; he slept with an expression of the most utter abandonment to slumber": willing passivity. After the disastrous incident of the English lesson, at which not only the students but their ineffectual teacher are ruined, Hanno reviews his future with Kai. Music? Well, his family would never consent to his travelling around as a performing artist. He complains of a tiredness deep in his body— "I'd like to sleep," he tells Kai, "and never wake up. I'd like to die, Kai!" Hanno simply cannot confront living—life is static to begin with; it is the process he cannot handle. "One day," he confides, "I heard Pastor Pringsheim tell somebody that one must just give me up because I come of a decayed family." Kai wants confirmation, showing a "deep interest." As the boys continue to speak, Kai begins to relate how he looks forward to writing "something marvellous"; Hanno will play his music, not practice his sonatas and études but "play." Although he feels guilty because such play (clearly erotic in its abandonment) "only makes everything worse" and fails to accomplish anything even on this level, he nevertheless seems powerless to resist.

At the same time Mann is parodying what to a cultivated German reader was easily recognizable as Schiller's *Spieltrieb,* his "play instinct"; for Schiller this had been a serious concept (derived from Kant) which freed the spirit towards authentic ethical commitments, even social good, while for Mann it has become a substitute for any action, a mere titillation in Hanno. At first Kai is puzzled, but gradually he understands. What for Schiller was specifically an aesthetic education has in Hanno become a sexual *frisson*; it will lead to the grave, not to ethical imperatives. Abandonment of consciousness also prepares for its annihilation, and Hanno finds that pleasurable self-destructiveness in the suspect realm of music.

After the wretched day, the two boys walk home together, Kai as usual without an overcoat, despite the snow. They part, but at the last moment Kai, putting his arm on Hanno's back, tells Hanno: "Don't give up—better not play!" Yet Hanno plays; improvisation on a simple motif leads to a "festival, a triumph, an unbounded orgy"; artistically, Mann's commentary is almost intrusively obvious: "The fanatical worship of this worthless trifle, this scrap of melody . . . had about it something stupid and gross, and at the same time something ascetic and religious—something that contained the essence of faith and renunciation. There was a quality of the perverse in the instability with which it was produced and revelled in . . . cynical despair . . . a yielding to desire . . . till exhaustion, disgust, and satiety supervened." Such a transparent metaphor for masturbation is the mark of the young writer, but it was essential for Mann to make certain the point was clearly understood: Music becomes a symbol of sexual waste in Hanno, and it is clear that he will never be able, even should he live, to sire any more descendants for the Buddenbrook family.[12]

The distinguishing difference between Roderick Usher and Hanno Buddenbrook is the degree of consciousness which in turn responds to a corresponding degree of conscience. Usher is wholly conscious of what is happening to him, to his "House," for he is after all his own executioner. Hence the full horror is upon him, to quote Hopkins, like "the fell of dark" ("I wake and feel the fell of dark") and the pain of consciousness, everywhere stressed in the story, stimulates an equally painful conscience: the interment of

Madeline is in great measure not merely an exorcism of awareness but also, ironically, an act that insures that awareness will not, *cannot* be subdued. Usher knows he buries his sister alive; his great fear at the end is largely the tension of awaiting her return—it is a vigil. For young Hanno the horrors are quite different. Guilt (a "bad conscience") also ensues from a consciousness of faults and failures: procrastination, lack of vital energy, "playing." But, unlike Usher, Hanno is not master of his own dialectic; although he realizes that slovenliness will yield nothing but grief and pain, the narcissistic impulse, the lure of abandonment, is too strong, too pleasurable to resist. Furthermore, the risks of guilt do not seem to Hanno as metaphysical as they did to his father, who read Schopenhauer (or to the reader). It must be admitted and remembered that on the most fundamental level Hanno is still a child. Usher in some sense plans his own retribution; Hanno merely succumbs to it. For all the nervous exhaustion of Poe's hero, meticulously analyzed by the visiting friend, the narrator, there remains nevertheless that inevitable strength of debility, that intensity of neurosis, which gives Usher the chance to act out both roles— victim of consciousness and victimizer (of himself) in the guise of conscience. Hanno has no such energies, except the energy to "play"; and his final resistance to life is so feeble that the typhoid takes him without a struggle. Although this, too, may be seen as a form of assertion, inherent in all self-destructive acts, it is a far more advanced stage of decadence than Usher's, whose struggle Poe sees, as usual, in more general terms as individual swallowed up by large abstractions, the forces that compel men to fall within themselves into the contracting and annihilating power, the escape from "gravity" that means certain and sudden collapse.

Why does Hanno Buddenbrook, sole male survivor of the House of Buddenbrook, surrender to the death which he embraces, almost *Liebestod* fashion, by wasting his seed through the medium of music, enervation, and ennui? Mann's book is more complex than it might seem, and the answer to this question is not to be found in any single glib formula. For the purposes at hand, however, one may say that certainly one of the driving forces behind Hanno's submission was his tormented sence of *Pflicht,* duty, a force that swirls like a storm over the whole book. Progressively, every male Buddenbrook becomes heavily burdened with the responsibility of preserving the family name, the family firm, the family tradition, and the equally progressive realization that he cannot do it. This sense of failure overshadows almost everything else, and life becomes not a patrician pleasure but a *duty*; conscience ultimately destroys consciousness, or perverts it, or, to continue the sexual relevance of the theme, wastes it in a kind of lust. To show this one must view the whole novel, not merely Hanno, but especially one must focus on the true hero, Thomas Buddenbrook, Hanno's father, the man in whom the conflict is still truly a conflict and who is the only figure to approach the tragic condition in this often Dickensian novel. If the book may be said to be "about" something, it is about the failure of will, most agonizingly revealed in Thomas Buddenbrook, in spite of that man's most desperate attempts to invoke that will, almost to the moment of his death.

Schopenhauer was neither the first nor the last philosopher to worry over the question: "Is the will itself free?" (which is a far more sophisticated question than "is there free will?"). But he carried his argument along the most precipitous pathways feeding finally into that larger contemporary concern of much of "existential" philosophy, where the question emphasizes not so much the concept of will as of free. I do not intend to follow this intricate route, but a few clues from Schopenhauer's important "Essay on the Freedom of the Will" help us considerably to understand poor Thomas Buddenbrook, who incidentally would have fared better had he read that essay in place of the dangerously misleading piece which Mann actually does have him read, "On Death and Its Relation to the Indestructibility of Our True Nature." For in the essay on will, Schopenhauer makes some very bold statements, in effect answers to rhetorical questions: "What is freedom?" "What is the self-consciousness?" or "does the Will retain complete freedom either to will or not to will?" What Thomas Buddenbrook would not have given to know the answers to such questions!

For Schopenhauer freedom lies not in the actions of men ("*operari*") but in their full being ("*esse*"), a turnabout, he claims, of traditional concepts, that is, that man is what he is but that he demonstrates his freedom in what he does. "Everything," Schopenhauer contends, "depends on what one is; what he does will follow therefrom of itself": it is severely deterministic. So men like Thomas Buddenbrook, or for that matter any number of Poe's heroes, are doomed to fail because they do not understand where freedom lies, searching for it in choice of action rather than in *esse*: "In a word: man does at all times only what he wills, and yet he does this necessarily. But this is due to the fact that he already *is* what he wills. For from that which he *is*, there follows of necessity everything that he, at any time, *does*."

There is something ancient and modern here, something of Sophocles and something of, say, Freud. Self-consciousness, as against mere consciousness, Schopenhauer defines as an inner-directed state, "the consciousness of one's own self in contrast to the consciousness of other things"; self-consciousness is, almost "exclusively, occupied with willing," which is, as has been noted, the product of what one is. Hence "conscience" is defined as "really this closer and progressively more intimate acquaintance" with self, with consciousness of the outer world, with the empirical knowledge of actions.[13] In this way conscience is the product of reflection on things done or the anticipation of doing things done which have previously caused a feeling of guilt. For Thomas Buddenbrook, his whole life becomes at its unceremonious end a pang, a sense of failure engendering a very "bad conscience" without allowing him any religious machinery with which to requite it. It is a "bad conscience" for not having lived up to the ideals which he had with the utmost futility sought to uphold by the exercise of his will. Despite this, Thomas Buddenbrook is unable, and unwilling, to accept the greater power of the Schopenhauerian will and thereby expiate himself by faulting the world rather than himself. This becomes his last act of *Pflicht*, his "duty" to accept his failure as his and his alone, his nagging suspicion on top of this that somehow someone else might have done more with his will than he, that stubborn patrician pride that would never allow individual responsibility to melt into cosmic causes beyond a single man's control. Life becomes finally a tragic experience for this man: a deepening consciousness paralleled by a deepening conscience and receding power of will, indeed a feeling of impotence. Only once does he attempt to justify release from his individual responsibility, and this attempt, too, is doomed to fail.

Mann continued to be interested in this aspect of Schopenhauer's philosophy. In the 1938 essay he returns to it: "Freedom, like the will, was beyond . . . the phenomenal," and common sense did no good when confronting the problem of freedom. For that elusive freedom "lay not in doing but in being, not in *operari* but in *esse.*" Doing was, inevitably then, deterministic; whereas Being was metaphysically free (precisely Arnold's point in "Hebraism and Hellenism"). Hence a man who did wrong "had indeed so *acted* of necessity . . . But he could have *been* different; and his fear, his pangs of conscience, also had reference to his being, not his doing" (Arnold never went *that* far). Mann was quite correct in calling this both a "bold" and "at the same time a harsh thought."[14] Its harshness was, I think, already clear to him when he created Thomas Buddenbrook. Yet he could never side with Schopenhauer's archenemy, Hegel, who saw the relation of will to duty and conscience in quite a different light. "What is right and obligatory [duty]," he proclaimed, "is the absolutely rational element in the will's volitions and therefore it is not in essence the *particular* property of an individual." Therefore conscience must be judged as a universal not a personal and subjective phenomenon; furthermore conscience "is the expression of the absolute title of subjective self-consciousness" to determine the nature of the "right" and of the "obligatory." Indeed conscience is "this unity of subjective knowing with what is absolute . . . a sanctuary which it would be sacrilege to violate." For Hegel the will is not malign but "good," and the nature of "duty," in its absolute garb, is to express itself through the proper avenues of conscience. Schopenhauer (and Mann) judge Thomas Buddenbrook harshly; Hegel would not even permit him to come to court.[15]

The Passion of Thomas Buddenbrook (although his decline is slow, steady, and foreshadowed throughout) occupies most of Part X of the novel. From the opening sentence, "Often, in an hour of depression, Thomas Buddenbrook asked himself what he was, or what there was about him to make him think even a little better of himself than he did of his honest, limited, provincial fellow-burghers," to the last sentences describing the burial of this sorely tormented man, the dissolution is described like the progress and the process of an illness. Upon his hero Mann had, by his own admission, placed both the glory and the burden of insight and vision. To his "suffering hero" he proffered "the dear experience, the high adventure" of reading Schopenhauer's famous essay on Death. He had tried, he said in later life, to make Thomas Buddenbrook "find life in death, liberation from the bonds of his wearied individuality"; and most of all to instill in him a sense of "freedom from [playing] a role" of the martyred bourgeois, a role which had "never satisfied his spirit or his hopes and had been a hindrance to him in achieving something other and better."[16] High and noble aims these—but to no avail. A quick glimpse into a strange and forbidding world of release, the illusion of salvation, the delusion of having resolved the intricacies of life and death—and then it is over with Thomas Buddenbrook, dead after having a decayed (naturally!) tooth *partially* removed.

In these remarks about the Schopenhauer episode, written nearly four decades after the publication of the novel, Mann suggests what the book might have been about had he been able to do more than weave the subject of death, philosophically speaking, "into the narrative," "only close to the end," where it almost seems anomalous. Because *Buddenbrooks* is, among other things, a novel about the failures of will and the terrible struggle to justify those failures, it must, however briefly, anatomize the agonizing moments when its hero becomes aware of his defeat, his brief and vanished vision, and his bondage to a conscience which has enslaved him all his life. And all of this must, and is, accomplished without having Thomas Buddenbrook aware of this final tragic defeat until it is much too late, even to clutch at the awareness itself.

Ostensibly the House of Buddenbrook is collapsing because of its refusal and inability to compete in the new, aggressive mercantile world in which Pietism and gentlemanly business practices have been supplanted by the fruition of the Protestant ethic. According to Lukács, Mann was seeking "bourgeois" man—that is, those who would replace the inevitably declining patricians, like the Buddenbrooks, as the truly representative class of German life. Thomas and his brother Christian represent a further struggle, Thomas wishing to stave off for as long as possible the early and total decadence of his dilletante brother. For this Mann gives Thomas "composure," but Lukács admits that this composure fails in the end to prevent that "emotional anarchy" against which it was initially mobilized. The Buddenbrooks fall because they have no sense of class identity and because moral values are lost with that identity.[17]

Nothing about such a reading of the novel is wrong, but it tends to ignore the actors within the drama, especially the individual heroics—ironically as they are often presented—of the actor of the penultimate act, Thomas Buddenbrook. Long before the crisis of this man's life is given full attention, the reader is made aware of the little things that add up, year by year, to thwart Thomas Buddenbrook's will. Hanno, the last hope for the Buddenbrooks, has turned out to be a bitter disappointment almost from the moment of his birth. Listless, delicate, sickly, shy, with no great propensity for anything but "play," Hanno simply will not (and cannot) be what his father wishes. This battle is lost before it is really joined. Little Hanno in fact writes the obituary of the Buddenbrooks by taking the family Bible, in which all the births and dates have been carefully charted, and drawing after his name a "clean double line diagonally across the entire page"—as if he were saying *finita la commedia*! When his father confronts him, the boy answers simply and no doubt quite honestly: "I thought—I thought—there was nothing else coming." Earlier, during the centennial celebration of the "Firm," Hanno botches his role in that already outdated event by not remembering properly "The Shephard's Holiday Hymn," which it was to be his responsibility—his *duty* to recite.

So when Thomas Buddenbrook enters the final stages of his defeat, he has already been badly shaken: a mysterious wife, more and more devoted to music, and even playing duets with a handsome army officer behind closed doors; a son who has failed in every way to take up the standard intended for him; a sister who remains after two unsuccessful marriages a "child," and whose own daughter has followed in her footsteps towards a disastrous marriage of her own; a brother well on the road to insanity and eventual confinement; a business beaten to its knees both by the onslaughts of a new and rapacious economic climate and by its own outmoded methods which hamper growth and vitality. Within himself a much sinned against Thomas Buddenbrook is made to carry, by his creator, almost the sum of nineteenth-century *taedium vitae,* the spent spirit, the thwarted will, the capitulation of utter desolation and isolation, annihilation and subsequent alienation from the mainstream of life. The failure of his one and only "risky" business venture, incautiously embarked upon more out of stubborness than business wisdom, followed an internal struggle of titanic proportions. This struggle resolves itself only by defying the fates: " 'I will do it!' he said in a passionate whisper, even stretching out one hand and shaking the forefinger. 'I will do it!' " He ought to have known that he was not master of his will in that naïve sense inherited from his forbears, where the individual action seemed determined by trust in God and stiff resolve, in just about equal proportion. Only a few years before this debacle, when the business had lost money without his decision being first asked for, Thomas Buddenbrook had fumed: "He could have prevented it if he had only been told! But events had taken their course without him. It was this which he felt could not have happened earlier— would not have dared to happen earlier! Again his faith tottered— his faith in himself, his luck, his power, his future."

When, therefore, Thomas Buddenbrook finally takes up that volume of Schopenhauer, he is a vanquished man looking for solace and freedom from bondage to the eternal sense of conscience which had driven him beyond endurance. He searches also for release from the grip of that duty to be always willing his individual and family fortunes in a world in which men like him now become slaves, not masters of will. What do such men do? They cultivate already entrenched habits of fastidiousness, in dress and manner, in life style; they tend to become irritable and compulsive about time—punctuality of meals becomes a ritual; they pose, after much care, for a world outside as if that world would or could not penetrate *eau de colonge,* stiffly ironed shirt collars, or brilliantine on the mustache. Such a man was Thomas Buddenbrook, of whom Mann says that his existence "was no different from that of an actor," on the wrong stage. And, as with the actor, the makeup only conceals while the process of death goes on unchecked, in this case even accelerated. Failing in health, stubborn in following doctor's orders, "His will-power had grown flabby . . . He slept late . . . though every evening he made an angry resolve to rise early . . . And the constant effort to spur on his will, with the constant failure to do so, consumed his self-respect and made him a prey to despair." Through the shutters of this ailing patricians's "self-consciousness, his ancestor-worship," begin to shimmer the ominous shadows of death. He had a conviction that a man must, "before it was too late, wring for himself a pious readiness before the hour of death"; yet even here he is spurred on by a "bad conscience," seeking solace not for personal relief but because he feels it to be his *duty.*

"On Death and Its Relation to the Indestructibility of Our True Nature"—what did Thomas Buddenbrook find in those pages which offered him that momentary ecstatic vision of relief and release? Mann singles out as the most important discovery the realization that individuality is an illusion: "Where should I be were I not here? Who, what, how could I be, if I were not I—if this my external self, my *consciousness,* did not cut me off from those who are not I? Organism! Blind, thoughtless, pitiful eruption of the urging will! Better, indeed, for the will to float free in spaceless, timeless night than for it to languish in prison, illumined by feeble, flickering light of the intellect!" (Italics mine.) And, as the "walls of his native town, in which he had wilfully and consciously shut himself up," now tumble, he attains a brief vision of eternity, immortality, the "endless present" which makes him weep with joy and whisper into his pillow the inevitable *Lebenslüge* (life-lie) as he understands it, "I shall live"—beyond any personal death which is but the death of a body. Already the next morning, "the vision . . . quenched," he feels remorse (a "bad conscience") for his "emotional extravagances of the night," and the "precious volume" is eventually returned to the bookcase without ever being opened again.

A pity, for had Thomas Buddenbrook reread Schopenhauer's essay he might have fastened onto stronger thoughts: "But consciousness consists in knowing; therefore, for consciousness death is no evil"; "For consciousness has always showed itself to me not as the cause, but as the product and result of the organised life"; "although the individual consciousness does not survive death, yet that survives it which alone struggles against it—the will"; "As now the *will* does not *know,* so conversely the intellect, or the subject of knowledge, is simply and solely *knowing,* without ever *willing.*"[18] No doubt Thomas Buddenbrook would have had difficulties understanding such fine maxims, and he cannot be blamed for that. Despite the fact that in this particular essay, as elsewhere, Schopenhauer repeatedly insists that consciousness is knowledge divorced altogether from "the will," a true Buddenbrook, like Thomas, would have continued to insist that somehow an individual's "will power" determines his fate. Clearly he blames himself for his defeat, his increasingly flabby will which, he thinks, through greater effort by means of a more capacious consciousness he could have strengthened. Events tell against him: The more conscious he becomes of his impotence, the more helpless he seems to be against its progress. Awareness only paralyzes will, over which, as Schopenhauer would insist, he can never have control. He is enfeebled; he sinks "now weakly back to the images and conceptions of his childhood." The doctor diagnoses this general debility as a case of "nerves," warns him against excessive smoking, and packs him off to the seashore.

So there he finds himself at the waning part of a summer, among a decaying, self-indulgent colony of prematurely old men (like himself), including brother Christian. And there he spends the last moments of battle, convinced now that introspection has brought about his decline, that after all it was the sin of thought, of self-consciousness, that has made him a moral invalid forever, enervated, done with the strength to carry on with life itself. "What sort of men prefer the monotony of the sea?" he asks his sister Toni, rhetorically; "Those," he replies, ". . . who have looked so long and deeply into the complexities of the spirit, that they ask of outward things merely that they should possess one quality above all: simplicity." In a given sense this is not untrue, for had he not asked for simplistic answers to the conflicts which consciousness first revealed? "Health and illness," he concludes, "that is the difference. The man whose strength is unexhausted climbs boldly up into the lofty multiplicity of the mountain heights [Hans Castorp finds that, too, is not simple]. But it is when one is worn out with turning one's eyes inward upon the bewildering complexity of the human heart, that one finds peace in resting them on the wideness of the sea."[19] And that monotony of the sea, that endlessly captivating rhythm of the waves, mesmerizes one into the final sleep. Shortly after this brief sojourn by the seashore, Thomas Buddenbrook dies, not at all as he might have wished it but quite unceremoniously, his body splattered with dirt, lying face down in the rain and mud-soaked streets of his town, his own confines, beyond which—with one brief and misunderstood exception—he could never really go. In his essay "On a Chapter from 'Buddenbrooks,' " Mann, looking back, concedes that he had learnt the "psychology of dissolution" (the German editions all carry the subtitle: *Verfall einer Familie*) from Nietzsche. However he "rejected or simply did not take seriously" what the "drunken vitalist" said about life, namely that "there was 'no fast point . . . from which it is possible to contemplate existence, no instance in which life could be *ashamed.*' " This sentiment Mann finds perhaps German but not European. In Mann's riper humanism such a "point," such an "instance" exist, though they may indeed be interstices in the midst of the freedom man cherishes even as it is destroyed.[20]

At the very end Thomas had perhaps finally accepted fate, in the sense of his treasured philosopher's definition, "nothing but the conscious certainty that all that happens is fast bound by a chain of causes, and . . . with a strict necessity, that the future is already ordained with absolute certainty and can undergo as little alteration as in the past."[21] One must suppose that Thomas Buddenbrook "forgot" his vision of Schopenhauer's attractive conception of a de-individualized death because he suspected the deep pessimism that lay beneath its surface: man's impotence in the face of life, as simple as that. Now how closely Mann means us to read his *Familienroman* in that spirit I am not sure; but his hero epitomizes the theme of the thwarted will, consciousness of one's progressive diminution, and the losing struggle of conscience in attempting to drive a man into a tide which rolls inexorably towards him and finally engulfs him. That tide, to which the *Zeitgeist* of Pietism and gentility must inevitably yield, is more than the mercantile chicanery of the new class of businessmen; it is also the new and relentness awareness that survival depends almost entirely on one basic premise: Conscience is something a man cannot afford to indulge any longer. All conscience implies a check, a momentary retreat, and in this brave new world there is no time for such a moment. But man cannot survive without such moments, not for long, for awareness always seems to lead back to conscience. Even a relentless surge ahead requires open eyes, and open eyes will, eventually, again begin to see. How to have the best of both—a driving force and halting moral sense—without surrendering either? In the 1860's and 1870's, in England, Matthew Arnold thought he had found a solution. But Henry James, an older contemporary of Thomas Mann, and a disciple of Arnold, proved his master wrong, devoting a lifetime to the sorting out of the intricacies of consciousness and conscience. Indeed James tortured himself, at times into virtual incoherence, on this one troubled point: how to be aware to *enjoy*—and was *that* granted?—the fruits of that awareness?

Poe's concern was quite different, for his interest in conscience was not in its function as the avenging agent but in the process— how consciousness became conscience through *thought*; how will drove men either to resist or to succumb—or how they were overcome by that irresistible urge of the abyss, not half-pleasurable as in Mann, but terrifying, a life burial. The question of enjoying the fruits of knowledge never seriously arises is Poe's work, for it is a foregone conclusion that the process of thought counters and betrays, that ratiocination is often the prerequisite for the irrational. Mann, of course, intellectualized the problem, refined it, historicized and "placed" it within a particular context, one which Poe simply had not lived through (and even if he had would not have bothered about). Lukács writes eloquently of Mann's position vis-à-vis conscience: "The fact of conscience as a force in life gives both expression and acknowledgment to the discrepancy between things as they are and things as they ought to be, between appearance and essence . . . Conscience then is simply the injunction: 'Become what you are; be your essence, develop the essential, living core within you, whatever the disruptive influences of the inner and outer world.' "[22] But Lukács cannot forget that this very freedom-giving conscience can be, and for Mann often was, a tyrannical force; here is where Arnold and James sought means of rapprochement, James incidentally looking, initially, to the same type as Mann—the artist. "Become what you are; be your essence"; Arnold agreed, but called this "Consciousness." Nietzsche agreed and created his Zarathustra. James agreed and asked the question that seemed to him uppermost: Once we do become what we are have we the right to be what we are for our profit, or must we take solace in simply having become our essence and renounce our sharing it, for would not this be a gross egotism?

VI. The Tyranny of Conscience:
Arnold, James, and
Conrad's *Lord Jim*

[Conscience] is man's knowledge . . . concerning what he has done . . .
—Schopenhauer

Arnold's Search for a "Cultured" Zarathustra

Between Arnold and James the connections are clear and on record.[1] Conrad, of course, was no stranger to James (whom he greatly admired); and who could have avoided Arnold? While Conrad's direction as a novelist was quite different in some respects from that of James, and his posture distant from what Arnold's appeared to be, his Lord Jim is a man whose plight Arnold would certainly have understood and James might have created: the hero enslaved by conscience. There were times when Arnold would have counseled resignation (as we shall see), while James would decidely have favored a renunciation less dramatic and less reluctant than Conrad carved out for Jim's life. And this difference accounts for the aptness of linking Arnold and James with Conrad, for Conrad accepted neither Arnold's resignation nor his later Hellenism ("spontaneity of consciousness") nor James' renunciation, so often a dénouement based on the promise of freedom and moral purification.

Of the three men Conrad was the most metaphysical; he would agree to engage the great theme—what I have called "the tyranny of conscience," but his Jim neither resigns nor renounces: he resists. Within that resistance, it is true, both resignation and renunciation operate, but they are symptoms not aims, and there is no approval (implicit or explicit) of Jim's final controversial act (in effect, suicide) as there is approval of, say, Lambert Strether's or Isabel Archer's final acts.

In the *Empedocles on Aetna* (withdrawn for reasons that now seem questionable), Arnold blamed man for his foolish desire to see the world as created to shape destiny in accordance with his will. (Not much later in time, Hardy would make a similar point.) Empedocles' long sermon, accompanied by doleful harp music, is sometimes versified philosophy but it is clear: Man, to find answers, must "sink" in himself, for only there can he hope to find "light." The problem which Arnold faced (or did he face it?) was that his Empedocles, having looked inward and found light also had despair intensively illuminated; so the question (unresolved in Empedocles) became: can a man sink inwards, find light, and withstand despair? Empedocles himself says that man asks too much:

· · · · ·

Why are men ill at ease?—
'Tis that the lot they have
Fails their own will to please;
For man would make no murmuring, were his will obey'd.

And why is it, that still
Man with his lot thus fights?—
'Tis that he makes this *will*
The measure of his *rights*,
And believes Nature outraged if his will's gainsaid.

Couldst thou, Pausanias, learn
How deep a fault is this;
Couldst thou but once discern
Thou hast no *right* to bliss,
No title from the Gods to welfare and repose;

Then thou wouldst look less mazed
Whene'er of bliss debarr'd,
Nor think the Gods were crazed
When thy own lot went hard.
But we are all the same—the fools of our own woes!

(Act I, i, 148-166)

Arnold is not saying that man can never be happy, but he insists it is foolish for him to behave as though that happiness were a *right,* owed him by an indifferent "nature":

> He [Man] errs because he dreams
> The world does but exist that welfare to bestow. (I, i, 175-176)

For Arnold life is a darkling plain—"we are strangers here; the world is from of old." Indeed Man is but a "rude guest" who expects the world to reflect his image and resents it when it does not, a creature who thinks his will can bend fate and who wants "inward peace/Yet will not look within," and, equally naïve, "would have misery cease/Yet will not cease from sin." We blame Fate, the Gods, and our fathers in an unending process of attaching "blame elsewhere," inventing "Stern Powers" which embitter our existence. Empedocles' solution (and that of the younger Arnold, 1849-1852) was a Goethean *Beschränkung* (limitation): "Make us, not fly to dreams, but moderate desire." Borrowing, perhaps, from Dr. Johnson's "Vanity of Human Wishes" throughout this long sermon, Arnold nevertheless wishes to leave us on a note of comfort, cold comfort as it may be. If we do not cultivate "extravagant hope" in the face of so much "ill," then we will not be so perplexed at the pain of life. Yet even in the speaking, the speaker belies his own counsel, for he jumps into Aetna's crater reasoning that he alone being dead to life and joy projects upon all thing his "own deadness." (Arnold probably suspected that this reasoning was fraudulent.) The patient has diagnosed himself too well; if he is capable of such insight, the crater might not have beckoned. Mind and thought become, in the end, entities, "lords," who "keep us prisoners of our consciousness/And never let us clasp and feel the All"; like Keats's "think," mind and thought (as opposed to instinct) are danger signals for Arnold, pulling us inevitably back to the "reality," rallying our natures "for one last fight—and fail"—:

> And we shall sink in the impossible strife,
> And be astray for ever. (II, 389-390)

Between dreams and reality, then, only the crater seems an alternative, because the dream and the reality are both unbearable. What Arnold sought most during the painful years of struggle with his poetic Daemon was what he called in Wordsworth that poet's "healing power," a power which, he lamented in "Memorial Verses" (1850), seemed destined to be absent from European poetry for a long time to come. Inevitably torn asunder between the contrary impulses, or "desires," one "the world without" and the other "solitude," the poet, it seems, had no option but to abrogate everything for his art:

> He only lives with the world's life,
> Who hath renounced his own, ("The Author of 'Obermann' ")

words Yeats remembered when he wrote that

> The intellect of man is forced to choose
> Perfection of the life, or of the work . . . ("The Choice")

Yet even with that renunciation man is not, for Arnold, solely in charge of guiding the direction he can take—

> Can neither, when we will, enjoy,
> Nor, when we will, resign. ("The Author of 'Obermann' ")

A standoff best describes this condition, and poetry has not fared well under that kind of stasis. In turning to criticism, in *his* sense, Arnold was more honest with himself than some have thought. "Rugby Chapel" dates originally from 1857 (its completion has been dated as late as 1867), the year in which Baudelaire and Flaubert, each on trial for his own art, signified that their lot would forever be with the poet, however accompanied by irreconcilables. The year 1857 was also, coincidentially, the birthdate of Conrad who was to write in his famous preface to *The Nigger of the Narcissus,* that the "artist descends within himself, and in that lonely region of stress and strife, if he be deserving and fortunate, finds the terms of his appeal." But for Arnold it was a time to recall his father and the values he had harnessed from life; it was a time to pray—"Order, courage, return . . . /On, to the bound of the waste,/On, to the City of God." In the often quoted lines from the "Stanzas from the Grand Chartreuse" (1855), Arnold was now "between two worlds," though he was perhaps less bewildered than his critics have made it sound. To know that you are between two worlds is already a step beyond confusion. In fact the suspicion is aroused by the very clarity of his expressed precarious perch which seemed to have made possible the move from poetry to criticism. Freedom was not, at least for Arnold, to be wrung out of poetry, that is, not out of his own. Yet freedom was what he devoutly wished to possess, to win, "Till free my thoughts before me roll . . ." "Obermann Once More," inspired by a trip abroad in 1865, when the essays for *Culture and Anarchy* were already taking shape, is a farewell not so much to Obermann once more as to Arnold's poetic self. In the "vision" of the French poet (contrived and not happily brought off) Obermann's spirit speaks to Arnold as Arnold no doubt spoke to himself:

> 'Though more than half the years be past,
> And spent thy youthful prime;
> Though, round thy firmer manhood cast,
> Hang weeds of our sad time
> 'Whereof thy youth felt all the spell,
> And traversed all the shade—
> Though late, though dimm'd, though weak, yet tell
> Hope to a world new-made! ("Obermann Once More," 305-312)

It seems now a rather awkward exit; still perhaps it was needed just in this way. For Arnold would comply with this rousing call—he would "tell," and the first thing he had to tell his fellow-men, especially his countrymen, was that they had better begin to realize the tyranny of conscience that had for too long weighed them down with a sense of sin; that they had better prepare *now* for a spirit of consciousness, free though not frivolous, spontaneous though not anarchic. That is the clarion call of "Hebraism and Hellenism," the second essay in the book-form version of *Culture and Anarchy*.

In his call for Hellenism Arnold codified the schism which had preceded his decision by several decades. If the early Tennyson, the Pre-Raphaelites, Swinburne, George Moore, did indeed represent a kind of continuum of Romantic Hellenism, more pagan than Hellenistic, then Arnold rescued that tendency from the associations of a libertine heresy and hoped to direct it towards respectability. And for some time the respectability associated with Arnold's name obscured the implications of the essay for everybody—for the intellectuals, who summoned up images of pure classicism, and for the new generation of dandies, who were not to be considered very respectable in their day. Arnold, it must not be forgotten, provided much for what became central not only in Pater and Wilde, but in Yeats, Eliot, and Joyce. Although he might well have shuddered at the comparison, he was in certain respects the English Nietzsche (Carlyle never succeeded in that role); we are too often misled by his measured prose, his restraint, his Olympian equanimity (despite his ability to engage in polemics). But, as T. S. Eliot almost regretfully discovered, Arnold positioned himself into center stage by the end of the sixties, and from there he delivered a major blow against the very foundations on which he stood. If there was mischief in this it was not in what others might do with his ideas (no one should be held accountable for that) but in his separation, however much couched in dialectical terms, of Hellenism from Hebraism, consciousness from conscience.

Now Arnold's general orientation was, as is well known, generously directed from the continent, especially from Germany: Kant, Goethe, Schiller, Heine—and Hegel. In his 1882 Rede Lecture, "Literature and Science," when he asks, rhetorically, "But how, finally, are poetry and eloquence to exercise the power of relating the modern results of natural science to man's instinct for conduct, his instinct for beauty?" we know that Kant, Schiller and Hegel rather than, say, Shelley, stand behind such conjunctions. Moral and aesthetic values were, it is true, also for Shelley projected towards a millennium where all is unified; but the German idealist aesthetic differed in one important respect: it envisioned, as Arnold did, a climate that would make it possible for the "instinct for beauty" to become an equivalent for the "instinct for conduct." Each domain would retain separate but equal status. Such a condition described accurately what Arnold seemed to have striven for in his phrase "criticism of life"; he urges upon us not the utopia of Shelley but a cultural soil in which beauty might take root because conduct permitted, indeed fostered, its vitality and growth.

In his recent study of Hebraism and Hellenism in Victorian England, David J. De Laura correctly traces to German thought the English Hellenism revived in such figures as Arnold, Pater, and Wilde. He sees the effort as an attempt to transcend the "dualisms" of Christianity and Platonism. What results is a "search for a new basis of life compatible with the exigencies of modern thought and experience, and yet ensuring fullness of consciousness, 'fullness of being.' " This transcendence De Laura sees perhaps excessively anchored in the "aesthetic," deriving from Winckelmann, Hegel, and Heine; the collective effort to revise Christian values was embedded in the aesthetic "norm" of German Idealism, but it was also the nature of that Idealism to be highly *moralisch,* especially in Schiller and Hegel, but also in Heine, and even in Goethe. Aesthetic paganism is not quite the same as pagan aestheticism, at least not in the way Arnold or Pater interpreted it. However, De Laura is quite right in stressing Arnold's Hellenism as a genuine search for an alternative to the existing Christianity, and he phrases the texture of *Culture and Anarchy* with great delicacy when he describes that book as "symptomatic in hesitating between synthesis and a Hellenism *above* Christianity." In this context he concedes that Arnold's Hellenism is more in the tradition of an "ethical humanitarianism" than an "aesthetic humanism."[2] Like Schiller's, Arnold's conception of the aesthetic education must be seen as two-pronged, aesthetic *and* ethical, beauty *and* conduct, with perhaps one important distinction of priority, for Schiller (following Kant) put the aesthetic first, while Arnold chose to concentrate initially on man's ethical, or cultural, self out of which aesthetic sensibility would, he thought, inevitably follow. Arnold was following historical precedent: first create a proper culture, and then the aesthetic refinements will follow; Schiller relied more on the ontology of the problem, feeling that the sensitivity of man's aesthetic feeling would be a necessary prelude to any understanding of ethical conduct. To date neither position has proved its point.[3]

In this light, then, Arnold's Hellenism becomes comprehensible as more than an aesthetic domain: Hellenism is clearly, as the title of the work suggests, subsumed under the rubric of "culture." One of the few writers to have taken seriously the modernity of Arnold's "Hebraism and Hellenism," William Barrett, suspects that Arnold got his concept of the serene Greek ("radiant and harmonious") from eighteenth-century classicism. Insofar as this refers to Winckelmann, from whom all subsequent German philosophers and poets, including Nietzsche, proceeded, he is correct. But Winckelmann's "serenity" hardly stays intact, under heavy attack from the very beginning from Lessing and others. Even the disciples modify as they shape their own interpretations. Already in Schiller it may be assumed that "serenity" is a metaphor to describe what is only a possible condition (for example, as in *Naive and Sentimental Poetry*) rather than to suggest that serenity is (or was) a historical reality. Certainly Arnold took both Hebraism and Hellenism as metaphors, symbols, huge abstractions, which blocked out for him, in some sensible fashion, the historical paradigm from Greece to "Puritan" Victorian England. Nor do I think, as Barrett does, that reason was the essential value in the Hellenism whose cause Arnold now pleaded. In focusing on reason (as against faith) as the prime value in Arnoldian Hellenism, Barrett maneuvers his argument so that he may attack the Greeks—and Arnold's concept of them—as having wrought the mischief of sundering the "pristine wholeness of man's being," and for not realizing what he says we have learned only in this century, "how precarious a hold consciousness may exert upon life." So too Nietzsche (Barrett's hero) had attacked Socratic rationalism in *The Birth of Tragedy* (1871-1872), realizing, however, in later life the distortion of history and the partiality of vision embodied in that book.

To push the Greek too far into the posture of *"detachment,"* versus the Hebraic *"commitment"* (faith), "The passionate involvement of man with his own mortal being," is dangerous and does not correctly represent Arnold's view, either of Hebrew or Greek. "Essential in Hellenism," wrote Arnold, in "Hebraism and Hellenism," "is the impulse to the development of the *whole* man, to connecting and harmonizing all parts of him, perfecting all, leaving none to take their chance." But Barrett's general reading of the Hebrew-Greek dualism is accurate and sharp: "The Greek pursues beauty and goodness as things . . . coincident . . . The Hebraic sense of sin, to which Matthew Arnold alludes, is too much aware of the galling and refractory aspects of human existence to make this easy identification of the good and the beautiful."[4] And, we might add, the "Hebraic sense of sin" not only is incapable of a "coincident" view of beauty and goodness, it is the divisive agent between the two, since for the Arnoldian "Hebrew"—as for Heine a term including the nineteenth-century "puritan" Christian—beauty is a beast endangering the path of goodness, impeding its existence, and therefore dangerous and marked for extinction.

Neither Arnold nor Nietzsche made any real distinctions between Hebraism and Christianity.[5] Nietzsche favored the Old over the New Testament and often felt that Christianity was merely a deterioration of Hebraism. The real distinction, however, was Hebraic-Christian versus Greek (Hellenic). Arnold thought in more dialectic terms, seeing Hebraism and Hellenism as two polar forces, each having an ascendancy from time to time: the guiltless intellectualism of the free Hellenic spirit or the haunted corrective moralism of the Judaic-Christian culture. Both Arnold and Nietzsche (who seemed totally unaware of each other) derived their distinction from Heine, a poet both men admired. Heine had suggested the Hellenic-Hebraic division in his memoir of the Jewish philosopher Ludwig Boerne, where he also speaks of the strange but understandable antagonism between Boerne and Goethe (Germany's great champion of Greek Classicism). Boerne, said Heine, was a "Nazarene," and he views the struggle with Goethe in larger terms as a "duel which is not yet decided and may never be fought to the end: the little Nazarene hated the tall Greek, who was a Greek God as well." Then, justifying the appellative Nazarene for a Jew, Heine writes: "Boerne betrayed his Nazarene limitations. I say Nazarene in order to avoid such expressions as either 'Jewish' or 'Christian,' as both expressions are for me synonymous and are used by me not to specify a faith but a [specific] nature. 'Jews' and 'Christians' are for me totally related terms in contrast to 'Hellene,' with which name I also do not mean a particular people but a direction of spirit, a manner of seeing, both intrinsic and acquired. In this connection I would say that all men are either Jews or Hellenists, men with ascetic, anti-intellectual desires which seek spiritual objectification [*vergeist-igungs-süchtigen Trieben*] or men of a joyful, realistic nature, proud of their growth."[6] As will become evident, Arnold and Nietzsche are very close to this definition of the perpetual duel, Heine's "*Zweikamp.*" I am not suggesting that Arnold and Nietzsche were consistent allies, but on this issue and a good many others they journeyed a remarkably similar course, motivated by strikingly parallel impulses. An understanding of some of the literature which roughly paralleled their period of influence, extending well into our century, needs first to recognize their affinities; and their common roots especially in Goethe and Heine, serve only to strengthen what otherwise might be attributable merely to parallel currents of the *Zeitgeist.*

Heine's influence on Arnold has been documented, although some of Arnold's notions about Hellenism might well have been derived from Hegel.[7] In an essay on Heine, first delivered as an address in 1863, the forthcoming distinctions between "Hellenism" and "Hebraism" are prefigured. Arnold correctly pays tribute to the "Jewish element" in Heine, and, perhaps with some benevolent envy, he shows Heine to have had the best of two worlds, for Heine "has excellently pointed out how in the sixteenth century there was a double renascence—a Hellenic renascence and a Hebrew renascence—and how both have been great powers ever since. He himself had in him both the spirit of Greece and the spirit of Judaea; both these spirits reach the infinite . . .; the Greek spirit by beauty, the Hebrew spirit by sublimity. By his perfection of literary form, by his love of clearness, by his love of beauty, Heine is Greek; by his intensity, by his untamableness, by his 'longing which cannot be uttered,' he is Hebrew."[8] It should also be added that such a sympathetic view of Hebraism was to be somewhat tempered in "Hebraism and Hellenism."

Arnold sees Hebraism and Hellenism as the antipoles of Western history: "doing" and "thinking," "energy" and "intelligence." Thus "the uppermost idea with Hellenism is to see things as they really are; the uppermost idea with Hebraism is conduct and obedience." What most markedly characterizes the spirit of Hellenism is *"spontaneity of consciousness"*; what characterizes Hebraism is *"strictness of conscience."* The ideal of Hellenism is the perfection of beauty; its attainment, Arnold feels, is presently being impeded by the Hebraic sense of sin, which Arnold notes was greatly strengthened during the (justified) puritan reactions against the excesses and moral deficiencies of the Renaissance. Yet, without being unfair to Arnold, it would appear that, despite precautions implied in his argument, the way out of the impasse is to overcome its complexities: Consciousness must once more become a more important priority than conscience; but what of conscience? Fear not, Arnold reassures us, conscience will once again have its supremacy—it is the inevitable swing of history.

Henry James's Renunciation Fables: <u>Roderick Hudson</u>, an Example

Yet Henry James, an early reader and lifelong admirer of Arnold, was to spend his lifetime seeking individual conscience which he felt no amount of historical blocking out of abstractions in dialectic form could conveniently subdue. Seeing things "as they really are" was for James a more difficult exhortation to follow than Arnold had envisioned.

James, too, would emphasize seeing, and the pursuit of beauty was to become one of his major themes, but also his bête noir. If one were to make a concordance of James's fiction, the word "consciousness," so persistently associated with James's technique, would show up in abundant numbers; but "conscience" might come in a very close second, for I cannot think of a single major novel or tale in which "conscience" or the consequences of conscience fail to appear with regularity and point. A book would be needed to explore the subtle and complex development of James's use of that word, especially on the meanings that "conscience" is intended to convey in four or five of the major novels. Austin Warren has already explored *The Ambassadors* in the light of what "conscience" meant for James and in the context of the

Puritan conscience in general; what I wish to achieve here by means of a very brief glimpse at those always pertinent *Prefaces* is a very general and selective survey of the meaning of the *idea* of conscience in some of the major work. Lest one think that the idea preoccupied James only in the "major phase," I have chosen to take a close look at the very first novel in the New York Edition, *Roderick Hudson,* a book which not only deals squarely with conscience and consciousness but owes direct debts, I believe, to Arnold's essay on "Hebraism and Hellenism" and which sets the course James was to travel.

The *Prefaces* are always of value; though concerned more with the sheer delight of the novelist's role as master puppeteer than with interpretive insights, they nevertheless reveal how closely James interwove—the metaphor is his—the manner and the matter. No reader of *The Portrait of a Lady* can escape Isabel Archer's periods of brooding; James's characters are a brooding lot. They engage in what James called in the Preface to *The Portrait of a Lady* a "vigil of searching criticism," *self*-criticism he might have said. Invariably they are hard on themselves and ascetic, stoic, even prideful renunciation becomes more often than not a resolution. Daisy Miller and Isabel Archer, Fleda Vetch and Lambert Strether, Maggie Verver and Milly Theale, Morton Densher and Kate Croy are representatives of what R. P. Blackmur called the "conscience and motive for everybody else taken separately and, taken together, for the human action as well."[9] And, he adds, "each, naturally, is destroyed," his remark covering only Strether, Maggie Verver, and Milly Theale but applicable to the other heroes and heroines named and to many others not named (I have deliberately selected from the better known). James himself would have argued, did argue, that these consciences ought not to be regarded as losers: their triumph lies in the very freedom they gain by "giving up." So in writing of Fleda Vetch, the heroine in *The Spoils of Poynton* who foregoes the material and human "spoils" within her reach, he remarks: "The fools are interesting by contrast [to heroines like Fleda Vetch] by the salience they acquire, and by a hundred other of their advantages; and the free spirit, always much tormented, and by no means always triumphant, is heroic, ironic, pathetic or whatever, and, as exemplified in the record of Fleda Vetch, for instance, 'successful,' only through having remained free" (pp. 129-130).

Whether this analysis holds for Isabel Archer or Lambert Strether has been the subject of much critical debate, but we must recognize in what light James conceived "freedom"; his light may not be ours yet it is unwise to ask of him a vision of life he could not and did not have. He justified the sacrifices of his characters in terms of the personal freedom they won through renunciation; of Milly Theale, perhaps the greatest sacrificer of them all, he writes: "There goes with it, for the heroine of 'The Wings of the Dove,' a strong and special implication of liberty, liberty of action, of choice, of appreciation, of contact" (p. 292). She is considered the "last fine flower—blooming alone, for the fullest attestation of her freedom," the very same vision, from a different angle, which he had already positioned for the heroine of *The Portrait of a Lady* (p. 292).

Others, less heroic than Isabel Archer, Lambert Strether, or Milly Theale, also "sacrifice," renounce (like Charlotte Stant in *The Golden Bowl*), because in the end James, in effect, leaves them no choice. In some cases he makes them "pay" enough to earn his admiration which, in the *Prefaces,* he then asks the reader to share. Of Kate Croy and Morton Densher in *The Wings of the Dove* he is moved to write: "Heaven forbid . . . we should 'know' anything more of our ravaged sister than what Densher darkly pieces together, or than what Kate Croy pays, heroically, it must be owned, at the hour of her visit alone to Densher's lodging, for her superior handling and her dire profanation of" (p. 301). Such heroic payment is, of course, what he had in mind for Charlotte Stant and Adam Verver, who must beat a retreat in *The Golden Bowl* in what can hardly be called a happy ending to that trial. Trial—it is not inappropriate to see much of James's fiction as a series of "trials": the accused and the accusers, the crime itself; the process of argument, deliberation, confession, cross-examination; the jury deliberating and the judge sentencing, these are basic ingredients of many novels and tales. So much of James's major work proceeds along such judicial (and judicious) architectural lines, that the House of Fiction James built looks more often like a Hall of Justice, within whose walls governs a penal code for human behavior as intricate and as subtle as any dreamt of in the Middle Ages.

A good deal has been written about *The Sacred Fount,* a novel that has baffled readers from the beginning. The main question appears to be whether the narrator, who attends a weekend gathering at a country house, is "an intelligent man gone wrong" and quite "crazy," or, as he sees himself, engaged in a "high application of intelligence," an adventure in which the very process of sharpening his consciousness is scientifically explored as in a detective story.[10] One may better resolve the question the novel poses by paying more attention to the narrator's own expressed doubts, for it is possible to read the entire book as an allegory of the conscience-consciousness conflict. Ostensibly, the aim of the narrator is to follow leads and clues in order to confirm suspicions of certain liaisons among the various people gathered for the weekend. Much of the novel is centered on the narrator's curiosity, his sheer unabashed snooping, really, which he hopes will lead him to discover who is sleeping with whom. But the more the narrator (unlike Kafka's heroes, this man is not even given an initial, let alone a name) wants to find out, the more he *thinks* he finds out, the more he opens that insatiable consciousness—the more guilty he feels. The nameless narrator appears as a kind of projection of an undisciplined consciousness.

Now the guilt does not appear to be the result of becoming privy to great scandals or even to the discovery of his own unconscious libidinous desires, because James is careful never to reveal any substance to any scandal and leaves the whole unresolved and highly ambiguous. In fact the story is a teaser with no dénouement. Perhaps James could find none; more likely he realized that his narrator was one of his frequent types, the curious intruder whose capacity for meddling is rewarded by an uncomfortable sense of guilt. Such guilt proceeds not so much from the impropriety of meddling as from the realization that the privacy of others, prodded and pried into, reveals more than merely the shock of something discovered by the temerity of the meddler, whose manipulations can produce self-consciousness followed by shame and self-disgust: it reveals an immoral invasion into the sanctity of self. (This is precisely what happens in *The Aspern Papers.*) Commitment is one thing; interference is something else. Admitting to have "scruples," realizing that in his attempt to make for himself a receptive, sharpened consciousness he invites the retribution of a reluctant conscience, the narrator attempts to propitiate that conscience by periodically delivering himself of doubts throughout *The Sacred Fount*: he resolved to rid himself of his "ridiculous obsession," and he felt it absurd to have immersed himself so deeply into the lives of others.

Such scruples, such doubts, are by no means unique in James's fiction: they figure largely, in various forms, in many tales, some examples of which are: *The Aspern Papers, Daisy Miller,* "The Author of 'Beltraffio,' " "The Pupil," "The Figure in the Carpet," and, of course, "The Turn of the Screw," in addition to the major novels already named. The "curious intruder" is a Jamesian theme, and James examined, over and over, the ethical propriety and the psychological risks of a curiosity so avid that it turns into a selfish and insatiable greed to *know,* to become involved, at times, in unwanted manipulations of the lives of others. One of the investigated characters in *The Sacred Fount* tells the narrator precisely the nature of the problem when she urges him to "give up" his pretense to providence, for a genuine providence "knows" and need not labor towards such knowledge. That finding out is apt to develop an "imagination of atrocity," a severe judgment perhaps, but preparatory to the last three major novels an appropriate one.

In the first of James's novels (he preferred to think of it as his first), *Roderick Hudson* (1875), the problem is much more gently handled because nowhere is there any conscious evil; the obsession in that story remains fairly unconscious until the end, and the accessories to the crime of meddling number at least three beyond the main curious intruder. Also *Roderick Hudson* operates on a larger outer geography—the "problem of the artist"—and this tends to give it a wider scope in some areas while, of course, depriving it of the fine intensity of the later work.[11]

The Romantic's urge for vague and infinite abstractions; the realist's awareness that such a course is futile; and the artist's struggle to resolve this impasse, these are all carefully delineated in the novel. What makes *Roderick Hudson* a special case is not the treatment of a Romantic artist who fails (romantically), but the special conflict leading to that failure, both within and without the hero, who is unwillingly made to participate in the dialectic.

One way to describe this dialectic is Romanticism versus Realism. Certainly the consistent change of a word like "picturesque" (in the early versions) to the word "romantic" for the 1907 New York Edition provides some evidence for James's apparent desire to underscore the novel's involvement in Romanticism, particularly as James saw the book retrospectively.[12] Another possible approach to the dialectic of the novel is the strongly suggested Faustian theme: defiant action and defiant despair. A year before writing *Roderick Hudson,* James reviewed a French translation of *Faust.*[13] Several indirect and direct allusions to *Faust* found their way into the novel: the young man who sculpts a Water-Drinker called "Thirst," for "knowledge," he says; the betrayal of the fiancée; the pursuit of Ideal Beauty in a woman; the debauchery of the Baden-Baden episode, even the final thunderstorm, a kind of *Walpurgisnacht.* There are references to the sculptor Gloriani as resembling Mephisto and to the black poodle in Goethe's *Faust.* All these allusions, however, do not add up, except in a general way. Indeed Roderick is less a Goethean Faust and more a Byronic Manfred—the Manfred who, Gérard de Nerval thought, personified remorse. As a variation of the Faust-Manfred theme, Roderick may be seen as suffering from an imagination too quickly spent, for, like Coleridge's, Roderick's decline of genius is not merely a dissipation of character but a paralysis of creativity: "My mind is like a dead calm in the tropics, and my imagination as motionless as the blighted ship in the 'Ancient Mariner!' "[14] Here in his dejection Roderick echoes Coleridge:

> But oh! each visitation
> Suspends what nature gave me at my birth,
> My shaping spirit of Imagination . . .
> ("Ode to Dejection")

But there is yet another and a far more explicit set of terms to describe Roderick's dialectic, for the terms are James's own as he undoubtedly took them from Matthew Arnold: Hebraism (conscience) versus Hellenism (consciousness). From this dialectic there can never result any synthesis, only mutual annihilation.

In Chapter VI of *Roderick Hudson* James describes an elaborate party of artists and friends who have come to be guests at Roderick's debut as a sculptor. They are rewarded with life-sized statues of Adam and Eve and with a confident and ebullient young genius. It is Roderick's high point (a figure of speech that fits in several ways). On this occasion he announces a creed which to any cultivated English reader would undoubtedly have been a topical allusion: "I'm a Hellenist; I'm not a Hebraist!" That James was here alluding to Arnold's famous distinction is almost certain, although James reinterprets Arnold's terms and applies them to serve his own purposes. Encouraged by Henry James, Sr., James had from early youth been a sympathetic reader of Arnold. We also have evidence that in the year *Culture and Anarchy* (which contains the section on "Hebraism and Hellenism") was published in book form, 1869, James was in London, where he probably first heard of the new book, then the talk of the hour: it was his "thrilling opportunity to sit one morning, beside Mrs. Charles Norton's tea-urn . . . opposite to Frederic Harrison, eminent to [him] at the moment as one of the subjects of Matthew Arnold's early fine banter."[15] James's first review of Arnold (the *Essays in Criticism,* First Series) was published in the *North-American Review,* July 1865. In his biography of James, Leon Edel records a meeting between James and Arnold in 1873. Though the personal confrontation was a disappointment (due apparently to the "little glass [Arnold] screws into one eye"), Edel stresses the intellectual kinship between the two men. He also records a letter from Arnold to James in 1879, congratulating James on the achievement of *Roderick Hudson.* Clearly, Arnold was an early, strong influence, and, I should think, a permanent one.[16]

Although neither Roderick Hudson nor his patron, Rowland Mallet, perfectly fits one or the other of Arnold's principles, Hellenism or Hebraism, each behaves according to certain basic patterns which a knowledge of Arnold's dualism helps to illuminate. Rowland, by and large, is a puritan, a man long habituated to "conscience" of the kind Arnold meant by "Hebraism"; Roderick is largely a creature of consciousness, and his own aesthetic aims towards the perfection of ideal beauty identify him as something of an Arnoldian Hellenist. (It is true that Roderick's Hellenism is very Romantic and less "classical" than Arnold's, and that, unlike Shelley, whom Trelawny took to see the dirty Grecian ships, Roderick never discovers what Trelawny said—that Hellenism can be Hell.) These distinctions are not, of course, rigid in the novel, and the complexities of character and story happily prevent one from forcing an almost allegorical interpretation on the book. Still, in that very complexity James seems to have caught the duality of the problem with a very firm grip: The century was, after all, characterized by a mixture of inclinations between Hebraism and Hellenism. Goethe, Schiller, Wordsworth, Shelley, Carlyle, Hopkins, Ruskin, Nietzsche, Tolstoy, and, indeed, Arnold and James—were they not all (sometimes alternately) moral aesthetes or aesthetic moralists?

From the first pages of the novel, James makes us aware of Rowland Mallet's conflict between his puritan heritage and his acquired taste for a form of irresponsible dilletantism: "[Europe is] always lotus-eating." Rowland had a "lively suspicion of his [own] uselessness," which coincides with his cousin Cecilia's suggestion that there may be some positive harm in a man who is *not* doing some "positive good." This inner state of disaffection puts Rowland on the track of some "errand," something to *do*; and in his "frequent fits of melancholy," he declared that he was "neither fish nor flesh . . . neither an irresponsibly contemplative nature nor a sturdily practical one." Indeed, the two impulses divide him to make an "awkward mixture of moral and aesthetic curiosity," and Rowland can obtain "happiness" only in one of two directions: "either in action of some thoroughly keen kind on behalf of an idea, or in producing a masterpiece in one of the arts." Since he confesses himself as being incapable of achieving either, being "a man of genius half-finished" with "the faculty of expression . . . wanting," but "the need for expression" remaining, the reader is very early alerted to Rowland's fate, which Rowland himself predicts: to "spend [his] days groping for the latch of a closed door" (like Morris Townsend in *Washington Square*).

Rowland's conception of the artist, which is central to the shaping of Roderick's fate, is a "strong conviction that the artist is better for leading a quiet life": Creation is the fulfillment of a *duty*. The artist, then, must *do*. What is to feed the imagination towards execution is a question that does not exist for Rowland; or, to put it more positively, any contact with life as a source of stimulation will, in Rowland's view, merely contaminate the artist.

Rowland's sole prescription for artistic success is work: "You've only to work hard," he tells Roderick before they set sail for Europe; and, much later, after a stormy scene during which Roderick pleads the special case of genius, Rowland's only response is: "tumble to work somehow." Virtue always lies in the act, in "the resolution *not* to chuck [it]," in making "the effort necessary at least for finishing [the] job," after which one is free to destroy it, the moral fibre having been tested by chafing it against the grain. When Roderick's collapse is imminent and he pleads for Rowland's companionship, the latter offers to bargain his affection on familiar terms: "If I go with you, will you try to work?" To this he gets a bitter reply: " 'Try to work!' [Roderick] cried, 'Try—try! work—work! . . . Do you suppose I'm trying *not* to work?' " James may very well have been divided on the question himself; all artists have found, sometimes to their dismay, that work is an inseparable adjunct to creativity. Nor am I suggesting that, in the special case of this novel, Rowland's advice was always and altogether wrong. But James also courts sympathy for the artist's desperate need to rejuvenate himself, an activity of "play" and "purposelessness" (using Kantian terms) with which Rowland's "work" has little in common. The somewhat sudden decline of Roderick's creative productivity, James shows very clearly, is not due to a lack of work, as Rowland repeatedly thinks, but to the idealization of Christina Light—of reality—and to a misunderstanding of Hellenism.

To counter Roderick's Hellenism, James creates an antagonist, the sculptor Gloriani, strictly a realist, both as man and artist. Gloriani warns Roderick against "trying to be Greek" and suggests that he sculpt Judas, to which Roderick replies (in the revision) that though such a figure might have "a great deal of character," it is not the sort he cares for: "I care only for beauty of Type."

Roderick complains that his contemporaries have forsaken the "beauty in the large ideal way," and that he means to restore it, to "go in for big things; that's my notion of my art. I mean to do things that will be simple and sublime," an unconscious echo perhaps of Winckelmann's famous phrase about Greek sculpture—"noble simplicity and calm grandeur." For the 1907 revision James puts into Roderick's mouth a pure late Jamesian language to propose what the young sculptor means to do: "I want to thrill you, with my cold marble, when you look. I want to produce the sacred terror."

Against the idealistic Roderick, James marshalls all the resources of the new realism (including cynicism), embodying them in a point of view which admires the naïveté and spontaneity of a nineteenth-century Hellenistic imagination, while recognizing all the inherent weaknesses and dangers of an epigone: a point of view neither Hellenist nor Hebraist. When Rowland asks Gloriani to judge a photograph of the "Water Drinker," an early piece done in Northampton, the experienced sculptor admires but issues a warning that Roderick won't be able to keep up this sort of thing; to which Roderick replies that he won't merely keep it up but do even better. Gloriani's answer is straight to the point: "You'll do worse. You'll do it on purpose. This thing wasn't done on purpose. It couldn't have been. You'll have at any rate to take to violence, to contortions, to romanticism, in self-defence. Your beauty, as you call it, is the effort of a man to quit the earth by flapping his arms very hard. He may . . . jump about very gracefully, I admit; but you can't fly; there's no use trying."

It takes only a week for Gloriani's prophecy to come true; Roderick suddenly becomes restless and he ceases to work. Here occurs the interlude at Baden-Baden (Roderick is reluctantly released by Rowland to make the trip himself and James never reports what happens except indirectly). When he returns he seems to have forgotten all his grand abstractions. Instead he sculpts "a woman leaning lazily back in her chair, with her head inclined in apparent attention, a vague smile on her lips and a pair of remarkably beautiful arms folded in her lap," which Rowland "was not sure he liked," but which Gloriani admires, happy that Roderick is "coming around." Had he not prophesied he "couldn't keep up that flapping of his wings in the blue, and . . . [would have to] come down to earth?" Rowland remains unconvinced; he does not like this fruit of experience at Baden-Baden. "That's because you yourself try to sit like an angel on a cloud," replies Gloriani; "This . . . is full of possibilities, and he'll pull some of them off; but it isn't the *sancta simplicitas* of a few months ago . . . I congratulate him on having found his feet." Baden-Baden, then, has not been merely an episode of debauchery, nor has it led to declining creative powers. On the contrary, experience with life has now put to rest some of Roderick's grandiose abstractions ("I mean to do the Morning . . . Night . . . Ocean") and inspired a new inventiveness and a new art, a new consciousness.

Although Rowland has an "uncomfortably sensitive conscience," his consciousness is another matter; we must not confound, as he does, a Hebraistic sense of sin with a Hellenistic capacity to see the object as it really is. Rowland is a connoisseur, that is all; and even in this role his "Puritan" taste remains an unconscious censor. He tells his cousin Cecilia that to care for something or someone is now his only aim, for as a man he is totally insufficient; his search is for love. James allows Rowland to fall in love (in the Jamesian manner) with Roderick's American fiancée at the very start of the novel, yet he proceeds to have Rowland remove not only the future bridegroom but himself. While the young James might well have been struggling with plot and structure, there is already the self-punitive economics as well as the punishment-of-others at work in his character of Rowland, essentially a form of "emotional cannibalism."[17]

In fairness, Rowland does not undertake his mission of "educating" Roderick lightheartedly: "when he reflected that he was really meddling . . . he gasped, amazed at his temerity." Yet this very sense of duty, of responsibility, nails down his relationship to Roderick with ambiguously gained rights, to which the victim objects: "I think that when you expect a man to produce beautiful and wonderful works of art you ought to allow him a certain freedom of action . . . to give him a long rope . . . to let him follow his fancy and look for his material wherever he thinks he may find it . . . An artist can't bring his visions to maturity unless he has a certain experience. You demand of us to be imaginative, and you deny us the things that feed the imagination . . . When you've an artist to deal with you must take him as he is, good and bad together . . . If you want them to produce you must let them conceive. If you want a bird to sing you mustn't cover up its cage."

When it is the artist's turn to reproach his sponsor, he asks bitterly: "What am I . . . but a desperate experiment?" The word "desperate" James added in the 1907 revision perhaps to balance the characteristic noun of the century—experiment—with an adjectival corrective from the world of feeling (Hawthorne had written a score of stories about "desperate experiments"). Roderick prepares his brief against the future with a typically Romantic weaponry: "Do I more or less idiotically succeed—do I more or less sublimely fail? I seem to myself to be the last circumstance it depends on." The Romantic hero invariably feels that "circumstance" is his greatest enemy, and he himself the least effective of circumstances. Although only ten pages earlier Roderick had in effect accepted the responsibility for success or failure, he now implies that *Zeitgeist* will play the ultimate role in his fate.

In making of Roderick a self-conscious Romantic increasingly aware that he is an anachronism presiding over his own extinction, James has opened the question of free will, essential in the case of the artist who must decide whether he can triumph over such preying monsters as ennui, one thoroughly catalogued and described by a variety of nineteenth-century writers.[18]

For James "consciousness" seems almost always *intended,* at least, as the liberated state; yet in this novel, as elsewhere, it is clear that consciousness, in the end, can be a dangerous, even barren, condition. In spite of James's insistence on living to one's greatest capacity, few of his heroes or heroines, even when they achieve such desired awareness, are permitted to enjoy the fruits of their struggle. From Roderick and Rowland to Isabel Archer, from Strether to the Ververs, conscience prevents, thwarts, aborts; renunciation is James's ultimate virtue, but it is an expense of spirit, a waste, a highly questionable triumph at best.

Feelings of helplessness, excessive self-pity, regressive and petu-
lant moods, passions and quiescence alternating—all are standard
symptoms of "Romantic Genius" whose consciousness of life
brings not freedom but imprisonment, bondage. Certainly Roderick
still belongs in the tradition of Werther: the gesture towards
sublimity, the empty response, the paralysis of imagination,
the tendency to self-dramatize, the fears of a devouring world,
and the final plunge into the abyss (which incidentally Roderick
appears to take during the inevitable Alpine thunderstorm,
rejecting Werther's more orderly suicide by revolver). The end of
the novel moves swiftly toward the dénouement.

During the last interview between Roderick and Rowland the
pains of the sufferer, that final mark of the sensitized aesthete's
conscience, are fully bared in a final bitter outburst against his
patron. Now the economic aspect of his relationship to Rowland
(a theme James was to explore many times in later works) mirrors
itself in the most vulgar images, translating itself from the currency of coin to the currency of emotions and spirital loans:
"What I resent is that the range of your vision should pretend to
be the limit of my action. You can't feel for me nor judge for me,
and there are certain things you know nothing about. I have suffered, sir! . . . I've suffered damnable torments. Have I been such a
placid, contented, comfortable creature these last six months that
when I find a chance to forget my misery I should take such pains
not to profit by it? You ask too much . . . for a man who himself
has no occasion to play the hero. I don't say that invidiously; it's
your disposition, and you can't help it. But decidely there are
certain things you know nothing about."

This attack against Rowland and those against Mary Garland are
strengthened in the 1907 revision, where Mary herself blames
Rowland for having in part destroyed her lover. When it becomes
clear that Roderick will not return from the night of the storm,
"Mary stood there at first without a word, only looking hard at
[Rowland] "—a hard look she does not give in the earlier versions.
Hebraism, too, James seems to have felt, needed its atonement.
And if Hellenism failed Roderick, he dies like a hero, imperfect
but admirable. There is a suggestion of the Icarus myth in the

circumstances and descriptions of Roderick's death, a myth thoroughly Romantic but already foreshadowing a more famous portrait of the artist.

Alone amidst the stony Alps the morning after the storm, Rowland searches for his lost friend. "The silence everywhere was horrible; it mocked at his impatience, it was charged with cruelty and danger. In the midst of it . . . sat a hideous *crétin* who grinned at him over a vast goitre." Looking down into the "ugly chasms" below, Rowland "was to consider afterwards, uneasily, how little he had heeded his foothold." Rowland's sense of guilt works hard upon his imagination: With a bright sun penetrating the "depths and heights" of a lonely and "stony Alpine void" Rowland feels "sick to his innermost soul." Finally, in a gorge, he and a friend find "a vague white mass," but James almost ritualistically avoids gory details. This Icarus "had fallen from a great height, but he was singularly little disfigured. The rain had spent its torrents upon him, and his clothes and hair were as wet as if the billows of the ocean had flung him upon the strand."

Though attacked by some as melodrama, the final pages of this novel, seen in the perspective I have tried to place them, reinforce the elegiac note of the last Romantic's death and the survivor's guilt for his victim. Again James added sentences for the 1907 edition to strengthen Rowland's guilty conscience as an instrument of Roderick's death. Alone, waiting for the stretcher-bearers to take Roderick to the village, Rowland feels at the very least an actor in a tragedy of Fate: "The great gaunt wicked cliff above them became almost company to him, as the chance-saved photograph of a murderer might become for a shipwrecked castaway a link with civilisation: it had but done *its* part too, and what were they both, in their stupidity, he and it, but dumb agents of fate?" Of the surrogate nature in his relationship to Roderick, Rowland is now aware, for he now "understood how up to the brim, for two years, his personal world had been filled [with Roderick]." This world now comes to a close in the appropriate metaphor of the stage (added for the 1907 edition), for the world seems to Rowland now "as void and blank and sinister as a theatre bankrupt and closed." In spite of vast economic advantages he has been driven to seek domination over another: It is a sinister parable in nineteenth-century literature, and James was not alone in being fascinated by it. When the patron becomes the conscience of his protégé's consciousness, neither can prevail.

Hebraism and Hellenism, conscience and consciousness, play a central role in the lives of countless nineteenth-century heroes and their authors. As consciousness is permitted to expand, experience often corrupts it (Rowland Mallet's fears are not entirely unfounded); then conscience, or guilt, begins to destroy from within and from without. The Romantics never fully resolved this problem—how to allow a receptive consciousness to lead to fruitful experience and free will (many of Ibsen's early plays are variations on this particular theme, especially, of course, *Peer Gynt* and *Brand*). Schopenhauer's blind and malign will (though often misunderstood) was ubiquitous, haunting scores of heroes in fiction and drama and turning them into helpless victims. It was not until 1887 that Nietzsche struck out in *The Genealogy of Morals,* attacking the whole Judaic-Christian system of "guilt" and "conscience." Throughout the nineteenth century the Faustian urge to "experience" seems converted (or perverted) into the compulsive urge to repent (even as Faust himself sometimes repents). Something holds back; something negates what is being affirmed; from *Werther* to the last of the Buddenbrooks the theme of conscience versus consciousness is often a source of art itself.

This theme James treated largely, I think, by adapting Arnold's distinctions between Hebraism and Hellenism, for here he seemed to have found the perfect dialectic for describing his hero's conflict. As a late Romantic, an epigone, Roderick is already overtaken by a new art and a new time, a situation that makes Roderick's struggle to reach a compromise with reality pathetic and futile. Hebraism—work, conscience, renunciation—served James perfectly in fashioning his Puritan Hebraist, Rowland; while Hellenism—freedom, spontaneity, the free pursuit of beauty, consciousness—created the perfect foil in drawing the portrait of his artist-hero.

James was a Romantic pragmatist, something which Roderick tries but fails to become. What finally frustrated Roderick was not only Rowland, the Puritan Hebraist (his alter-conscience), but his illusory belief that the artist's consciousness can go slumming and then return to its rarefied Heaven. Clearly once the artist has had true intercourse with life he has fallen and no return to innocence is possible. To see the object as it is requires, at least for the artist, a seeking out, a process of "doing." Thus, whether or not he intended it, James's novel is a critique of Arnold's distinctions, for implicitly James insists that the artist cannot survive them.

Arnold's opposition of Hebraism and Hellenism, conscience and consciousness, was well intentioned; and it served for a time as a useful historical paradigm that highlighted the negative of a striving society too dedicated to the virtues of a materialistic "doing." Yet he was perhaps too optimistic in thinking that he might divide and conquer a habit which he had recognized and berated in the Romantics even before he saw and feared the worst in the conduct of his contemporaries. For between "knowing" and "doing" there can never be a true choice, only a continual oscillation. Doing, when translated to the life of an artist, must always precede knowing or being (Arnold was no Existentialist); and the road to Hellenism leads from the imagination to Baden-Baden, to Christina Light, to life and experience. Like Emerson's, Arnold's moral vision was sometimes misleading and incomplete; in separating Hebraism from Hellenism, doing from knowing, conscience from consciousness, he perhaps ultimately rendered a disservice to the culture of his day. It is perfectly true that, in "Hebraism and Hellenism," Arnold saw in both Hebraism and Hellenism the same aim, "man's perfection or salvation," and, though he stressed Hebraism, he would, in time, return to correct any Hellenic excesses; for his age he wanted Hellenism and, in the tradition of Goethe, a Hellenism both guiltless and free, yet full of "order" and "authority." From the outset, James's view of the imagination was that it could not sustain itself on itself, that it needed, besides its own spontaneity, stimulation from without, a conviction shared, somewhat later, by James Joyce.

In *The New England Conscience,* Austin Warren has analyzed James's particular concept of conscience (and consciousness), singling out for special attention *The Ambassadors.* Warren feels it was James's purpose to educate Strether's conscience, to make his story "the development of conscience into consciousness"—a significant reversal of how some of the other authors discussed in this book have treated the subject, that is, developing a consciousness into a conscience. Yet even here the circle comes 'round again, for to "develop a conscience into a consciousness" amounts to having Strether revert to his conscience, however "educated" it now is. "The novel," (*The Ambassadors*) writes Warren, "is a novel of initiation, a *Bildungsroman.*" While showing such a conscience as Strether's as educable, James did not free it to enjoy anything for itself except, of course, the awareness of its own freedom, no small victory. Pointing to the controversial ending, when Strether refuses the hand of Maria Gostrey, Warren shows how this *had* to be so, being perfectly consistent with Strether (and with James): "Miss Gostrey's question remains—Why does Strether have to be so 'dreadfully right' [that is, "good," self-sacrificing and "true to type"]?. . . . Strether's emancipated conscience in judging others, an emancipation painful to him in the process and hardly joyful in the end, has still left him pride—his pride in the supererogatory rigors of his own, his New England, conscience."[19]

Readers (especially when young) have found the ending to *The Ambassadors* needlessly unrewarding and sterile for "poor Strether." It seems that James was determined to have conscience prevail, although he was increasingly willing to let consciousness educate conscience as Warren has so aptly phrased the "strategy" of the novel. To educate it was, indeed, to free it, at least in Strether's case, from a narrow, joyless, ignorant sense of guilt and sin to an aware sense of self-sacrifice and renunciation. In the last Big Three of the major novels James came very close to a Goethean concept of renunciation as best illustrated in that psychological masterpiece, *Die Wahlverwandtschaften* (*The Elective Affinities*) which James probably, and regrettably, had not read.

In *The Wings of the Dove* "conscious," "consciousness," "consciously," and "conscience," when added up, occur over one hundred times, certainly the sign of a preoccupation, if not an obsession. This story of two lovers planning a consummation in marriage when their prey, the young and fatally ill Milly Theale, dies leaving her fortune as a gift for deceptive love—such a story is an "atrocity of imagination" for which we might well hold James accountable. What James recognized as all the vulgar possibilities, the "risks" as he might have said, he candidly put down in his *Notebooks.* Only those rejected possibilities measured against the published version allow *The Wings of the Dove* that consideration of high value which some critics have bestowed upon it. R. P. Blackmur interprets *The Wings of the Dove* as a problem of conscience in process of being created. In his Preface to the Laurel Edition, he sees the fineness of the book in the moral dilemma that is finally embodied in the young man upon whom the fiancée has urged the plot: make love to this dying girl and thereby help make her remaining life more generous; there can be no harm in that. Then, once she dies and leaves her money, we shall have both freedom and means. All can be gainers. But the young man, Densher, gradually awakens to the brutality of this scheme proposed by that harsh-sounding lady, Kate Croy. Finally, in all his splendid defeat, the young man triumphs: "Densher comes out not with a bad conscience or a good conscience . . . Densher comes out with created conscience—the very 'agen-bite of inwit'—and the assertion of conscience is his form of action . . . Densher's conscience prevents at the same that it invites. His weakness is that he is incapable of his own conscience when it is confronted with the conditions of life. This is the course of the last two hundred pages of the novel: the realization and assertion of conscience in the name of, and at the same time destroying, the joy of life."

Densher woos the dying girl—up to a point. When she discovers how she has been used and betrayed, she turns her head to the wall, dies, and with a last gesture of largesse leaves the major portion of her fortune to the man who has deceived her. In constructing his conscience, in realizing it, Densher learns; he learns so much, as his consciousness is flooded with past actions, that he renounces not only his fortune but his fiancée. They shall never again be as they were; this Kate Croy agrees with as she leaves Densher behind her. They have indeed "won"; yet they have lost everything, not only each other but parts of themselves. Densher atones by renouncing. Success of such atonement is not the issue, for James had no obligation to take his story any further. By the time James leaves Densher alone in Venice, paying court to the dying Milly, the man's very isolation is sufficient to work upon him the birth of his conscience. Thinking over at one point all the implications of the duplicity he has heaped on his character, James writes of his young man sympathetically: "Never was a consciousness more rounded and fastened down over what filled it." When it is full to overflowing that consciousness has metamorphosed into conscience. That very subtle and refined treatment of the issue was, however, already foreshadowed when Roderick Hudson, that pirate of his own consciousness, proclaimed that he was a Hellenist, not a Hebraist.

Lord Jim's "Romantic Conscience"

Conrad also was a student of conscience. Like James's, his major tales and novels are excursions into the subject from different directions, but their theme is sometimes the same: man's response—and his responsibility—in the face of trial, and the margin of error permitted to salvage oneself, fallible but necessarily committed to strict moral engagement. Although in style and setting no two novelists could be more apart than James and Conrad, both men admired and liked each other, not only personally but with respect to each other's art. Coming of literary age almost a generation later than James, and being fourteen years his junior, Conrad tended to be overawed by James, at least if the letters that survive are any indication. Even after they had met and had formed a pleasant association and Conrad's reputation was assured, Conrad's letters would still begin *"Très cher maître,"* signed *"A vous de coeur."* To the end Conrad professed veneration for James, and when James once criticized him in print, Conrad was hurt. Essentially, aside from the difference in age and the established reputation which James had earned (Conrad was long fighting off his fame as storyteller of sea adventures), he must have felt in James a kindred spirit, not in the intricate theories of the

art-novel, which Conrad avoided while he respected their importance, but in a common concern with human defeat and victory in
the large arena of moral battle. However different their milieu,
both saw the possibilities of man's actions and consequences in
terms of self-conscious choice (and, in Conrad, chance) and the
attendant heavy duty of a man to fulfill his selfhood selflessly.[20]

The recognition of these concerns has recently placed Conrad
among what had previously been a more select "modern" company: Ibsen, James, Mann, Gide, Joyce, Hemingway, Kafka, to
name only a few invoked in M. D. Zabel's fine introduction to *The
Portable Conrad*. Even the "French Existentialists" are heirs to
Conrad, suggests Zabel, for they, too, have given "heroism a new
setting in the absurdity of society and the universe." It is especially "the processes and structures of the moral experience,"
imposed on "the form of the plot" that Zabel most admires in
Conrad's work, an area whose "dramatic version," he feels, might
have been surpassed only by Kafka. "Even in James, whose genius
also took this direction . . . the ratiocinative element" (as in Poe?)
prevented the "equal coincidence of sensibility with form" from
reaching fulfillment. In any event, an "instinct of guilt and moral
recrimination" (whatever its autobiographical causes) does by
common consent exist in Conrad's major work; he bestows upon
his characters a heroism—attenuated and ambiguous as many
critics of Conrad have admitted—"expressed in acts of expiation,
self-vindication, or secret moral victory," attenuated or not. A
man's salvation seems always the thrust of any major tale or novel,
"the test of experience," "the recognition of selfhood"—all that,
but, first of all, a deep fear of the "irresponsibly abstract faiths,
and the moral nihilism to which the modern world encourages
[man] to surrender himself." Even "alienation" applies to Conrad's heroes who, as Zabel eloquently expresses it, "must serve as a
focus of worth and honor when the world forgets what these
things mean."[21]

A year after the publication of *The Magic Mountain* in 1924,
Thomas Mann (in an introduction to the German translation of
The Secret Agent [*Der Geheimagent*]) touched on Conrad's par-
ticular western freedom-oriented and anti-Russian bias, as he saw

it then, in *The Secret Agent,* Conrad's equivalent of James's *The Princess Casamassima.* Exiled and embittered by his early years under Tsarist and revolutionary terror, Conrad is seen as rejecting that world for the ambiguities and uncertainties of individual freedom. While Mann was, even then, grinding an ax, his comments on the novel are often very shrewd; and his conclusion is important and probably very close to the truth, namely that Conrad's severe objectivity, though chilling, is a "passion—because it is love of freedom," the same lust for freedom which drove the young Conrad to seek the open sea and Turgenev to Paris. "I think," writes Mann, "that his art will protect him from having this sense of freedom equated with a liberal bourgeois position, his complete lack of sentimentality making it doubtful that he can be accused of 'aestheticism.' "[22] One may have doubts whether Conrad was all that objective and unsentimental, yet Mann means to clear up even the possibility of a dangerous misunderstanding. In his eyes Conrad was a lover of freedom without recourse to the idealistic rhetoric of his own Settembrini, epigone of nineteenth-century bourgeois liberalism, chatterbox and organ-grinder of pious sentiments that left individual man ultimately absolved of responsibility, a mere victim of institutionalized repression. That is a valid point, and it is astonishing, in a way, that Mann should have made it so early; it applies with equal meaning to a Joyce or a Yeats or to the best of D. H. Lawrence, as well as to those later "French Existentialists," particularly Camus, whom Zabel couples with Conrad. Man's personal freedom must be won afresh each day, to paraphrase Faust; the responsibility is each man's, yet each man may or may not be "one of us"—which phrase inevitably leads us to *Lord Jim.*

Of all James's heroes the one who most closely resembles Jim is young Hyacinth Robinson of *The Princess Casamassima.* Both men are young and, in Shakespeare's sense, foolish; both commit the greatest mistake of all—a false image of man reflected back intensively in a false image of themselves; both are not cut out for the life-experience fate presses upon them but which their own choice, falsely guided, makes them hold fast. In current idiom, both withdraw, yet neither is able to redeem himself because neither understands what conscience really is; both exaggerate the consequences of their moments of cowardice, their holding back from fulfilling their *duty*, but both fail to measure the meaning of their actions for themselves. So both, finally, commit themselves to the pistol, Hyacinth by pulling the trigger himself, Jim by permitting himself to be shot as payment for still another failure. One might carry the comparisons further, but this much will do; only kinship is suggested, since the two young men are very unlike in many important particulars. Yet their false sense of atonement, long a point of hot debate in Jim's case, is of central importance to an understanding of this particular problem in the fiction of both James and Conrad.

Jim's false sense of martyrdom is, perhaps to Conrad's credit, seldom stated explicitly but on the whole only suggested; James, usually by far the more subtle of the two writers, in the instance of Hyacinth Robinson, the hero of *The Princess Casamassima,* pushes the point home unerringly: "He [Hyacinth] suspended, so to say, his *small* sensibility in the midst of it, to quiver there with joy and hope and ambition as well as with the *effort* of renunciation" (italics mine). Smallness of sensibility (or consciousness) is a central feature in both young men, for it is upon such insufficiency that the faulty structure rests and therefore is doomed to totter and fall. Any saint can tell us (and any "tragic" hero) that renunciation requires no "effort," no deliberate "quiver" of joy, hope, or ambition; renunciation is the very absence of *that* sort of effort. Yet most conspicuous in *Lord Jim* is precisely the enormous "effort" that Conrad's young man exercises, an effort always directed towards vindication, not expiation.

To see things in their "reality" and "beauty" was, said Arnold, the aim of Hellenism; such desires, however, were obstructed by those features of Hebraism most inimical to "reality" and "beauty." "Under the name of sin, the difficulties of knowing oneself and conquering oneself which impede man's passage to perfection, become, for Hebraism, a positive, active entity hostile to man": what a paradox Arnold sees here! That same aim in both Hebraism and Hellenism, self-knowledge, is in the case of Hebraism sabotaged; the recurrent sense of sin stands in the way of self-knowledge, a state to which a man, according to Arnold, can only attain given free play of his spirit, *Spieltrieb*. This is certainly one of Jim's handicaps. Raised in a parsonage and taught to see things as they ought to be, rather than as they are, taught above all to see *himself* as he ought to be rather than to discover of what he might be capable, Jim is the most unlikely candidate for the tale that embodies him. He is already a confirmed Hebraist, in the Arnoldian sense.

In a preface affixed to *Lord Jim* in 1917 (first published in 1900), Conrad relates the story of a woman who disliked the book because it was "too morbid." He regrets that judgment but consoles himself with the thought that this woman could not be a European, certainly not a "Latin temperament" else she could never "have perceived anything morbid in the acute consciousness of lost honour." Conrad's sensitivity on this point is interesting; the European mind, he reasons, has after all always grappled manfully with the problem of "honour," won or lost, and certainly the "acute consciousness" of honor lost or stained or impaired struck Conrad as anything but a morbid subject. (In addition, it is true, that on such subjects as honor Conrad tended to be puritanical in the continental tradition.) Although admitting that Jim might not be "commonplace," he feels on solid ground with respect to his theme.[23] Preface aside, however, the lady who called *Lord Jim* "morbid" had a point, which Conrad himself supplied. Morbidity is perhaps a state of the reader's mind, but Jim's pursuit towards the recovery of his lost honor is suspect because of his "acute consciousness" (the "effort" to which I earlier alluded), a consciousness that tends, as the book progresses, to inflate the wrong kind of conscience, what Nietzsche would describe as a "bad conscience," a sense of having failed to please oneself rather than the recognition that pleasing oneself has really little, if anything, to do with the cultivation of a genuine conscience. (Jim's kind of conscience Schopenhauer called "spurious" and I will have more to say about that later in this chapter.) "I shall always remember him," says the narrator, Marlow, "as . . . taking, perhaps, too much to heart the mere consequences of his failure."

In his youthful daydreams, Jim makes of himself exactly the hero he will fail to be, "an example of devotion to duty, and as unflinching as a hero in a book." When failures prefigure the lapses of the future he doggedly persists, in spite of being quite aware of failure, indeed, *because* he is aware of it. The first incident involves the mishap at the Maritime School where he witnesses, helplessly, the destruction of a ship. Whatever he might have wished to do during that episode he did not do; it is too late then as it will be too late in times to come. Conrad's comment, through Marlow, his narrator, is that "Jim looked up with the pain of conscious defeat in his eyes." This fragment of a sentence seems to be the *leitmotif* of Jim's story; the "pain of conscious defeat" never leaves Jim, and hence it never frees him long enough to discover other options for redemption than the abuse of self, supererogatory demands on the ego, and finally a highly questionable renunciation. The goblins that haunt Jim's soul are always magnified by his scrupulous "effort"; "imagination," says Marlow, is "the enemy of men, the father of all terrors"; but, as Wordsworth asked rhetorically nearly a century earlier, whatever the risks with imagination, consider man without one? Still imagination is Jim's enemy because he uses it towards destructive ends. Even the final piece of drama is stage-set, when he "sent right and left at all those faces a proud and unflinching glance." There is more kinship between Jim and Werther than a rather carefully executed pistol shot (even though, of course, Jim lets himself be shot rather than shooting himself). Recognizing the failure of the idyl Jim sought to create during his sojourn in Patusan is a key factor in the decision to die. Like Werther, Jim sees what had promised even fleetingly to be possible become impossible; Paradise is invaded by the evil Mr. Brown, whom some critics have suspected of being a kind of *Doppelgänger*. And when failure becomes clear, the final act of imagination is the almost ritual submission to death: "Then Jim understood. He had retreated from one world, for a small matter of an impulsive jump, and now the other, *the work of his own hands, had fallen in ruins upon his head*" (italics mine).

In Conrad's own final and perhaps bitter words, spoken through Marlow, and at the center of controversy over the ending of the book, Jim leaves life and love "at the call of his exalted egoism ... to celebrate a pitiless wedding with a shadowy ideal of conduct." Werther was far more sophisticated in the knowledge of that "shadowy ideal of conduct" (in Werther's case merely a "shadowy ideal" would explain the matter); but neither is aware of that "exalted egoism," the great scourge of all idealists to which Ibsen devoted a lifetime of subtle study, and which artists from *Antigone* to Camus's *La Chute* have recognized as a monstrous, alluring, fatal disease. Those who defend Jim at the end sometimes insist on the wrong point: It is not the ideal of conduct which Conrad casts into doubt, but the manner and the reason why Jim pursued it.

Already under official questioning, Jim makes the fatal mistake of interiorizing what is external, building up a posture of defensiveness not against the questions his judges ask but against himself. This distinction is subtle, but Conrad is equal to shaping this point exactly as he wants it: Jim's voice, while responding to his questions, "was very loud, it rang startling in his own ears, it was the only sound audible in the world, for the terribly distinct questions that extorted his answers seemed to shape themselves in anguish and pain . . . like the terrible questioning of one's conscience." Prior guilt: that is what Conrad needs to establish, that Jim *feels* guilty long before the jump from the ship, as he must, as any man must who prepares for tomorrow with an imagined conduct set down today and the memory of a failure of conduct yesterday.

No, Conrad does not suggest that a man dispense with a system of personal values, only that he not indulge it either with too much imagination or with "exalted egoism." The captain at the court-martial who calmly jumps to his death at sea after the proceedings (Brierly) has understood this danger and taken, one may say, irreversible evasive action; he won't even chance what he fears might happen. For Conrad, I believe, Jim and Brierley—both ending up in rather the same way, suicide—represent the extremes of action vis-à-vis the question of man's conduct and his potential to carry it out. Brierley is not a "fool" like Jim and refuses to allow himself to become entangled in what Marlow describes candidly as "a little ridiculous . . . those struggles of an individual trying to save from the fire his idea of what his moral identity should be."

When the time might have been at hand for Jim to rouse the sleeping pilgrims and warn them of their imminent danger, he suffers a paralysis: "This is . . . what people mean by the tongue cleaving to the roof of the mouth. 'Too dry,' was the concise expression [Jim] used in reference to this state." Soundlessly Jim makes his way to the deck, some time before the jump becomes obsessional, when it really was only a culminating symptom, not the cause of his "case." (So, too, the narrator of *La Chute,* as we shall see, fails to respond to the splash in the water, the cry in the night, which he is certain indicates that a woman has jumped from the bridge he has just crossed.)

The long retelling of Jim's actions to Marlow takes up much of the novel (too much, as readers complained from the very start), but the overriding theme of that lengthy confession is the persistent rationalization of how this or that action would have been, at the time of the crisis, useless. Jim never really explains why he did things as he did, rather why he did not do them. It is omission that actually preoccupies him in the broadest sense, but commission of particular acts which fill out his long story surrounding the jump from the ship. Omission is much more difficult to account for; actions, if they do not speak for themselves, can at least be spoken for; "I saw," says Jim, "as clearly as I see you now that there was nothing I could do." This is a premise; it is not a fact.

And the more Jim broods on this premise, the more he needs to extricate himself; the more need to do that, the more need to call upon his imagination. "He must have had an unconscious conviction that the reality could not be half as bad, not half as anguishing, appalling, and vengeful as the created terror of his imagination. I believe . . . his heart was wrung with all the suffering, that his soul knew the accumulated savour of all the fear, all the horror, all the despair of eight hundred human beings . . . else why should he have said, 'It seemed to me that I must jump out of that accursed boat [the small boat he shares with the others who have abandoned the *Patna*] and swim back to see . . . to the very spot . . .'? . . . . to see—as if his imagination had to be soothed by the assurance that all was over before death could bring relief?" Marlow's observation is very astute; to paraphrase what I think it implies is important to an understanding of how Jim's case is here being viewed. If we consider (as I think we can) that imagination, especially in this context, is synonymous with consciousness, then what Jim is doing is establishing the premise of his helplessness. In effect, Conrad suggests that Jim, in a state of deep remorse and shame, wishes to confirm what his imagination has conjured up, to rationalize his projections. To confirm or to deny, that is the essence of the conflict. Jim would like to shape reality to conform to his deed: He has left the ship because he was helpless to do otherwise, and eight hundred people have died even before being aware that death was at hand (probably, he feels, thereby escaping any lingering horror in the process of dying). Such convictions might assuage his guilt. But in fact Jim does *not* leave the little boat to swim back to the spot, to see; unconsciously he must have suspected what he might see—drowning people by the hundreds or even the truth, the ship still afloat without command; and, more important, not seeing anything gives further license, at the time, to his imagination. Speculation is now a better course of therapy than the truth, whatever it is. A bad conscience he can readily admit to because a man may more easily say I *should* have than I *did*.

To err is human: Jim takes full advantage of that; and to the very end it is the error he concentrates on rather than the man who erred. Such a distinction is no verbal nicety but a major factor in his subsequent behavior after the inquiry. Sitting in that boat he suddenly feels a silence descending: He hears nothing; he makes this an essential point in his defense, that he heard nothing at all. Finally the silence frightens him and he begins hearing "shouts for help . . . Very faint screams—day after day." For those screams, as "imaginary" as the silence that obliterates everything, must be heard; they become his only salvation in place of the ocular proof he had forfeited when he did not swim back to the *Patna* to see whether, indeed, the boat had actually sunk. Either way he needs truth. Marlow recognizes this and pronounces Jim "guilty and done for"; yet he decides to help Jim for much the same reasons he recognizes the failures in the young man: "If he had not enlisted my sympathies he had . . . reached the secret sensibility of my egoism."

That egoism is not so different from Jim's "exalted egotism" which Marlow describes at the close of his story; as others have seen for a long time, Marlow's education is here (as in other stories he narrates) as much a process and function of the theme as the tale he unfolds. Perhaps it is one of the ironies of *Lord Jim* that Marlow's involvement is almost as much a testing of Marlow as of Jim: "If [Jim's] imaginative conscience or his pride; if all the extravagant ghosts and austere shades that were the disastrous familars of his youth would not let him run away from the block, I, who of course can't be suspected of such familiars, was irresistibly impelled to go and see his head roll off." Even Marlow knows that he indeed must be suspected "of such familiars," that he comes, initially, to see the execution from the classic motive of superiority: There by the grace of God I might never be! This is "exalted egotism" from a different angle or, as Marlow later describes it in Jim as a variation, "idealised selfishness." Both agree on one thing, though they see it differently at various points: "All the same," says Marlow, questioningly really, "one is responsible"; "And that's true," answers Jim.

Stein, that enigmatic man with the butterfly net and the pistol, diagnoses Jim as a "romantic." That again has led to much critical debate, but it is fairly certain that Stein does not mean a Byronic or Wordsworthian Romantic, not a hero who merely feeds on phantom dreams or seeks affinity with the repose of natural elements. Stein means rather a Blakean figure (Blake recognized the figure and suffered for it): "He wants," says Stein of Jim and his type, "to be a saint, and he wants to be a devil—and every time he shuts his eyes he sees himself as a very fine fellow—so fine as he can never be." This phenomenon Freud explained repeatedly as one of the experiences of conscience. The ego, guilty and disappointed with itself, intensifies the ideals against which measurement becomes, predictably, increasingly hopeless. What fails for Jim is a proper marriage of saint and devil, heaven and hell; the subtleness of such an arrangement lies beyond his range, and so Stein quite correctly sees him as neither saint nor sinner but a self-indulgent, self-congratulatory, overly righteous youth creating impossible moral standards for himself, so that, by failing to attain them, he can still be a "fine fellow." For only look at the *effort!*

Other than this, Stein's contribution to Jim is more a function of the plot than the deep philosophic import attached to him and his utterances about submitting oneself to the "destructive element," and Stein is clever enough to know that. His advice is, therefore, less directed at Jim and more at the human predicament, accentuating the failure of that specimen, the Jim-Romantic, who fails to do warfare with the waves.

In any case, sending Jim to Patusan is hardly preparation for immersion in any destructive element (if anything it is protection from it), except as it turns out literally to become for Jim a self-destructive experience, hardly what Stein had in mind. "To follow the dream," go the famous words, "and again to follow the dream—and so—*ewig—usque ad finem*." The trouble is Stein is, or at least has been, too much like Jim, and hence fails to be of real help, for both follow the dream always, *ewig, usque ad finem*; one wonders whether those superfluous foreign tags are not part of Conrad's underrated irony, operating like the tags Thomas Mann so often appended to the long speeches of Settembrini in *The Magic Mountain* (also a dreamer *without* immersion) which help the young Hans Castorp of that novel about as much as Stein's semicoherent utterances, though spoken to Marlow, help Jim.

Marlow does somewhat better. All exiles, he says, all homeless ones, need something; to have "joy," "peace," "to face the truth," one must have, not a clear conscience but a "clear consciousness." He means one must risk it—"few of us have the will or the capacity to look consciously under the surface of familiar emotions." That will Jim did, according to Marlow, possess in abundance; it was an acuteness of his situation and highly sensitive antennae which made his case so exceptional: "He was aware of [his exile] with an intensity that made him touching"; a man's character is his fate. In this respect Conrad was a thoroughgoing Aristotelian. Nevertheless, although Jim's imagination, his consciousness, and its intensity, make him a victim, Marlow (like Wordsworth) argues that to be without illusions may be "safe" and "profitable" but also very "dull." The problem, then, is for Jim to balance his acute consciousness with something else, to leaven his dreams, to balance his butterflies, with a revolver, one he holds pointing away from him not one he faces, willingly, pointing towards him. That lesson Stein has been unable to pass on; yet it is the only one to make even survival possible for such "romantics." When Jim tastes happiness in Patusan he cannot accept it as being quits with his disgrace. As Marlow exclaims, "This is glorious!" at the new love and life in a paradise of sorts, Jim "sat with his head sunk on his breast and said 'Yes,' without raising his eyes, as if afraid to see writ large on the clear sky of the offing the reproach of his romantic conscience."

That "romantic conscience" seems to be what Schopenhauer skeptically called "*conscientia spuria,*" a "spurious conscience," which is "often confused with the genuine." In an analysis Freud would adapt to his own analytical vision of guilt, Schopenhauer makes a distinction between the guilt occasioned by genuine ethical concern or by simple fear. "The remorse and anxiety," he argues, "that are felt by many a man for what he has done are often basically nothing but the fear of what may happen to him." Such "conscience" is, therefore, better seen as remorse based on past performance in trepidation of future judgment. Schopenhauer concludes that our dissatisfaction and distress "over the suffering we have not *undergone* but have *caused,* is a plain fact that no one will deny." The problem is certainly more subtle, and we will have occasion to return to this idea in a later chapter. Jim's discomfiture is certainly also a case of what he has "undergone"; but it is true that his torment is basically the consequence of focusing on what he has "caused" and, in turn, a fear of what this has done to his reputation, his good name, his place in life. "Conscience," writes Schopenhauer, "is an acquaintance with our own unalterable character, which we make only through the medium of our deeds."[24] Jim's acquaintance with that medium is in doubt, for he fails to satisfy us that he has really come to understand his own "unalterable character," the prerequisite for genuine, not "spurious," conscience.

Dorothea Krook entitled her major study of James *Ordeal of Consciousness in Henry James; Tyranny of Conscience* might well be a companion volume. For James's characters it is imperative that they have "refined sensibilities," "delicate perceptions," and

that James "endow them with the supreme gift of consciousness—
especially self-consciousness." But, haveing been so blessed, these
characters, says Miss Krook (correctly), must now endure an
"ordeal."[25] If there is a paradox here it is certainly not novel, as I
have made it central to all the authors and works so far discussed:
man's ability to handle the gift of consciousness (or self-
consciousness) may vary, but what is invariable is the ordeal of his
efforts. Whether that ordeal is called "conscience," as it must be in
the case of James and surely in *Lord Jim* ("spurious" or not) does
not essentially matter. What does matter is that Arnold's hope of a
consciousness spontaneous, free, guiltless without "ordeal," was
from the outset a futile hope; Arnold, it must be said, underestimated what he called "sin" and overestimated man's capacity
to see things as they really are. This occurred partly because he did
not envision how consciousness in the modern world would reveal
such things as men had seldom dreamed of—the fear and trembling, the sickness unto death. As a cultural exhortation, the call
for Hellenism was both needed and appropriate; as a *Weltanschauung* it was doomed to failure. Arnold, of course, could not
have forgotten his own Empedocles; but, quite the contrary, he
tried to overcome him, even to suppress him, to remove the crater
from his own consciousness. If we do not (as we should not)
forget that Arnold always insisted on the dialectic nature of
Hebraism and Hellenism, we should still be quite clear that in this
dialectic there is never an equal partnership between conscience
and consciousness: one or the other is the "ascendant force" at a
given time. There lies Arnold's miscalculation, that the effort "to
see things as they really are" can be severed, even for a historical
instant, from the "effort to win peace by self-conquest." What
obstructs the Hebraist, says Arnold, from gaining a wider perception is his single-minded pursuit of an "*unum necessarium,* or a
one thing needful." Such a "victim of Hebraism" cannot allow
himself the perceptions of man's full instincts, but "There is no
unum necessarium, or one thing needful, which can free human
nature from the obligation of trying to come to its best at all these
points . . . Nothing is more striking than to observe in how many
ways a limited conception of human nature, the notion of a one
thing needful, a one side in us to be made uppermost, the disre-

gard of a full and harmonious development of ourselves, tells injuriously on our thinking and acting."[26]

There is little to quarrel with in these words; they would have pleased Freud. Yet between Arnold and Freud there still remained one more step. Through the tragic fate that was to be Arnold's he failed to recognize that he was guilty of the very thing he warned against, "the notion of . . . a one side in us to be made uppermost." His Hellenism, while it would last, would indeed be "uppermost," and even the excesses he feared would explode all too soon in the lives of yet unknown disciples. The English nineties would be remembered for a long time as excess of "thinking and acting," as too much "spontaneity" and no "conduct" at all, as a frivolous age playing with sin (to paraphrase the Hebraist T. S. Eliot from a review of Arthur Symons's translation of *Les Fleurs du Mal*) without even understanding it. Such assessments were exaggerated but that is what it all came to, Arnold not living to see the final humiliation of what had been clearly, once again, a "premature" hope.

On the continent one man, thinking much as Arnold did, and taking inspiration from some of the same sources, Goethe and Heine, would settle for no dialectic. Conscience, or the Hebraic-Christian crystallization of it, must be destroyed once and for all, not to make room for drawing-room Hellenic dandies but for a new breed of man altogether, strong, resolute, morally free. Very shrewdly, however, Thomas Mann has recognized Nietzsche's "aestheticism" and its relation to the English *fin de siècle:* "It is astonishing to note," he writes, "the close relationship between some of Nietzsche's aperçus and the attacks . . . with which . . . Oscar Wilde . . . shocked his public and made it laugh."[27] (If we think of Wilde as a *serious* student of Arnold and Pater, as by now we must, then the coupling of Arnold and Nietzsche will seem less outrageous.) Yet Nietzsche, too, would underestimate and overestimate; he, too, would err by failing to offer a believable substitute for what he passionately sought to remove by what can only be called radical surgery. The operation was surely unsuccessful; but the patient lived—to continue to encounter his "ordeal."

VII. Towards a Genealogy of the Modern Problem: Schopenhauer, Nietzsche, and Freud

—La conscience dans le Mal!
  —Baudelaire, *"L'Irrémédiable"*

I have chosen Schopenhauer, Nietzsche, and Freud because these three extraordinary men considered conscience-consciousness within the perspective of a historical continuity. It was their passion to explore the past from all kinds of unexpected directions; to create sweeping historical patterns; to hypothesize from the groundwork of such new territory as anthropology and myth. From their comments about the problem, which I have tried to gather together from many scattered sources, we get, I think, an overview of the genealogy of conscience-consciousness as it manifests itself finally in some of the major modern writers. In addition, these three men often shared major positions, though each succeeding figure made advances and generally attempted to minimize his debts to his predecessor.

For example, Schopenhauer actually made his most important remarks on conscience in what he called his "critique" of Kant, but obviously much of Kant remained. Nietzsche, whose ambivalence towards Schopenhauer is always clear, almost ignores his mentor on the point of conscience, although, as we shall see, he bases much of what he says, even when in opposition, on Schopenhauerian foundations. Freud's case, because it is Freud's, is the most curious of all. Although many recent commentators, such as Walter Kaufmann and Philip Rieff, have acknowledged a general similarity between Freud and Nietzsche on the question of conscience (as well as on other matters),[1] it is still generally accepted that Freud was entirely candid and accurate when he wrote in his *Autobiography* (1925)—his *Selbstdarstellung:* "I have carefully avoided any contact with philosophy proper. This avoidance has been greatly facilitated by constitutional incapacity . . . The large extent to which psycho-analysis coincides with the philosophy of Schopenhauer . . . is not to be traced to my acquaintance with his teaching. I read Schopenhauer very late in my life."[2]

Yet Freud mentions Schopenhauer in his first important book, *The Interpretation of Dreams* (1900), on three occasions with very specific references to some Schopenhauerian theories about dreams. These references appear in the first chapter, "The Scientific Literature on Dreams," in the *first* edition of the book.[3] Two references to Schopenhauer were added in subsequent editions, one in a note in 1912 and one in 1914. Schopenhauer is also referred to in: "Notes Upon a Case of Obsessional Neuroses" (1909), *Totem and Taboo* (1913), "History of the Psycho-analytic Movement" (1914), "A Difficulty in Psycho-analysis" (1917). On occasion Freud lauded Schopenhauer as a precursor, citing particularly the philosopher's theory of sexuality (see, for example, "The Resistance to Psycho-analysis," 1925). On the whole Schopenhauer tends to disappear from the work of Freud after 1925, so that most of the references appear early rather than late. One remark might be quoted for its specificity: "I know of no outside impression which might have suggested it to me [the theory of repression] . . . until Otto Rank showed us a passage in Schopenhauer's *World as Will and Idea* in which the philosopher seeks to give an explanation of insanity." This is from the "History of the Psycho-analytic Movement" (1914), but Freud's footnote to this passage refers back to the *Zentralblatt für Psychoanalyse,* 1911. Again Freud immediately disowns any influence: "Once again I owe the chance of making a discovery to my not being well-read"; he follows with a remark about how he avoided philosophy, especially Nietzsche, just because that philosopher was so close to his own thinking.[4] This he was to adumbrate in the *Autobiography:* "Nietzsche, another philosopher whose guesses and intuitions often agree in their most astonishing way with the laborious findings of psycho-analysis, was for a long time avoided by me on that very account; I was less concerned with the question of priority than with keeping my mind unembarrassed."[5] The remark is patronizing and misleading, for Nietzsche, too, is alluded to in the first edition of *The Interpretation of Dreams*. Ernest Jones even detects a "paraphrase from Nietzsche" in the remarks written during the writing of *Interpretations* as early as 1897.[6] Nietzsche is quoted in "The Psychopathology of Everyday Life" (1904), when Freud compares his view of memory with Nietzsche's aphorism #68 in Book II of *Beyond Good and Evil.* Zarathustra is quoted in "Psycho-Analytic Notes Upon an Auto-biographical Account of a Case of Paranoia" (1911); Nietzsche is further referred to in "Some Character Types Met in Psycho-analytic Work" (1915), where Freud speaks of a "friend" drawing his attention to Nietzsche's perception of criminality and guilt. The phrase "eternal recurrence of the same" appears several times, once in a letter to Ferenczi in 1917.[7] (In 1908 Freud had direct contact with Nietzsche's work, but I reserve this episode for later.)

It would appear, then, that while professing general ignorance, Freud was fairly well acquainted with Schopenhauer and Nietzsche very early in his career, and that his special efforts to disown such knowledge is suspect in the face of the references, at regular intervals, which I have cited. I do not suggest a conscious attempt to mislead, but the probability of ambivalence (to use Freud's own word in such instances) and self-deception is very high. Freud was, in fact, very well read; as a typically cultivated European living and learning in the civilized milieu of Vienna at the end of the nineteenth century, he would be expected to know some Schopenhauer and Nietzsche. Finally, as to the protestations against the difficulties of philosophy, neither of these men stands strictly under the rubric of philosophy: Schopenhauer was a great stylist and often wrote like a sophisticated essayist; Nietzsche has been called a poet. A mind such as Freud's need not have encountered undue difficulties in either man's works. The record should be clarified. Even Thomas Mann stated flatly that Freud "did not know Nietzsche" and "did not know Schopenhauer," while allowing himself the pleasure and delight of instructing his readers in how these two philosophers had anticipated the founder of psychoanalysis.[8] As I have said, I make this point because when the views of the three men are placed side by side, on the question of conscience (and consciousness), they show a remarkable sense of having been built up from one another, and even if Freud did not consciously build on Schopenhauer and Nietzsche, the sequential edifice of the views, especially on conscience, is worth delineating in detail as part of a general progress of an idea—and that is the chief reason for establishing the relationship here.

Schopenhauer's main argument with Kant on the question of conscience was the implied identity, in Kant, of conscience and the categorical imperative. These are not the same, Schopenhauer argued, since the imperative is a priori, operating prior to any man's deed, while conscience comes into view only a posteriori, after the deed: "Even the etymology of the word *Gewissen* (conscience) seems to me to rest on this, since only what has already taken place is *gewiss* (certain). That is . . . impure, base, and wicked thoughts and desires occur to everyone of us, even the best; but a person is not morally responsible for these and they should not burden his conscience, for they show only what *man generally*, not what *he* who thinks them, would be capable of doing."[9] There are other kinds of motives that penetrate our "consciousness" in opposition to those already lodged there; hence base motives do not always become base deeds, but indeed such "evil motives are like the outvoted minority of a meeting that passes a resolution." This being so, man learns of himself, finally, in deeds only, "and only *deeds* burden the *conscience*."[10]

As might be expected, Nietzsche varies these points just enough to reveal the link with Schopenhauer while clearly displaying his unique conception of the problem: "Nobody is responsible for his actions, nobody for his nature; to judge is identical with being unjust. This also applied when an individual judges himself. The theory is as clear as sunlight." Nietzsche's conception of man's moral freedom, although it takes off from Schopenhauer's, goes far beyond him. In fact, it is in the context of rejecting Schopenhauer's conception of "intelligible freedom" that Nietzsche wrote the above, having concluded that "therefore, it is only because man *believes* himself to be free, not because he is freed, that he experiences remorse and pricks of conscience."[11] Further still, a man who feels a *"pang of conscience"* is one who, in Nietzsche's opinion, has not yet developed a character "equal to his *deed"*—one, that is, finally willing to take on whatever deed might be decreed for him.[12]

In Freud the whole process of conscience is complicated by such specialized concepts as the superego (*über-Ich*), "repression," "ego-ideal," "guilt," "narcissism," and so on down the litany of psychoanalytic nomenclature. Despite this barrier, however, Freud's style, masterfully lucid, found ways of presenting his views on conscience, which are most elaborately discussed in two para-analytical works, the early *Totem and Taboo* (1913) and the late *Civilization and Its Discontents* (1930-1931). In *Totem and Taboo* Freud sets himself the rhetorical question, "For what is 'conscience'?" and proceeds to answer it: "On the evidence of language it is related to that of which one is 'most certainly conscious' [*was man am gewissesten weiss*]. Indeed, in some languages the words for 'conscience' and 'consciousness' [*Bewusstsein* in the original] can scarcely be distinguished." When we feel inside us a wish that we instinctively seem to repudiate, then we have hit on conscience. Now that instinct for rejection, says Freud, needs no appeal: It is "quite 'certain of itself' [*gewiss*]."[13] Schopenhauer had said of deeds that they differed from "thoughts" because thoughts are merely projections; deeds, he insisted were *"certain* [*gewiss*] "*; they are unalterable, and are not merely thought but *"known* [*gewusst*] ." And "only *deeds* burden the *conscience"* as they reveal, make known, man to himself. Schopenhauer and Freud agree on that quality of conscience both call "certain," or *gewiss,* both recognizing how in German that word is cognate with conscience (*Gewissen*). Conscience is "Man's *knowledge* [*das Wissen*] concerning what he has done."[14]

This certainty is what constitutes the consciousness of conscience or what Freud *almost* interchangeably calls "consciousness of guilt." I stress the "almost" because Freud does make a distinction between conscience and guilt, at least in this discussion: Conscience is the perception of rejecting a wish, while guilt is the perception of "the internal condemnation of an act by which we have carried out a particular wish."[15] So while generally agreeing with Schopenhauer's conception of a deed or act, Freud (at least in this context) seems to be suggesting a conscience when the deed is but a wish, but a sense of guilt when the wish has become, contrary to the wishes of conscience, a deed. As Freud explained, the violation of the conscience (a given, like the categorical imperative) is what induces guilt. Such a view is helpful in that it establishes the conscience as a mechanism already intact in the human mind, a sort of guardian, who need not necessarily be invoked—or provoked—in relation only to *bad* deeds; conscience exists to oversee what direction deeds will take. That is why, of course, we have "good conscience" and "bad conscience." And for Nietzsche, as we shall see, "sense of guilt" is synonymous, or at least coterminous, with "bad conscience."

In *Civilization and Its Discontents* Freud stuck to his claim that conscience exists prior to the deed, but instead of guilt he now speaks of "remorse" (*Reue*) and rearranges the "sense of guilt" so that it now is "in existence before the superego, and therefore before conscience, too." Even remorse precedes conscience, for now Freud views conscience more as a function of the superego— in short, the judging world that keeps watch over us and holds us to account. Guilt is a man's knowledge that the world watches, that conscience is there to judge. Remorse and guilt, then, become functions of conscience, which realizes itself after the deed but only in adjudicating what a man does vis-à-vis the world that judges (that is, the superego).[16] In the most succinct definition Freud offers in this context, conscience is "the readiness to feel guilty"; remorse and guilt, though responses to the deed, exist solely in the individual, lying in wait, as it were, to assert themselves when the great judge between self and world, conscience, gives the signal.[17] Schopenhauer had already argued that "the object of our satisfaction and dissatisfaction with ourselves is *what we are*": so, he queried, "How could guilt and merit lie anywhere else than in *what we are*? *Conscience* is the . . . *register of deeds* that becomes more and more filled up."[18]

Nietzsche had his own conception of the "superego" and the relationship of conscience to it. Men used to think, he says, that actions became reprehensible because conscience had judged them to be so. Not so, he declares; indeed, quite the contrary, "conscience condemns an action because that action has been condemned for a long period of time"; conscience only "imitate[s]," it does not "create" values. What led to the taboo of particular actions was either the "knowledge" or the "prejudice" against whatever possible *consequences* might ensue; it was *not* conscience itself that said "no." Even when we feel at peace with our conscience, we are no more acknowledgeable than the artist who experiences joy—"it proves nothing . . . We are far too ignorant to be able to judge of the value of our actions . . . we lack the ability to regard things objectively," precisely what Arnold had lamented. Even at the point when we repudiate our actions, "we do not do so as judges, but as adversaries,"[19] a crucial distinction, not only for Nietzsche, but for all those who followed him, knowingly or otherwise. Judge and adversary cannot have the same sense of "justice"; and in modern literature judges tend more often to be adversaries, to behave like them in any case. How this affects books like *The Trial, Steppenwolf,* and *The Fall* will be the subject of the next, and final, chapter.

It is clear that as Freud went forward with his work, conscience became increasingly regarded as the authority which rules whether guilt or remorse come to life or not. The deed, in either case, still is the ultimate mover, and that is the important issue. Obviously Freud's distinctions are further made subtle in the more technical analyses of neurotic states, and these cannot be aired here by the nonexpert. But for our purposes the several distinctions will be useful, both retrospectively and for what follows.

Now what had these three men to say of consciousness, especially as related to conscience? Again, philosophy and psychoanalysis have centered, quite naturally, on consciousness, whether as part of metaphysics or psychology. And even more than was the case with conscience, these disciplines explore consciousness with a technical apparatus so forbidding that it is entirely out of view for our purposes. Still, as with conscience, Schopenhauer, Nietzsche, and Freud engaged in some plain-speaking on the subject of consciousness; and no wonder, for consciousness must always be the prime source as well as the sine qua non for the discussion of anything else.

Schopenhauer was so intent on getting away from self-consciousness that he almost ignored the whole problem, except to indicate, as I have already quoted him, that the consciousness of conscience must come about in that order. One of his angriest outbursts against Kant comes when he testily remarks: "The ambiguity of the word *conscientia* . . . will not mislead me into loading the self-consciousness with the moral impulses known under the name of conscience or of practical reason together with its categorical imperatives affirmed by Kant." His reasons are first, as already stated, that conscience is not a priori and second that the "borderline between that in [these impulses] which belongs originally and properly to human nature and that which is added by moral and religious education, is not yet sharply and indisputably drawn."[20]

But Nietzsche broke with Schopenhauer on the issue of consciousness (among others), though the occasions for his view do not leave a consistent picture. Sometimes he appears to hail consciousness as preeminent, but most of the time—rejecting the Schopenhauerian depersonalization of self—he is impatient with consciousness (often, like Schopenhauer, he equates it with self-consciousness), and moreover he even blames the *maladie du siècle,* "nihilism," *taedium vitae,* and the general enervating state of European man on the consequences of consciousness. At the end of his life, in the unfinished *Will to Power,* he protested: "Where must our modern world be classed—under exhaustion or under increasing strength? Its multiformity and lack of repose are brought about by the highest form of *consciousness.*"[21] This was in keeping with Nietzsche's view that an overworked inner curiosity could, and did, soften man to self-pity and to undue pity for others, a cardinal sin in Nietzsche's view of life.[22] Modern man seems to have made a religion of consciousness (how right he was again in sniffing out the symptoms of a future he would not live to see), and Nietzsche complains that this fact has equated consciousness with "spirit," something that "now seems to us rather a symptom of relative imperfection . . . an affliction which absorbs an unnecessary quantity of nervous energy." Every purpose, it seems, must be a conscious purpose, but " 'pure spirit' is a piece of 'pure stupidity!' ": Nietzsche's distrust of rationalism, dating from the early *Birth of Tragedy,* is clearly the main leverage he uses against the modern fetish of consciousness, pointing out in the process that any studied and formal implementation of consciousness mitigates against whatever spontaneity might be inherent in it.[23] Consciousness also tends to make things generalized and therefore "shallow, meagre . . . a characteristic of the herd," by robbing us of instinct and individuality. Nietzsche was finally moved to warn that "the growing consciousness is a danger . . . a disease,"[24] something he may well have learned from Dostoevsky's Underground Man.

The most sustained and perceptive analysis of Consciousness appears in a long passage in *The Joyful Wisdom,* part of which runs as follows: "It is thought that [Consciousness] is *the quintessence* of man. . . . Consciousness is regarded as a fixed, given magnitude! Its growth and intermittences are denied! It is accepted as the 'unity of the organism'. . . . Because men believed that they already possessed consciousness, they gave themselves very little trouble to acquire it . . . It is still an entirely new *problem* just dawning on the human eye . . . *to embody knowledge in ourselves* and make it instinctive,—a problem which is only seen by those who have grasped the fact that hitherto our *errors* alone have been embodied in us, and that all our consciousness is relative to errors!"[25]

For Nietzsche, then, the great and urgent dilemma about consciousness was the smug acceptance of what he considered we had not even begun to probe, and the belief that somehow consciousness was given to man gratis. He deplored, here as elsewhere, our unawareness of the difficult task of developing and cultivating an authentic consciousness—"to embody knowledge in ourselves." The same unquestioning acceptance of conscience is also scored, for, contends Nietzsche, we tend blindly to accept the reproaches of conscience without ever really questioning: "But why do you *listen* to the voice of your conscience? And in how far are you justified in regarding such a judgment as true and infallible?"

Again Nietzsche steers his thoughts very close to what Freud was to call the *"über-Ich,"* the "superego" (*supra*ego, incidentally, would have served the layman better, eliminating the unfortunate connotations of "super" which are not necessarily inherent in the German *"über"*). We obey our conscience through habit; we accept judgment, however adverse, because we have never examined our "nature," that is we have never acquired genuine *instinctual* consciousness. A thoroughgoing examination of the nature of morality, Nietzsche feels, would quickly put an end to our being at the beck and call of "duty" and "conscience"; indeed, "the knowledge *how moral judgments have in general always originated* would make [us] tired of these pathetic words," as severe a judgment of idealistic *Pflicht* (duty) as he ever penned.[26] When put together, Nietzsche's critiques of conscience and consciousness are both eloquent and clear, but his habit of aphoristic organization has unfortunately not served him well. However, in *The Genealogy of Morals* he did finally commit himself (nonaphoristically) to that very question: How moral judgments have in general always originated. It is to this book that we must look for the most sustained position on the questions I have raised here.

First, however, a brief glance again at Freud, whose own analysis of conscience tended to travel some of the same subterranean forests as Nietzsche's: myth, prehistory, anthropology, religion. In *Civilization and Its Discontents* the picture of man's past and future is fairly gloomy. Eros and aggression are at war despite the fact that they are, at times, merely two faces of the same phenomenon. In any case, aggression must be subdued and controlled, and the price may be high but the risk worth it. The book ends with the expressed hope that "eternal Eros" will begin to "assert himself in the struggle with his equally immortal adversary," aggression. In 1931, when European politics began to discourage him, Freud added a final sentence, "But who can foresee with what success and with what result?"[27] Unfortunately the answer is now available. In the past, Freud argued, "the sense of guilt [has been] the most important problem in the development of civilization," and one of the aims of Freud's book is to "show that the price we pay for our advance in civilization is a loss of happiness through the heightening of the sense of guilt," *Schuldbewusstsein,* better translated as "guilt-consciousness," or our conscience-fear, *Gewissensangst.*[28] Obviously, in the larger context of *Kultur* (translated for the English title as "Civilization"), Freud was willing to gamble and accept that increase in guilt-consciousness as a price for keeping aggression at a tolerable level of destructiveness. It is true that this would in effect put us back where we began, fearing the authority of conscience simply because it is authority, with one significant difference: now we would *know* it, we would, in Nietzsche's words, *"embody knowledge in ourselves,"* be truly conscious.

Civilization and Its Discontents is a turning point, not only in Freud's thinking but, as he was to lead so much of our culture (and subcultures), in the thinking of others. Love became once more freshly endowed as a communal need, and the excess of guilt retained by thus curbing a rapacious appetite in aggression, would, surely to Freud's ultimate dismay, once more find ablution in religions, both formal and private. Freud's study would permit such a Freudian poet as the younger W. H. Auden to write the line which, despite his later removal of it, is quoted more often than any line of his poetry: "We must love one another or die" ("September 1, 1939"). Also, with *Civilization and Its Discontents,* Freud broke away from Nietzsche's main thesis, the necessity for unleashing what had become "interiorized," the necessity for suppressing all impulses to love or pity which threatened to weaken us further into some vision of effeteness, a threat of 'femininity' that always darkened Nietzsche's mind. However, the Nietzschean spirit, initially enriched and reinforced by Freud, held sway for better than a generation, and to say that Freud rejected any Nietzschean concept is to imply first of all the enormously influential nature of their combined views, not an entirely conscious severance. Nevertheless Freud was thoroughly aware of at least one of Nietzsche's works, the compelling *Genealogy of Morals* (1887) which, as I have indicated, features Nietzsche's most careful and sustained discussion of conscience.

On two occasions in 1908, the Vienna Psychoanalytic Society specifically discussed Nietzsche, and the recently published

Minutes, regrettably scant, still make interesting reading. The first of these meetings took place on the evening of April 1, 1908, and was devoted to the *Genealogy of Morals.* Dr. Eduard Hitschmann opened the proceedings by calling Nietzsche a "moralist" rather than a philosopher, a man of "unusual sagacity." He then introduced the *Genealogy* as another of Nietzsche's arguments in defense of "cruelty and vengeance" as being primeval "instincts." It seems surprising to learn that Dr. Hitschmann reviewed the first two books "very briefly," since these contain the important sections on "Good and Evil" and "Good and Bad" and "Guilt, Bad Conscience, and Related Matters." It is the third and last essay, "What is the Meaning of Ascetic Ideals?" that Dr. Hitschmann chose to read aloud, apparently in its entirety. At this point it would seem the subject of sexuality and Nietzsche's life were more intriguing to the gathered analysts and guests than his views on conscience; but, as Jones admits, the whole episode could not have been lost on Freud, even if some time elapsed before any influence would become manifest. According to the *Minutes,* "ADLER first stresses that among all great philosophers . . . Nietzsche is closest to our way of thinking. Adler once tried to establish a direct line from Schopenhauer, through Marx and Mach, to Freud. At that time he omitted Nietzsche." Presumably he would not now do that. In more recent times, such lines have been revised (and revived) emphasizing Hegel, Marx, and Freud and omitting both Schopenhauer and Nietzsche. Adler's list, with Nietzsche added, seems more accurate. The fourth speaker during the discussion period was Freud: "PROF. FREUD first emphasizes his own peculiar relationship to philosophy: its abstract nature is so unpleasant to him, that he has renounced the study of philosophy. *He does not know Nietzsche's work;* occasional attempts at reading it were smothered by an excess of interest. In spite of the similarities which many people have pointed out, *he can give the assurance that Nietzsche's ideas have had no influence whatsoever on his own work*"[29] (italics mine). Feeling it necessary to begin so defensively, Freud then makes some remarks that do not really bear on the *Genealogy* and the problems it has raised.

The Society again discussed Nietzsche on the evening of October 28, 1908. On that occasion they discussed *Ecce Homo,* and again some members were prompted to observe that Nietzsche, "without knowing Freud's teachings . . . has sensed and anticipated a great deal [that appeared in them]." Also Freud once again found it necessary to insist that "he has never been able to study Nietzsche, partly because of the wealth of ideas, which has always prevented [him] from getting beyond the first half page whenever he has tried to read him." It might be added that this disclaimer appears in the *Minutes* apropos of nothing in particular: it seems simply another instance of Freud's anxiety lest his ideas be ascribed to Nietzsche, something about which he was obviously very touchy.[30]

Now Nietzsche's general interest for the early psychoanalysts, quite aside from the pathographic fascination already indicated, was obvious and inevitable. As an investigator of what he considered the taboos of a Christianized culture, Nietzsche ranked preeminent; he was, of course, no scientist, dispassionately theorizing but, as Hitschmann correctly said, a "moralist." The subtitle of the *Genealogy* is a *Streitschrift,* a "Polemical Treatise." The book is more than that: it is a brilliant and vicious attack on the prevailing morality with an emphasis on the deleterious effect in particular of the concepts of "evil" and "bad conscience."[31]

Nietzsche begins by discounting the usefulness of experience as revealing ourselves to ourselves: we remain, he insists, essentially strangers to ourselves. Precisely how the men of the Psychoanalytic Society dealt with the problem of "cruelty" on the night of April 1, 1908, beyond the scant *Minutes,* no one has revealed. But one of the essential points in the *Genealogy* is Nietzsche's handling of cruelty as inverted pity. An inhibitive and repressive religion, intent on self-flagellation in the name of "sin," has, as Nietzsche sees it, destroyed men by denying life itself. Breaking with Schopenhauer's "veil of Maya," the grand illusion, Nietzsche finds the ascetic ideal a possibly acceptable way of the Buddhist but, like Yeats who learned from him, he feels an asceticism transplanted to Western man is unnatural and leads only to effeteness or, what is even worse, to nihilism.

His first aim is to distinguish good and bad from good and evil. With the decline of the aristocracy (Nietzsche fails to date it specifically) came the "herd-instinct" which, in its levelling process, resulted in pity (and piety) and a justification for "good" deeds. The opposition of egotism and altruism is an invention of this new value system: What was once considered heroic is now selfish, hence "bad"; what was once viewed as weak is now altruistic, hence "good." By executing a complicated maneuver with history, Nietzsche ascribes the effeminate nature of Christianity to the Hebrews, for he sees their resentment and hatred as giving birth to their antithesis, Christ, the savior and redeemer dispensing pity, love, and mercy. We now live under the Hebraic revenge, a smothering love born of hatred. Rome (the "Classicism" of Greece is anterior) versus Israel, that has been the struggle; but while the Hebrews were conquered, *their* Christ ultimately conquered Rome, Hebraism triumphed. The secret weapon, the thermonuclear equivalent in Christianity, was now ready to mature—not merely conscience but a *bad* conscience. (The comparison to nuclear weapons is not idle; Nietzsche considered conscience a coercive deterrent, man's superweapon against himself which inspired terror simply by existing, a view which Freud developed and refined into part of his analytic system.) Like Schopenhauer and Freud, Nietzsche liked to play with etymology, in this instance by pointing out that the German "bad" (*schlecht*) is related to simple (*schlicht*), bad having no *moral* connotations until Christianity created it; also "good" (*gut*) is related to godly (*göttlich*), the two having perhaps become synonymous. So a man who sees the "evil" as an enemy outside and the "good" in himself is not altruistic but, on the contrary, egotistic. "Bad" is of noble origin and "evil" has grown out of hatred; "bad" is merely a byproduct, but "evil" is "the original creative act" of what Nietzsche often called the "slave-ethic," that is, the modern Christian ethic, with its dialectic of herd-instinct and Redeemer. Now the noble and the powerful have become the "good."

Nietzsche acknowledges the cruelty inherent in aristocracies and sees it as the wild beast instinct which strong races must vent every so often in order to remain strong: "One may be quite justified in continuing to fear the blond beast at the core of all noble races and in being on one's guard against it: but who would not a hundred times sooner fear where one can also admire than *not* fear but be permanently condemned to the repellent sight of the ill-constituted, dwarfed, atrophied, and poisoned?" Had Nietzsche lived forty-five years longer he might not have felt the need to ask the question; still his point should not be lost: In the present culture he saw a cruelty far worse because it was predicated on an inversion, on hypocrisy, on lies—that is how he saw it and he was not alone. Hesse's Steppenwolf, as we shall see, must confront identical questions.

Nietzsche closes the first essay of the *Genealogy* by reminding us that "good-bad" was a purely social, amoral distinction, which Christianity turned, inverted, transvalued into "good-evil," a moral and religious distinction. Hebraism, sin, guilt, "bad conscience," all these are now symptoms of Rome's capitulation to Israel. In the Renaissance there was a brief stirring: "Like one buried alive, Rome stirred under the weight of a new Judaic Rome that looked like an ecumenical synagogue and was called the Church." But with the reformation, "Israel triumphed once again." This is exactly as Arnold had read the past, with this distinction, of course, that Arnold pitted against Hebraism not Rome but Athens, and that his aim was not to destroy Hebraism as much as to replace its influence—temporarily.

Nietzsche now follows with the middle and most devastating essay: the attack on "bad conscience" and "guilt." It is the virtuoso passage of this book, and it is also its fortissimo, though closely reasoned and brilliantly argued. In its way this essay looks before and after to the works discussed in this book. (For a long time I considered using it as an introductory chapter, but it seemed to resist this and now stands in its proper place with the remainder of the *Genealogy* of which, after all, it is an integral part.)

Oblivion, says Nietzsche, is a screening device, keeping from our consciousness the flood of all experience: oblivion acts like a "concierge," only letting up those visitors we give permission to enter. Thus we "close the doors and windows of consciousness for a time." Memory, on the other hand, acts as the opposing power reminding man in spite of his wishes of certain things he may wish to forget. The provenance of responsibility lies with emancipated, free man in full control of his will. Such a man can do more than make promises, he can keep them, and in the process he becomes conscious of, and proud of, this awesome power for which he will now seek a name: he will call it his conscience. Conscience, then, becomes initially an enforcer, who sees to it that forgetful man remembers—wherein lies the root of torture and pain as mnemonic devices to stir the memory.

Yet what is *bad* conscience? It is, says Nietzsche, playing skillfully with his German, payment for freedom and responsibility. To owe in German is to have *Schulden,* and to have guilt is to have *Schuld.* So a guilty or a bad conscience is that which man exacts, as he once did the pound of flesh, as payment: "The feeling of guilt, of personal obligation, had its origin in the oldest and most primitive personal relationship, that between buyer and seller, creditor and debtor." Since exacting payment was once quite literally a physical, cruel, painful act, guilt, now interiorized, has become the cat-o'-nine-tails flogging the human psyche into whimpering submission and leading to all those menacing states Nietzsche feared most: pessimism, denial of life, *taedium vitae,* shame, self-deprecation, decadence.[32] Moreover, "bad conscience" is an invention of vindictive man who needs to sublimate his lust for masochism by creating a system of "payment"; the strong have always had a clear conscience. Again the inhibitions, of modern civilized man's aggression, however outward they may be as facade, are responsible for a greater cruelty than any barbarian ever dreamt of in his free, aggressive state: "To speak of just or unjust *in itself* is quite senseless"; life is *"essentially"* rapacious, exploitative, and destructive, and it "simply cannot be thought of at all without this character."

This Freud too recognized, but in *Civilization and Its Discontents* (and thereafter) he was willing to risk curbing that aggression, not with a false facade of moral laws and codes but with an eros which Nietzsche's private life perhaps deprived him from ever seeing as possible. When man "found himself finally enclosed within the walls of society and peace," he had succumbed, according to Nietzsche, to the "serious illness" of "bad conscience." He goes on to diagnose the course of inhibitions in a passage so strikingly preemptive of Freud that Ernest Jones, once he had it pointed out to him, quoted it in its entirety in his biography. Here is the core of that passage: "All instincts that do not discharge themselves outwardly *turn inward*—this is what I call the internalization of man: thus . . . man first developed what was later called his 'soul.' The entire inner world . . . expanded and extended itself, acquired depth, breadth, and height in the same measure as outward discharge was *inhibited* . . . The man who, from lack of external enemies and resistances and forcibly confined to the oppressive narrowness and punctiliousness of custom impatiently lacerated . . . himself; this animal . . . who had to turn himself into an adventure, a torture chamber . . . became the inventor of the 'bad conscience.' "[33]

So since bad conscience is the result of a cruel turning in of man upon himself, any redemptive motives are suspect. The wish for self-mortification is, therefore, at the bottom of all altruism. Needing punishment, man invented religion to exacerbate his torment, under the sanction of expressing contrition. Insanely and inexplicably it would seem, man has succeeded in cultivating "a will to erect an ideal . . . and in the face of it to feel the palpable certainty of his own absolute unworthiness." The Greeks, making gods of their animal parts of themselves, had no compulsion to search for such self-torture. It is only "modern men" who "are the heirs of the conscience-vivisection and self-torture of millenia," resulting, it must be stressed, in a much greater implosion of cruelty, or what Freud called the anxiety resulting from its repression. Nietzsche's point can be and was oversimplified, but it is clear that he recognized instinct as having been subdued by the veneer of civilization, and in that course he saw nothing but a flaccid and yet cruel culture. W. B. Yeats, G. B. Shaw, D. H. Lawrence, Ezra Pound, Wyndham Lewis—a whole generation of major writers, not merely English-speaking, were to agree with Nietzsche (not so often with Freud, whom they mistrusted); none of these writers, or others kin to their views, can be fully understood without taking stock of Nietzsche's direct or indirect presence.

The third essay of the *Genealogy,* on Asceticism, the one Dr. Hitschmann read aloud, is really a recapitulation of the first two essays, with special emphasis, however, on the "ascetic ideal" as one of the chief results of the course Nietzsche had traced. Asceticism is essentially a release from torture, thinks Nietzsche, but in the end it is also a release from life, the draping of the Schopenhauerian veil, an escape from will. To the extent that the ascetic ideal achieves such a turning away from life, Nietzsche opposes it. But, he maintains, "any meaning is better than none," and insofar as "the door was closed to any kind of suicidal nihilism," even asceticism had a function. As long as man possesses a shred of his own will, though he might be "suffering under the perspective of *guilt,*" he was at least alive and *"saved."* Nevertheless asceticism exaggerates the anti-instinctual trend; it signals more "hatred of the human, and . . . animal"; a "horror of the sense"; it signifies *"a will to nothingness,* an aversion to life after all. But it remains, however negative, a *will,* and man, Nietzsche concludes, would rather will *nothingness* than not will."[34] Poe had made precisely the same point, while Mann, in *Buddenbrooks,* had shown what happens when man ceases to will. In effect, as I have said, Nietzsche both sums up and anticipates; he casts two shadows—one ahead and one behind. It is not until he himself becomes *an* alternative, rather than *the* alternative between nothing and himself, that conscience can once more be examined in a new light. But however new that light may be in the writers we take up in the last chapter, it is a light generated initially by Schopenhauer, Nietzsche, and Freud.

Thomas Mann, whose relationship to Nietzsche is documented by Mann himself, faced the inevitable task (as so many did) of reexamining Nietzsche in the light of the holocaust of 1939-1945. In the Library of Congress Lecture of 1949 he did so with extraordinary courage and, I think, equally extraordinary insight. One must suppose that it took one who knew and admired Nietzsche, one who was imbued with Nietzschean ideas from youth on, to make a proper reassessment.

To begin with Mann reminds us, rightly, that we must keep in mind Nietzsche's place in the history of nineteenth-century rebel-

lion against the "hypocritical morals of the Victorian, the bourgeois era." Also, for the sake of unremitting truth, like Ibsen's
Brand, Nietzsche developed an "immoralism" which Mann calls
the "self-cancellation of morality," that is, the deliberate destruction of traditionalism for the ability to see clearly and start anew.
Like Dr. Hitschmann, Mann considers Nietzsche preeminently a
moralist: "Who takes Nietzsche at face value, takes him literally,
who believes him, is lost." Mann also implies that Nietzsche's glori-
fication of instinct as superior to reason or consciousness (intellect) was merely a temporary solution; "the permanent, eternally
necessary correction remains the one exercised on life by the spirit
or . . . by morals." Finally Mann sees in Nietzsche's philosophy
"two mistakes" which "warp [his] thinking" and lead him into
the abyss he so much dreaded and sought to avoid. The first
mistake was a "deliberate, misperception of the power relationship
between instinct and intellect." The war still fresh in his awareness, Mann appeals to us to see how, unfortunately, "will, urge
and interest dominate and hold down intellect, reason and the
sense of justice" in most men. That being so, it is "absurd [to
think] that intellect must be overcome by instinct": the odds are
always in favor of instinct. In short, Nietzsche's outcry against the
embattled instinct is a bit of a red herring, for it is, alas, the
intellect that is embattled. Second, Nietzsche fashioned an
"utterly false relationship . . . between life and morals when he
treats of them as opposites." These two forces, says Mann, are in
fact kin; the "real opposites are ethics and *aesthetics.*"

This is, of course, in the German tradition, beginning with Kant
and Schiller, carried forward with intensity by Schopenhauer,
Wagner, even Hegel. "Not morality," writes the author of *The
Magic Mountain* and *Death in Venice,* "but beauty is linked to
death, as many poets have said and sung"—not only in Germany,
of course, but in nineteenth-century France and England as elsewhere. I have already mentioned Mann's perception of Nietzsche's
"aestheticism" (linking it in part to the style of *fin de siècle,* a
placing Nietzsche would have resented), and he clearly feels that
despite Nietzsche's struggles to free himself from Schopenhauer
and Wagner, he never succeeded completely in escaping the aesthe-

tic lure. To counteract it, it seems, he placed morality against life
when all the time he ought to have seen that not intellect (the laws
of rational men) but beauty (the impulses of men who may cease
to be rational) was the ultimate Trojan Horse of man's existence.
The point is vital, even if more convincing when related to Mann's
own preoccupations than to Nietzsche's philosophy. The latter
was the great enemy of death, the great defender of life, energy,
health: how could he have ignored the dangers Plato had warned
against? Because when " 'Socrates and Plato started talking about
truth and justice,' he says somewhere, 'they were not Greek any
longer but Jews—or I don't know what.' " Already with *The Birth
of Tragedy* (1871-1872) Socratic rationalism had borne the brunt
of Nietzsche's wrath: but, Mann suggests, Nietzsche had closed his
mind to history, for Greece, with its aestheticism, perished after
brief glory, while the Jews and their morality "have proven themselves to be good and persevering children of life . . . [surviving]
thousands of years,"[35] a remark aimed perhaps obliquely at
Toynbee as well.

Those who read Nietzsche closely know also (as Mann did) that
Nietzsche really did make a distinction between Christian Hebraism and the Jews; despite charges of antisemitism, any close reader
will see that he preferred the Jews of his time to Christians, that
he respected the Old Testament while despising the New. Nonethe-
less the "mistake" Mann sees is a real one: Nietzsche refused to
acknowledge the positive side of intellect (unlike Arnold) and,
however hard he tried to finesse his argument, he did embellish
instinct by making it victim instead of victimizer and by then
claiming its superiority on the grounds that its spontaneity would
permit man to exercise a liberty rather than a license. As Freud
came to see more clearly, in *Civilization and Its Discontents* especially, it is precisely instinct that needs conscious control; whatever freedom lost would be amply recompensed by a corresponding peace and communal strength which alone could save
civilized man from self-destruction—indeed allow him title to call
himself "civilized." Through *directed* eros man could achieve some
measure of this state, no Eden but no Hell either. Unchecked,
aggression would eat away at man from within until he was

hollow, while he practiced his cruelty, concomitantly, on others as well. That "Heart of Darkness" Conrad detailed in 1902 soon after Freud's *Interpretation of Dreams* (published the year of Nietzsche's death). For what is Conrad's tale if not the analysis of "the horror" implicit in an exchange in which consciousness is flooded by instinctual experience so that conscience (even according to Nietzsche, we recall, originally merely "responsibility") is swept away? Conrad's Kurtz is hollow not because he is unaware but because he is *all* awareness without any interpreter left. For all consciousness, lest it become merely a mass of instinctual response *only,* needs conscience to interpret. Conscience is the *response* to consciousness. And in German as in English response (*Antwort*) and responsibility (*Verantwortlichkeit*) are not, I would think, accidentally cognate.

Such a view, I feel, would lead us away from relating conscience only to sin, and it would indeed reinstate conscience as a moral rather than solely a theological concept. In the end Nietzsche's distinction between good and bad conscience is as dangerous as the distinction between conscience and consciousness. Actually he said so himself:

> The World without Consciousness of Sin
> —If men only commited such deeds as do not give rise to a bad conscience, the human world would still look bad . . . but not so sickly and pitiable as at present.
> —Enough wicked men without conscience have existed at all times, and many good honest folk lack the feeling of pleasure in a good conscience.[36]

Nietzsche (like Arnold) was right in emphasizing how we have become "heirs to the conscience-vivisection of two thousand years"; brooding on sin, as brooding too much on sanctity, can be dreary. But then the very men who so dwell on sin are often those least "conscious" of it. Schopenhauer had spoken of the ultimate expression inherent in freedom, not the expression of "doing as one likes," as Arnold dreaded, but the assessment of what we have done. Thus conscience becomes, in addition to being an interpreter of consciousness, a kind of guardian of what we are as well as of what we may have done: "*Freedom,* which proclaims itself alone through *responsibility* [*Verantwortlichkeit*], can be found only in the *esse* (what we are). It is true that the reproaches of conscience primarily and ostensibly concern what we *have done,* but really and ultimately what we *are*; for our deeds alone afford us conclusive evidence of what we are ... Thus guilt and merit must also lie in this *esse,* in what we *are.*"[37] For as Aristotle had long ago known: what we are will determine what we will, or will not, do. That is the modern lesson: Kafka, Hesse, Camus—only three of many one might name—returned to this problem in the new century and confronted its complexities anew, for despite Nietzsche, conscience had not gone away. On the contrary it stood poised like the great Boyg in Ibsen's *Peer Gynt* with no clear way through it or around it.

VIII. A Case of Conscience: Kafka's *The Trial*, Hesse's *Steppenwolf*, and Camus's *The Fall*

"All the same, one is responsible . . ."
"And that's true too . . ."
—Conrad, *Lord Jim*

Another of Schopenhauer's impatient responses to Kant is directed against the latter's conception of a "juridical dramatic form" in the matter of conscience. "There is brought to our minds," Schopenhauer complains, "a complete court of justice with trial, proceedings, judge, prosecutor, counsel for the defense, and sentence." If matters really stood that way, he asks, would it not be *"stupid"* for man "to act against his Conscience"? Indeed, if such a "secret tribunal" really existed in the "darkest recesses of our innermost being," would we not be struck down and become immobile, weighted down by "terror and a fear of the gods"? Actually, conscience is very ineffective, argues Schopenhauer, as we see in the fact that nations have always sought to reinforce it with institutionalized religion. Schopenhauer also denies Kant's assertion that within this "juridical dramatic form," the accused and the judge are *not* identical: "[Kant] says, 'That the man *accused* by his conscience is represented as *being identical with the judge* is an absurd way of picturing a court of justice, for then the accuser would lose every time' . . . I declare [this] to be a cunning trick. *It is not true* that the accuser is bound to lose every time when the accused is the same person as the judge . . . not in the *inner* court of justice." Kant's mistake, according to Schopenhauer, was to construe a "judicial conscience drama" in which the "inner judge" must be conceived as a person distinct from us, "as *another person,*" who has all the omniscience and power not only of a real judge but of an ultimate one, that is, of God.[1] All this the critical student of Kant rejects as specious—a "trick," as he says; in truth we have no such omniscient God, within or without, as regards our moral behavior. Presumably, then, in the "inner court of justice," accused and judge may well be identical and still the judge may sentence the accused (that is, himself) and hence allow the accuser to be victorious. This appears to Schopenhauer *psychologically* valid, and the literature that has appeared since he rendered these opinions tends to bear out his view rather than Kant's. Nietzsche was to agree with his sometime master. "The belief in authority," he conceded, "is the source of conscience"; but this is "not the voice of God in the heart of man, but the voice of some men in man."[2]

One matter that neither philosopher clarified was, of course, the identity of the accuser, who became in Nietzsche, and finally in Freud, synonymous with the accused and the judge, so that in effect the *dramatis personae* become a single figure with several masks. In the modern "*inner* court of justice" the accuser, the accused, the judge, and the executioner are likely to be all one, each assuming his role in sequential order. Such proceedings sometimes lead to annihilation and death, sometimes to perpetual exile, and sometimes to ambiguous redemption. *The Trial* is an example of the first resolution, *Steppenwolf* of the second, and *The Fall* of the third. In each case there is an implicit indication that conscience is identical most obviously with that which (or whom) it accuses. As Nietzsche observed in a sentence that might serve as the epigraph for this chapter, "Believe me, my friends: the sting of conscience teacheth one to sting," or, "When one trains one's conscience, it kisses one while it bites."[3] Conscience and self, in the absence of a deity, at least outside us, are merely verbal distinctions. Self usually splits into various personae (two is standard) necessary to enact the "judicial conscience drama"; but the distinctions among personae are symbolic, not real. In the works discussed here, heroes are split into selves *they* create.

The Judicial Conscience Drama of Josef K.
and Hegel's Version of The Trial of Socrates

However one views the three books under discussion, no one can deny that each is a "judicial conscience drama," in one respect or another; that all explore the "juridical dramatic form" of the *"inner* court of justice" in man. Needless to say, Kafka's *Trial* (both in title and substance) falls most conveniently into these categories. Critics of Kafka have so systematically cut down one another's views that they have inevitably receded somewhat from the text itself; perhaps this has left a book like *The Trial* receptive to some new remarks.[4] It is in this spirit, fully aware that my angle is chosen to view *The Trial* as illustrative of the theme that binds the present book together, that I will try not to suffer the fate of the aspirant to the law in Kafka's celebrated fable. We recall that this man, after waiting endlessly before the gateway, is finally told that it has been open to him alone all this time but that now it will be closed, forever. There are, of course, scores of entrances to *The Trial,* but the analogy to Kafka's fable is not idle: Each reader will have his own door to enter, but lest he be so busy wagging his finger disapprovingly at all the other doors first, he may suddenly discover his own entrance shut—a condition that leaves him to criticize the critics rather than the novel. So damn the fleas and straight ahead!

The Trial, whatever else it may be, is also a novel about conscience, though the word is not once used in its pages—"guilt," of course, occurs several times. Being about conscience it is also about consciousness. Like *Steppenwolf* and *The Fall,* its essential characteristic is the presentation—indeed the drama—of how a man, either suddenly or by degrees, becomes conscious of his conscience; how the *process* (it has been noted that the German *"Prozess"* means both "trial" and "process")[5] of such an event results in a kind of inner trial, however rendered, *and* a judgment *and* a sentence. This much seems incontrovertible; the question whether or not, or even in what manner, Josef K. is really guilty, or of what he is guilty, if he is, seems secondary. It needs no repetition that Kafka was deeply, abidingly obsessed with guilt;

but despite the autobiographical index, he was, I think, more concerned with the stages of a man's "inner" trial than with either its reasons or justification (or lack of either). All men possess conscience and, one day, like the Everyman of the morality play, each man is accosted and asked to give account. In modern contexts death is no longer the dreadful stranger; conscience appears. That figure, born out of the "innermost" in man, and assisted, as Freud stressed, by the midwifery of a societal or communal judge, can never be confronted as an alien force: Conscience is always a figure too familiar to one's own self.

During the interview with the priest in the cathedral, Josef K. is given one of the final clues to his dilemma; it may even be the source for the change in Josef K.'s approach to his trial, evident only in the last chapter, in the final paragraphs. "You cast about too much for outside help," says the priest, adding that this was true especially in the case of the women Josef K. had befriended. "Don't you see that it isn't the right kind of help?" the priest asks rather sternly. For the moment, Josef K. agrees only partially, but by the time the chapter ends (it is still considered even by those who have rearranged chapter sequences as the penultimate chapter), we get the distinct impression that the priest's words have been better understood.[6]

There is clearly a paradox in Josef K.'s relentless pursuit of his "case," and his avowed disinterest, or something like it, which he seems intent on displaying when confronting the various emissaries from the Court. Critics have seen this paradox in different ways, as death-wish, sexual repression, or (more imaginatively) as the Oedipus syndrome. It may also be a case of confused conscience. Josef K. tells the lawyer, whom he dismisses, "you must have noticed on my very first visit here, when I came with my uncle, that I did not take my case very seriously; if I wasn't forcibly reminded of it, so to speak, I forgot it completely." This is both bravado and fraudulent; the reader knows it is certainly not in any literal sense true that Josef K. has not taken his case "very seriously." In fact one might argue he has taken it *too* seriously, that if he really could forget it, it might forget him. Yet in another sense Josef K. is telling the truth; it is really not the "case" he takes seriously but its unpredictable consequences; his one defense against panic has been to minimize or dismiss the gravity of his situation because of its overpowering implications. Josef K. knows that any admission of how serious or possibly valid the case against him might be would be tantamount to a full awareness of a state he struggles to keep from consciousness. It is also arguable that he succeeds, up to the last chapter, in not committing himself either to consciousness or to abject surrender; the end comes with such inexorableness, with such rapidity and ruthless and mechanical clarity, that it is one of the amazing feats of Kafka's art that we are *not* taken by surprise; we knew what was coming all along. But when it happens we gasp nevertheless. There is a good reason for the swiftness and brutality of the end, aside from those already suggested by critics, ranging from castration to crucifixion. That reason may lie in the so-called unfinished chapters and fragments, but I doubt that had they been completed they would have changed the effect. It seems clear that Kafka is busy from the very first sentence in making Josef K. as defensive as possible in order to give us that somewhat unflattering portrait which has led critics to characterize him as an irritable, calculating, officious, and loveless bachelor who is ungrateful even to such well-meaning people as his landlady or his uncle. The nature and the particular artistry of the ending is, I suggest in the paragraphs that follow, well justified.

It may seem remarkable but we must admit that Kafka does not psychologize *about* his hero (one supposes this to be one reason why so many have sought to take up the slack); we know almost nothing about Josef K.'s soul, and relatively little, really, about his outer life. The attempts to fill in the details of Josef's life—trip to the mother, relationships to an intimate lady friend or the Assistant Director—were all abandoned, as the fragments testify. Although *The Trial* may be unfinished, its general style of presentation is probably the same as it would have been had more been written. It seems fair to compare the unfinished material to Joyce's *Stephen Hero,* realistic, full of details and dialogue, relationships and situations, while what we have resembles the *Portrait of the Artist as a Young Man*—laconic with lyric interludes, sparse, and inevitable in progress. (I think there are some very real resemblances between

Josef K. and Stephen Dedalus: both have been severely judged as selfish prigs, aloof and distant; the comparison is interesting, though there is no space to develop it here.) But despite the sparse, bony outline, and the equally hard and factual style, we feel that we know a great deal, or at least that we should, about Josef K. How does Kafka achieve this effect? I think it is by a technique of capturing the "fruitful moment," which Lessing thought possible only in the plastic arts. Laocoön's mouth, half-open, is between pain and scream. Metaphorically, that is how we catch, or Kafka catches for us, Josef K.: between pain and scream.

Josef K.'s pain is not the result of his arrest, nor of the mysteries of his "case," nor even of the irrationality of his being accused of an unspecified crime. The best description of Josef's reaction to his "case" would be to say he is self-righteous; and the pain is the alarm he registers at the outrage of being charged with a wrongdoing from which he wants to feel immune. In short, the pain evolves from the insult of the "case" against what he wants to convince himself was an irreproachable character; for whatever else Josef K. might be there is ample evidence that in his everyday life he was by and large a man who did his duty. (Again, the specified negligence of his mother and other such incidents were excised and clearly not meant as part of the presentation of Josef K.) When accused, Josef K.'s conscience is unprepared; it rebels and fails to muster what Nietzsche called the "intellectual conscience," the "conscience behind [one's] 'conscience.' "[7] It is accurate to say that from the beginning, Josef K. is a disoriented man; yet as with other of Kafka's heroes, the disorientation does not become overtly apparent in behavior. Josef K. responds normally to what seems to us an absurd situation. He is disbelieving, indignant, vain, superior, shocked, curious; he is all that and more, yet each response is but a moment's attempt to gain reprieve from the certainty of the final chapter, a certainty Josef K. at least suspects, one supposes, from the fruitful moment of his precipitous arrest. Hence his actions, right up to the end, seem rational, even systematic responses to an irrational, ambiguous, and haphazard condition. That is the main technique with which

Kafka achieves the effects of the ending—a dénouement sudden yet expected, shocking yet without alternatives.

Josef K.'s struggle is that of the fly in the marmalade;[8] and although he may sense his doom from the start he neither displays that knowledge nor acts upon it. What he does invoke is the first line of defense: the display of his dutiful life of obedience, correctness of demeanor, in short his primary conscience, not the conscience "behind the 'conscience.' " For this reason he utters those often quoted words to the priest: "But I am not guilty . . . it's a mistake. And, if it comes to that, how can any man be called guilty? We are all simply men here, one as much as the other." To which the priest answers, very pointedly, "That is true . . . but that's how all guilty men talk." This is what the tough detective says in the old gangster movie when the suspect pleads his innocence. But the priest's admonition, and it is that, has a double meaning: one is like that of the tough detective—the guilty always scream they are innocent; the other is that there are no hard and fast lines between guilt and innocence, none clear enough to permit such certainty of guiltlessness as Josef K.'s, not if men looked honestly within. Why should men look? The priest might say for the sake of his heart or soul; Nietzsche said for the sake of his conscience, though he amplified considerably.

Nietzsche insisted that men examine the real impulses behind their conscience, especially when they regard it as bad. The decision that one's conscience is speaking truly is, he suggests, the response of unconscious habit: "But *that* you hear this or that judgment as the voice of conscience, consequently, *that* you feel a thing to be right—may have its cause in the fact that you have never thought about your nature, and have blindly accepted from your childhood what has been designated to you as *right* . . . that which you call your duty . . . your 'moral force' might have its source in your obstinacy—or in your incapacity to perceive new ideals! And to be brief: if you had thought more acutely . . . and had learned more, you would no longer under all circumstances call this or that your 'duty' and your 'conscience'."[9] The relevance of this passage to Josef K. is that Nietzsche here describes a hero like Josef K. as a type who has not thought about his nature, as one who has in fact accepted blindly what he deems as conscience or duty, and that in both areas he feels altogether vindicated. Therefore the sudden accusation that he has done something that may be an infraction of a good conscience or a sense of duty shakes his belief in himself to its very foundations. Obstinacy is one of Josef's character traits; he is determined not to prove himself innocent or guilty (though admittedly he begins by making attempts in both directions) but to return rather to the status quo ante in which the accusation ceases to exist altogether. He wants no part of any trial that will prove him innocent; we must keep in mind that in Kafka's experience of Continental law the burden of proving innocence lies essentially with the accused; until that is done the State will assume his guilt. He really wants the charges dropped; he wants them considered a mistake, because having done his duty in good conscience he cannot fathom why he should be charged.

It is, predictably, precisely this option which can never be offered; as the painter, Titorelli, explains, not even definite acquittal is possible, certainly not the dropping of charges. "I am completely innocent," Josef K. tells Titorelli; to which the painter answers quite calmly, "If you are innocent, then the matter is quite simple." Then, why, asks Josef, is the Court so reluctant to quit its proceedings, since he has heard that "once [the Court] has brought a charge against someone, [it] is firmly convinced of the guilt of the accused and can be dislodged from that conviction only with the greatest difficulty." The painter's answer, I think, shuts the final exit for Josef K., and even here, before the priest's parable, Josef must sense this: "The greatest difficulty?" Titorelli repeats; "The Court can *never* be dislodged from that conviction" (italics mine).

The trial of Josef K., though never more than a pretrial at best, resembles in some important respects Hegel's version of the trial of Socrates. Among the most essential points in Hegel's account is Socrates' refusal to admit his guilt by choosing an alternative punishment for himself, an option left open to the accused by Athenian law. This, not the crimes of which he was accused, says Hegel, led to the death sentence. Hegel's attitude is somewhat ambivalent: while recognizing the grandeur and courage of Socrates, he also wished to make clear how such a stand was destructive of the fabric of Athenian law and society, how, indeed, it led to the collapse of the Golden Age. Socrates had "refused to recognize the competency and majesty of the people as regards the accused," when he refused admission of guilt. *That* became the true crime leading to the ultimate of judgments—death. Relying on "his own consciousness," Socrates rejected the "external universal Daemon" that operated in Athenian law. Now by allowing the accused a choice of punishment (within certain guidelines) it was assumed when the guilty man made himself judge that "he submitted himself to the decision of the court and acknowledged himself to be guilty." Asserting his "moral independence," Socrates "disdained the juridical power of the people," a transgression that touched the heart of Athenian coherence: "Socrates thus set his conscience in opposition to the judge's sentence, and acquitted himself before its tribunal. But no people . . . has by this [the right to a] freedom to recognize a tribunal of conscience which knows no consciousness of having fulfilled its duty excepting its own consciousness . . . This miserable freedom of thinking and believing what men will, is not permitted, nor any such retreat behind personal consciousness of duty . . . Now law also has a conscience and has to speak through it; the law-court is the privileged conscience . . . the conscience of the court alone possesses any value as being the universal legalized conscience, which does not require to recognize the particular conscience of the accused."

Hegel's philosophic arrogance should not blind us to his theory of law, namely that a duly constituted and presumably "just" law must superimpose its conscience over every individual conscience, else anarchy is inevitable. Hegel is aware that Socrates was "still the hero," a man "who possessed for himself the absolute right of the mind, certain of itself [*das absolutes Recht seiner selbst gewissen Geistes*] and of the inwardly deciding consciousness," hence expressing "the higher principle of mind with consciousness." Still Hegel finds the Greeks unprepared for such utter "subjective reflection."

The exorcism fails. In summing up the whole "drama" of the trial, Hegel reaffirms his theory of tragedy as a collision not between good and bad but between good and good: "Two opposed rights come into collision, and the one destroys the other." One of these rights is "objective freedom" (embodied in the law and state) and the other is "subjective freedom" (embodied in the individual). Indeed such subjective freedom "is the fruit of the tree of the knowledge of good and evil," and Socrates merely objectified a period of Athenian history when "individual consciousness made itself independent of the universal spirit"—though it would recover in time (via the trial and death of Socrates) to become Hegel's "world-spirit." Nevertheless, the "principle of self-determination for the individual" became "the ruin of the Athenian people," not because it was intrinsically wrong but because it had "not yet identified with the constitution of the people," that is, in Hegelian terms, it has not yet become universal.[10]

If as Camus said of his stranger, Meursault, that he is the only Christ we deserve, it is tempting to think that Kafka is offering us the only Socrates we deserve. Whatever parallels exist between the "trial" of Josef K. and that of Socrates, as viewed by Hegel, are, of course, ironic. Josef K., too, refuses to concede guilt, and it seems fairly clear that this, rather than the original crime (whatever its nature), is what brings on the severe judgment. Josef K. likewise does not recognize the "objective conscience" of the Court and he, too, "sets his conscience in opposition to the judges' sentence," or their anticipated sentence. But Josef K. submits not with certainty but with doubt, not with defiance but with the acceptance of inevitability. The *Zeitgeist* of Josef K. fears, as regrettably it always does, any obstinate challenge to the authority of its "objective conscience" and, so threatened, it feels it must act, and does, like the Athenians, to remove the threat to the constituted fabric of the law. Only this time it is not a Socrates but a bank clerk, not a hero but a victim.

What happens to Josef K. is what Nietzsche described as once having been the state of ancient man when faced with "independence": he was utterly lost. Nowadays, says Nietzsche, a man feels responsible only for what he "intends and for what [he] does," and he takes "pride" in that schematic system of morality. It was not always so, for once "there was nothing more terrible to a person than to feel himself independent." Independence, "neither to obey nor to rule," was an aloneness which was considered "punishment"; one was "condemned 'to be an individual,' " and though modern man feels laws as constraint and loss against his freedom, in former times laws protected and "egoism," that is, independence, was felt to be painful: "For a person to be himself, to value himself according to his own measure and weight—that was then quite distasteful . . . All miseries and terrors were associated with being alone. At that time the 'free will' had bad conscience in close proximity to it; and the less independently a person acted, the more the herd-instinct, and not his personal character, expressed itself in his conduct, so much the more moral did he esteem himself."[11] At first this may not be clear in relation to Josef K., but is not independence precisely what Josef K. has too much of? The protagonist of *The Trial* has been charged with overbearing pride, even with *hubris*; he has been accused of taking no account of others (egotism) and of using people merely to gain help for his case. These are somewhat superficial charges. In fact, Josef K. has been living a life quite in tandem with the herd-instinct, at least insofar as that life revolves around some basic rules and regulations: a dedication to duty, punctiliousness, good and correct manners, honesty in his work. By any measurable social standard, he has certainly both obeyed and ruled. Although a bachelor, he has not been alone in Nietzsche's sense at all. When he is arrested he fully expects to be held in custody, even imprisoned, then tried and either sentenced or exonerated; in short he fully expects (as he should) to become part of the judicial process he knows.

From the moment he is told by the Inspector that he is *free* to go to the bank, indeed free to live an "ordinary life," subject only to being called by the Court at its pleasure, Josef K. begins to suspect his case, wondering quite naturally what sort of case this is accompanied by what appear to be very extraordinary conditions. "Then being arrested isn't so very bad," he tells the Inspector; but his actions following this apparent freedom belie that he really believes this. Actually once set "free," his anxiety increases, and it is his so-called freedom that spurs him on to pursue his case. In the light of Nietzsche's observations, Josef K.'s pursuit of his case seems like a symptom of terror *for not being pursued,* a desire to obey or to rule—anything but the condition of independence in which, like the patient in analysis, the patient and not the analyst is expected to make the next move—and the *right* move. Laws and regulations become for Josef K. the very nourishment of his life, while egoism becomes unbearable. Josef K. (no more than Raskolnikov) cannot contemplate the awesome possibility of no design at all, as Frost posed it in his sonnet "Design." After finding a white moth in the deadly embrace of a white spider on a white heal-all, the poet asks what brought these three white things together if not an evil design to "appall" us? But he refuses to leave us with that certainty, however dark it may be, adding in the last line:

> If design govern in a thing so small.

It is perhaps less terrifying to imagine an evil design than no design at all.

Also Josef K. does not value himself according to "his own measure," only according to what he measures vis-à-vis the charges, unspecified, against him. It is, therefore, quite true as Nietzsche said of such cases: Josef K.'s "free will," on which he insists so brashly when he turns the first interrogation into a tirade against the Court, is in "close proximity" to a developing "bad conscience." The herd-instinct is represented by the world of normal relationships from which Josef K. has not been officially removed. He does everything to make amends: with the landlady, with Fräulein Bürstner, with the clerks in the Bank, with the men who arrest him, whom he later sees whipped, even with the advocate whom he dismisses. It would appear that Josef K. is a defiant and arrogant man whose sole aim is to assert his independence of all restraints, but I think this is an illusion and a deception. Much of what actually happens after the first chapter would point to an opposite profile; despite verbal bursts of arrogance and defiance, Josef K. wants nothing more than dismissal of charges and a return to the life of duty and good conscience. The charges, followed by an apparent state of freedom, drive him to *act,* as nothing else could have driven him; and the futility of action at each step confirms the independence to which he has been condemned and whose burden he cannot bear. No one can be certain to whom Josef K.'s final pathetic pleas are addressed, whether to God, man, or the law itself, "friend," "good man," or "one person only." I am sure Kafka meant *that* uncertainty to be there, because when Josef K. thinks he is being asked to commit suicide and refuses to oblige, Kafka rather pointedly remarks: "He could not completely rise to the occasion, he could not relieve the officials of all their tasks; the responsibility [*Verantwortung*] for this last failure [*Fehler*: literally error] of his lay with him who had not left the remnant of strength necessary for the deed." That "him" is sufficiently vague to stir speculation: God? the Court? or Josef K. himself? I choose the last. Josef K.'s response to conscience has drained him of all power; submitting to the knife is now a consummation devoutly to be wished, because it would once more be an act within the scheme of obeying and ruling. But it would also be a surrender of self and individuality, and therefore a "shame" (*Schande*)[12] that might outlive him; now he dies like one of the herd, "Like a dog!" At that moment, and not before, does Josef K. glimpse clearly the conscience behind the conscience, the authentic conscience—total consciousness. "The great privilege . . . of absolving from guilt," said the painter Titorelli, "our Judges do not possess." Only Josef K. possesses that privilege, much as the applicant at the gate of the law possessed the power to recognize that the gate was opened for him; of all human privileges the power of absolution is the most frightening, and to the end Josef K. is unable to effect it. Socrates he was not.

The progress of Josef K. in *The Trial* can be seen as an experiment in which the will is pitted against the law. Such a clash moves towards inevitability, as so many of Kafka's works do; but one witnesses this process with the same helplessness as that experienced in dreams. Josef K. insists not only that he *will* do his duty but that he has *done* it. The Court, however, wants capitulation. In one sense it defines duty as Kant did—rigorously: "The consciousness of a free submission of the will to the law, combined with an inevitable constraint imposed . . . on all inclinations, is respect for the law. The law which commands and inspires this respect is ... the moral law ... The action which is objectively practical according to this law ... is called duty."[13] What a commanding, and demanding, definition of duty! Josef K.'s final submission is an ironic comment on Kant's definition of the moral law: Josef K. does his duty. But Kafka is himself a rigorist and does not let it go at that, for Josef K.'s death does not lead to freedom, because the submission of his will is not made freely but is imposed. It might be too charitable to suggest that he is not yet ready for the "consciousness of a free submission of the will to the law" but in any case Kafka gave him no more time and that speaks severely in itself.

Throughout the book, Josef K.'s posture is defiant, but the Romantic gestures are gone—those of Manfred, Faust, Werther, and even the Underground Man. Josef K.'s defiance cannot go beyond his despair; indeed it develops in step with it. "No despair," wrote Kierkegaard, "is entirely without defiance ... defiance is implied in the very expression, 'Not to will to be.' "[14] In Josef K.'s case the defiance is inherent in the expression of his will *to be*; the despair in his discovery that such will has limited reach.

So, perhaps, Theodore Ziolkowski's judgment is too harsh: "During his year of trial Josef K. has not reached the state of human freedom and responsibility."[15] On the level of Kantian judgment this is perfectly true; on the level of a Hegelian judgment Josef K. also fails, but only after one realizes that Josef K. has achieved sufficient "freedom" (like the Underground Man) *not* to fulfill its potential. Yet the Underground Man sinks into inertia; Josef K. exhausts himself in strenuous pursuit. In large measure his pursuit is a method of escaping pursuit: he appears at times frantic to be one step ahead of the step he hears behind him. The implications of such freedom, which are so brilliantly dramatized in "The Judgment," Kafka may well have gathered from many sources, combining them early with his creative talent and his painful life. At Frau Fanta's Salon, the Prague German Society, he joined with an august company: Einstein, Phillip Frank, Max Brod. Discussions ranged widely and specifically to include Kant's *Critique of*

Pure Reason, Hegel's *Phenomenology of Mind,* and Fichte's *Wissenschaftslehre.* According to Brod, Kafka had read Schopenhauer as early as 1902 and Frau Fanta, despite Brod's protests, expressed enthusiasm for Nietzsche.[16]

In Kafka's "The Judgment" the father who sentences the son to death by drowning is shown to be especially cunning because he allows the son just enough "freedom" to die. Pretending to be ill, almost senile, he permits the son to proceed with his wedding plans, to carry on his business affairs, and to fall into a false sense of liberation. On the fateful afternoon when the son carries the father into the sunnier room and places him on the bed, the father, that personified conscience in the guise of a human Jehovah, springs the trap. "So," says the son, "you've been lying in wait for me!" And so he has. The sentence follows after a final accusation that the son has been a consummate egotist: "So now you know what else there was in the world beside yourself, till now you've known only about yourself." This the son cannot accept; he must carry out the sentence. Like Josef K. he must submit—here, willingly, for here he has now been accused not of mere selfishness but of harboring within his innocence "a devilish human being!" In "The Judgment" the son plunges from the "bridge" that Camus's hero will cross, but their freedom will be equally contingent.

The Second "Bildung" of Harry Haller

The "editor" of *Steppenwolf,* in his preface to the "MS" left behind by Harry Haller, tells of a conversation in which the thesis of the Steppenwolf syndrome is explained by the patient himself. "Human life," he observes, "is reduced to real suffering, to hell, only when two ages, two cultures and religions overlap"; at times a "whole generation" is caught "between two modes of life," resulting in a complete loss of "feeling for itself," what today we popularly call "identity." A man like Nietzsche, Haller points out, was in the unenviable position of having to "suffer our present ills more than a generation in advance." "What he had to go through alone and misunderstood, thousands suffer today."[17] The "editor" is wise to give prominence to this idea, just prior to offering us "Harry Haller's Records." One of the most important matters it expresses, aside from signalling to us Harry Haller's affinities to Nietzsche, is that through Haller Hesse feels the condition of his hero to be not unique but rather the sign of a generational disease, not the suffering of a misplaced genius but of "thousands." In some respects, then, we are invited to regard Harry Haller as a symbolic figure of an entire age; given that scrutiny, his tale may lose the intensity of singularity, but it gains in weight and authority by representing a recognizable and common experience. The "editor" ends his remarks by saying flatly that in offering us Harry Haller's story, typical of those "caught between two ages," he neither approves nor condemns them. "Let every reader," he declares with more cunning than may be apparent, "do as his conscience bids him [*möge jeder Leser dies nach seinem Gewissen tun!*]."

As our conscience bids us? But this is bait, is it not, this is no less and perhaps is even more than Baudelaire's *"Hypocrite lecteur—mon semblable—mon frère!"* Our conscience is a little too sly, since the responsibility belongs to the "editor," who, in 1942, dropped his mask and in the name of Hermann Hesse explained his purpose to those of us whose consciences had misled us altogether. Harry Haller's suffering and despair, Hesse urges, are balanced by "matters of the spirit, of the arts and the 'immortal' men"; these offer a "serene, superpersonal and timeless world of faith . . . of a man believing," not "despairing." In any final view *Steppenwolf* was therefore intended not as a story of "disease and crisis," not as "leading to death and destruction, [but] on the contrary: to healing." Not the first (nor the last) author to append such explanatory notes to his works, Hesse acknowledges that he cannot control how readers read his work, admitting that by laying down what *he* intended, he may, in effect, be guilty of the "intentional fallacy." Still, the authorial explanation is noteworthy because (especially today with a vigorous Hesse revival) *Steppenwolf* remains a rather misunderstood novel among many readers; "intentional fallacy" or not, critics are more likely to tread with caution than before Hesse interfered. (Imagine such a definitive statement about the intentions of Kafka's *The Trial*! Would critics still insist on that book's "total ambiguity" or "total ambivalence"?)[18]

Demonstrably, *Steppenwolf* is not merely about despair, disease, or death; many voices speak throughout the book. In a way, *Steppenwolf* belongs to the tradition of the German *Bildungsroman*, with a significant difference: the hero is not a naïve novice being initiated into the adult world, but rather a man in the middle of his journey, beyond it really, at nearly fifty. This man must undergo, initially, a reverse process, an un-*Bildung*, forgetting what he has learned in order to revaluate himself. In the process he undergoes, so to speak, his second *Bildung*. As in the typical *Bildungsroman*, there are teachers, testings, mistakes, painful realizations, even comic interludes, and if not final wisdom at least the readiness for it in the new terms set forth. Those terms forego finality of any sort; the main point of the second education is to make Harry Haller realize the dynamic and multiple nature of the life process. Purged of a life style pretentiously allegorized by a simplistic dualism, wolf and man, Harry Haller, at the end of the novel, stands on the threshold of some new life, one that may indeed lead to "healing."

Both metaphorically and literally *Steppenwolf*, like Kafka's novel, is a "trial," a "judicial conscience drama." Self-contempt and masochism characterize Haller's existence before his encounter with his new teachers, and the obvious question is, Why does this man torture himself? Some answers are inherent in the conditions surrounding the hero, biographical and *Zeitgeist*. For instance, it is clear that he has lost the love of one woman by divorce and is in precarious relation to another; his health, in part due to bad habits, is deteriorating; and, sensitive and intellectual, he feels all the oppression and crassness of a modern, jazzed-up world which offends every nerve—and every bit as much as the intrusions of the world once disturbed Poe's Roderick Usher. So much is clear. But Hesse's insistence, especially in the early pages, on making Haller a kind of Baudelairean "Héautontimorouménos," arouses some further suspicions. Let us face it: Harry Haller overreacts; his bitterness, his self-torture, even allowing for a healthy dose of self-pity, go beyond mere spleen. Haller must have a very bad conscience. Familiar with the work of Dostoevsky and Nietzsche (among others), he seems intent on finding out just why he feels guilt, assuming for the present that he does. His exile and solitude, his identification with the *Heimat-losen* (homeless) of the world, make him a Romantic, both in the tradition of the angry and ironic Byron and the spiritual Novalis (whom he admires). There is the rub: the spirituality of Harry Haller is suspect; the anger, which he blames mostly on the wolf in him, is always subverting it. Shame seems to drive him underground; quite unlike Hemingway's figure who craved the illuminated night out of fear, Haller is a "night prowler" who fears the day, the approach of dawn. By his own admission he is suicidal, without ever making the attempt. To quote the Nietzsche he seems to know so well: "He who despises himself, nevertheless esteems himself thereby, as a despiser."[19]

Suicides are threatened egos, says Hesse; a man of that group stands as though anchored with but "the slightest foothold on the peak of a crag whence a slight push from without or an instant's weakness from within suffices to precipitate him into the void." Metaphysically speaking such suicides are "overtaken by the sense of guilt inherent in individuals," and hence they strive for union with mother, God, or "the All"; many never commit suicide because "they have a profound consciousness of the sin of doing so"—not the religious sin, but the metaphysical sin. Nevertheless such men nourish, even sustain, themselves on the knowledge of the "emergency exit," Death. Such a man rationalizes: "A man cannot live intensely except at the cost of the self." Yes, but which "self" are we talking about? That will be one of Harry Haller's chief lessons in his second *Bildung.* Until he begins to learn certain matters about self and selves, he merely lacerates himself and fights off suicide because in his heart he knows that suicide is a "shabby business." Possessed of a "morbid conscience," not so different from the "militant conscience" of those who think themselves contented, "the majority of suicides are left to a protracted struggle against their temptation." Why do they have such a "morbid conscience"? Because, Hesse suggests, they are *knowing* victims, acutely aware of the "consciousness of the sin," not merely of self-destruction carried to its ultimate but of waste and aridity, a sin against the sanctity of life, the sin of resignation without the faith of a saint or the denial of a sinner.

The primary rationalization of such men is the illusion that a simplified dualism can explain life; for Harry this becomes wolf and man, "a very great simplification." Granted, this attack on the Steppenwolf thesis occurs in the so-called *Treatise,* the piece within the piece within the piece—twice removed from the encasing "editor." But I think the story of Harry's reeducation bears out the critique in the *Treatise. Steppenwolf* is not really a novel about a "man, the detached and cool evaluator of values . . . locked in deadly battle with the animal, whose ambition it is to break all 'civilized' fetters"; it is about a man who rather foolishly thinks that. It is not about a "schizophrenic duel" but about someone who keeps deceiving himself into believing this.[20] As the *Treatise* points out, any attempt on Harry's part to apportion wolf and man engaged in any act he undertook would be sufficient for "his whole beautiful wolf-theory [to] go to pieces." Men are not the "sum of two or three principal elements"; it is a "childish attempt" to so try to explain human existence, for there are "a hundred or a thousand selves, not . . . two." To think of himself dualistically, the *Treatise* charges, is a "lie," a "delusion," a "simplification," a "fiction."

Goethe, who plays a major role in the novel, is singled out in this context for permitting Faust the line "immortalised among schoolmasters," the famous "Two souls, alas, dwell in my breast!" because Faust (and presumably Goethe) has momentarily "forgotten Mephisto and a whole crowd of other souls that he has in his breast likewise." Harry Haller's division of himself into wolf and man is a convenience for explaining, by means of a dialectic, his contradictory impulses: the impulses towards love are ascribed to the man, but those towards hate can be hung on the neck of the beast. In fact, Harry is a classic case of "narcissism," a man whose suffering fulfills him without committing him to corresponding obligations. The narcissist's pleasure may, and often does, lie in the economics of suffering, a subject on which Nietzsche and

Freud made some penetrating remarks. Even when Harry Haller looks skeptically at his "double image," or becomes dimly aware that his suffering may be a kind of sustenance (vide Kafka's *Hungerkünstler*), the case does not alter. As Freud pointed out, "the idea of the 'double' does not necessarily disappear with the passing of . . . narcissism," since the ego develops a "special agency" in opposition to its parent-source, an offshoot that achieves a censorious independence: and this "we become aware of as our 'conscience.' "[21] So being a "double" serves Harry's purpose rather well; he can even maintain a moral posture with a conscience that is a direct result of both the original "double"-dialectic and the narcissism that acts as a function of fulfillment. It will be only through a transformation in The Magic Theatre that Harry Haller can be finally redeemed and made to see the essence of his deception.

Suffering under "his ludicrous dual personality," Harry, the *Treatise* diagnoses, seeks ways back that are forever barred: childhood or innocence in a kind of animality, "wolfhood." These are not opposites, only different names for the same narcissistic impulse—freedom from inhibition. But, the *Treatise* concludes, the road towards innocence does not lie in back of us but rather in front, "further into sin, ever deeper into human life," ever more, thinking of *Lord Jim,* in the "destructive element." That truth is the essential part of Harry's dreams; Goethe and Mozart, who invade his dreams, both try to impart some of this wisdom to a slow learner, for the Steppenwolf is obstinate, not stupid. Finally it is Hermine, another kind of "double," who instructs Harry and tells him the truth more succinctly than the *Treatise*; it is she who allows him to see by degrees the enormous selfishness of his renunciation, for which he is finally duly punished: "You, Harry," she says with accuracy, "have been an artist and a thinker, a man full of joy and faith . . . But the more life has awakened you and brought you back to yourself, the greater has your need been and the deeper the suffering and dread and despair . . . And all that you once knew and loved and revered . . . has been of no avail . . . and [has] gone to pieces." The more conscious of beauty and thought, the more conscious he has become of himself and the more despising of that conscious self. "Even sin," says Hermine, "can be a way to saintliness, sin and vice . . . Ah, Harry, we have to stumble through so much dirt and humbug before we reach home . . . Our only guide is our home-sickness." Dirt and humbug tend to make us guilty, but to partake of any life, always moving through time, we must make our peace; "home" is a moveable quality, a state of mind, not a place. One mistake Harry Haller makes at the beginning is to look for "home" in what he has lost, whether a wife, the smell of clean hallways, or "ideals." Henceforth he is instructed to look for "home" in what remains to be found and discovered, an unending process. Consciousness alone can reveal what lies ahead; to be discouraged on the way is to be conveniently martyred, and such guilt remains merely indulgence. Authentic conscience reckons with the *unknown* consequences of living, as well as with the known.

Pablo, jazz player, procurer, mystic, recognizes the symptoms of Harry Haller's wish to "forsake this world and its reality" for a transcendental reality. During the carnival scene, near the end of Harry's reeducation, he, too, advises Harry not to look for such a reality outside himself: "I can give you nothing that has not already its being within yourself," the theme, also, of Hesse's *Demian* (1919). To conquer time or "escape" reality means merely to escape from "personality," explains Pablo; but such escape is like struggling with a hydra, a "mistaken and unhappy notion" for man is never an "enduring unity" but consists of "multitude of souls, of numerous selves." What is the point of insisting on such multiplicity? In part it appears to be a method of demonstrating to the "Steppenwolf" the hopelessness of deluding oneself into escapes from time or *a* self; one can only slip into that space in time, and that self in time, which obtains at any given moment in man's salmonlike struggle against the stream. Also self must not be confused with "personality," which is mere facade. Guilt and bad conscience only hide things; they, not death, are the real "emergency exits"; true conscience permits the process of Becoming to divide the self into multiple selves, some saints, some sinners. It is a more updated version of Stein's butterfly-pistol dualism which Conrad, too, exposed as a totally inadequate dualism, not only for Jim, who did not know this, but for Stein, who did.

In the final pages, Mozart appears in a dream and explains that men pay not only for personal failures but for those of their times. Collective guilt is as real as personal guilt (Hesse was preoccupied with the lack of war guilt among his countrymen following the first World War). That may be what men mean when they speak of a "national conscience." When Harry expresses some shock, Mozart comes back with a sharply worded admonition: "Certainly. Life is always frightful. We cannot help it and we are responsible [*verantwortlich*] all the same. One's born and at once one is guilty." Both remarks are echoes, the first of Lord Jim's importunate assertion that we are, all the same, "responsible"; the second of Josef K.'s equally importunate question, put declaratively, that—after all—we are all "guilty." Harry Haller reacts predictably: he is in despair; he sinks into a fit of self-revulsion and self-pity. Mozart will not allow it. The "murder" of Hermine in The Magic Theatre is not yet disposed of and there must be a formal trial. "Or do you think," Mozart asks, "of evading the consequences?" Outraged, Harry again falls into the trap. "I evade the consequences? I have no other desire than to pay and pay and pay for them, to lay my head beneath the axe and pay the penalty of annihilation." But of course: annihilation brings forgetfulness, evasion, and erases all responsibility. Werther and Roderick Usher; Manfred, Roderick Hudson, and Hanno Buddenbrook; Lord Jim and Josef K.—had they not all wanted "to pay and pay and pay" and lay their heads beneath the axe? Mozart will not permit it; before sentence is pronounced, he looks at Harry Haller with "intolerable mockery." Harry is accused of misusing The Magic Theatre, of confounding art with reality, of using the Theatre as an instrument of suicide and murder, and of being "devoid of humour." "Wherefore," say the judges, "we condemn Haller to eternal life," and promise him no escape from the indignity of being laughed out of court. Mozart delivers further blows; he mocks Harry for being "ready for everything" except for "what will be required of [him] "—"ready to mortify and scourge [himself] for centuries together." Still Harry cringes: "Oh, yes, ready with all my heart," he cries out, still hoping for oblivion in the wrappings of martyrdom. Mozart will not let go, will not permit him to play the tragedian: "I don't care a fig for all your romantics of atonement . . . You are willing to die, you coward, but not to live! The devil, but you shall live!''

That is the real sentence. Like a drug, death is witheld; and the agony of life becomes meaningful only when a fully free and receptive consciousness permits life to flow freely through one's ever-changing self; when one is prepared to pay the consequences not of dubious deeds, or while indulging in the comfort of guilt and self-degradation, but when one dares to live, to be, to refuse conscience its easy success of making cowards of us all. "Good conscience," wrote Nietzsche, "has bad conscience for its stepping-stone, not for its opposite. For all that is good has at one time been new . . . strange, anti-moral, immoral, and has gnawed like a worm at the heart of the fortunate discoverer."[22] This constitutes the real lesson of Harry Haller's second *Bildung*.

The Paradox of the Fortunate Fall of Jean-Baptiste Clamence

Camus's *The Fall* opens with a question and ends with an exclamation mark, but this coincidence should mislead no one into supposing that Camus poses a problem which, at the end, he has resolved. Quite the contrary may be the case: the question mark is perhaps merely a pro forma punctuation to a rhetorical remark; the exclamation mark at the conclusion may in fact be a question placed in the form of an exclamation, a totem erected by the speaker for his, and our, momentary comfort. *The Fall* propounds no doctrines; although it is far less mysterious than *The Stranger*, it is nevertheless a difficult book to be certain about, because the credibility of its narrator is always in doubt, and there is no authorial intrusion, no *Treatise*, to counterpoint the essentially uninterrupted monologue of the narrator.[23] Answers are offered by the narrator to an interlocutor's occasional questions, and we must take even the existence of such an interlocutor on faith. I feel myself there is a good deal of evidence to challenge the "dialogue" of Jean-Baptiste Clamence (an admitted pseudonym); a sufficient number of references to "doubles" suggests that the ostensible interlocutor is Clamence's *Doppelgänger*. What we can be certain about is that Camus has taken the problem of conscience-consciousness to its ultimate contemporary arena; by the very ambiguity of the novel, he has shown that a case of conscience is inevitably a case of consciousness and that guilt and freedom, so long supposed mutually exclusive, are in fact interdependent.

The Fall both challenges and yet agrees with one of Nietzsche's most controversial ideas, the problem of compassion. "Is it to your advantage to be above all compassionate?" Nietzsche asked; "And is it to the advantage of the sufferers when you are so?" We must suffer alone according to Nietzsche, and he was not the first nor the last to ask that of us. In any other kind of suffering save that which we endure alone lies danger: "I am . . . certain that I need only give myself over to the sight of one case of actual distress, and I, too, *am* lost."[24] The problem *The Fall* explores is precisely what it may mean to be lost or, put conversely, what it may mean *not* to be lost, having resisted the "sight of one case of actual distress," the condition Clamence defines as his own during the course of his narrative. Clamence also fits well the definition Nietzsche offered of the sufferer whose sole purpose is to enlist not only our sympathy but an accompanying share of his own travail: "the tyrannical will of a . . . tortured being, who would like to stamp . . . the very idiosyncrasy of his suffering . . . on others; [one] who . . . takes revenge . . . and brands *his* image, the image of *his* torture, upon them."[25] Sufficient numbers of readers have come away from Camus's Ancient Mariner's confession feeling implicated and included in his transgressions to lend credence to Nietzsche's idea, which, incidentally, he called "*romantic pessimism* in its most extreme form," a sign of his rejection of certain Schopenhauerian and Wagnerian strains.

The story of Camus's romantic pessimist, who sees himself as a "judge-penitent," is simple enough to recapitulate. A brilliant *bon vivant*, a successful lawyer, who argues with particular success (sometimes without fees) the cases of the indigent, Jean-Baptiste Clamence appears to live a self-indulgent life full of pleasure and self-approval until one night, quite unexpectedly—but then again not so unexpectedly—he hears laughter. From then on this laughter grows louder and also turns derisive and persistent; Clamence begins to lose grip of his smug life. Before ending up as defense attorney for the underworld of the Amsterdam waterfront, where in self-imposed exile he is doing his penance, he descends by stages: debauchery, sexual adventures, self-destructive forays into his once safe society. In effect, he initiates a counterrevolution in which he plays the role of a guerrilla fighter against his former but still partially intact self; as such battles tend to be, it is a dirty, bruising, and inconclusive *bellum intestinum.* As he recounts the story of success in the opening pages, he observes that "after all, I was on the right side; that was enough to satisfy my conscience."[26] His good conscience would be satisfied until it became a bad conscience—until he became conscious of it in the first place, after which, of course, good and bad no longer mattered. Almost precisely in the middle of his account, he tells the story of how he once crossed a bridge on the Seine, saw the shape of a woman, heard a splash, hesitated, walked on, and for the next several days abstained from reading the newspapers. Ostensibly this incident precipitates his guilt. At the conclusion of his confession he asks for a second chance to relive its alternative possibilities—to relive it otherwise. But his plea is ironic because, as he says, it is too late: "Fortunately!" Confess he must. "No man," wrote Kierkegaard, "who has a bad conscience can endure silence."[27]

It is essential to reconstruct the chronology of *The Fall.* At first it may appear that the laughter preceded the episode of the girl on the bridge, because in the progress of the novel we know about the laughter quite some time before we hear the details of its ostensible cause. But the sequence is quite clear: "That particular night in November, two or three years before the evening when I thought I heard laughter behind me, I was returning to the Left Bank." What happened, not only in the two or three years between the incident on the bridge and the laughter, but in the years antedating the life of the *bon vivant,* is embedded in Clamence's memory. And it is the process of remembering what he has assiduously tried to forget which occupies the major portion of Clamence's confession. In *The Will to Power* Nietzsche explained how in the " 'inner world,' " the chronological order of cause and effect is inverted. "The fundamental fact of 'inner experience' is," he argued, "that the cause is imagined after the effect has been recorded . . ." This is also true for "the sequence of thoughts" where we "seek for the reason of a thought, before it has reached our consciousness; and then the reason reaches consciousness first, whereupon follows its effects."[28] For example we may say that in Clamence "inner experience," the *effect* of the laughter (indeed the laughter itself) is recorded, brought to consciousness, before its *cause,* the episode on the bridge, punctures through the lid of a suppressed consciousness, or memory. The girl's apparent suicide causes the laughter, but it is only "two or three years" later that the effect surfaces; when it does the original cause is *not* manifest in Clamence's mind. When he first hears the laughter he appears to be totally ignorant of its cause, indeed is "taken by surprise"; he now intends to take the reader by surprise by witholding the story of the girl (there are hints) for at least another thirty pages. The time that elapses between the laughter (effect) and the conscious manifestation of the girl on the bridge (cause) in the life of Clamence is not specified except that it has clearly been spent on one effort: to suppress the cause while battling the effects. But effects don't exist forever without causes—they demand them. "Suppressed dives," says Clamence, "sometimes leave one strangely aching."

Clamence has been accused of shame and hypocrisy and his confession has been regarded by some as evidence of a man even vainer and more selfish in penance than the man who is supposedly being remorsefully atoned for. Some truth lies in this, but it is surface truth; Clamence is human, all-too-human. "We get on with our bad conscience more easily than with our bad reputation,"[29] said Nietzsche; therefore Clamence's exile is in part an inner offensive launched against an expected attack from without. Since such offensives are always disguised as defenses, Clamence's tone is necessarily ironic, his self-deprecation suspect. Very early in his account he confesses his "nostalgia for the primates," for they "don't have any ulterior motives," as he so clearly has. Calling himself "judge-penitent" is a maneuver to cover his flanks; he is neither judge nor penitent. Throughout his account he stresses his real aim, avoiding judgment, for which he retains the talisman of the stolen panel of "The Just Judges" severed from van Eyck's "Adoration of the Lamb." There are no more just judges, he says, and justice has been separated from innocence (that is, the lamb). In Clamence's world, as in Josef K.'s, there is no outright exoneration from guilt, no "definite acquittal."

Like Josef K. and Harry Haller, Clamence is a bachelor, free of what an intimate sexual relationship might offer under the auspices of conjugal union. Like them, too, he is attracted to women, uses them for his purpose, but finds no lasting solace in femininity. Man, he says, "can't love without self-love," not a very scandalous remark (Pope said, in *The Essay on Man*, "Self-love and social are the same"); but his "self-love" allows him to avoid obligation, except, of course, to himself. One assumes from his repeated assertions that he likes "all islands" because "it is easier to dominate them" that such a choice is not accidental. Slavery is an obsession;[30] he insists that all men secretly desire for the state of gangsterdom in order to rule the world, the vicarious wishes of the adult for the life of the comic-strip outlaw, not James Bond but his adversaries, SMERSH, the independent slaveholders who seek to rule the whole world. We should never admit this but simply keep smiling and so "maintain our good conscience." However, silence is not possible; "I, I, I is the refrain of my whole life," he says accusingly, and we are tempted to ask for the rest of the "poem" to which the refrain is appended. The answer would undoubtedly be that he does not, or at the least did not, remember.

Until the laughter, he had "an extraordinary ability to forget ... Everything slid off—yes, just rolled off me." He neither had to implore spirits to give him oblivion, like Manfred, nor did he need the intercession of spirits to purge him of unpleasant thoughts, like Faust. "Gradually," he confesses, ". . . my memory returned," but then he adds, "or rather, I returned to it, and in it I found the recollection that was awaiting me." The distinction is no case of hair-splitting, for it confirms what Freud observed about guilt, that man does not await it but seeks it out. Again Clamence seems to say that effect precedes cause, that he felt the laughter drawing him to the bridge, the "adventure" that he "found at the heart of [his] memory." Like Lord Jim, Clamence hesitated; while Jim jumped away from obligation, Clamence walked away from it: it comes to the same thing at that point of their intersecting dilemma. But Jim attempts to reconstitute the scene of his disaster, however uncertain the method may be; Clamence spends his life explaining how ("fortunately!") it cannot ever be reconstituted, and how he has "accomplices," indeed, "the whole human race." Jim seeks to convert the world to his innocence; Clamence seeks to convert it to his guilt. In order to achieve this he must become the penitent, even if only a hyphenated one: "I had to submit and admit my guilt. I had to live in the little-ease." Subverting the recognized desire that we are all ready to prove our innocence at the expense of the world's guilt, Clamence finds a subtler method: a double strategy of self-accusation and world-accusation. He is too smart merely to try to offer himself as did Harry Haller; "it is not enough to accuse yourself in order to clear yourself; otherwise, I'd be as innocent as a lamb." And if that were so he would have no need for "The Just Judges" separated from the adored lamb. He readily concedes that men want to be rid of guilt without the effort of "cleansing"; in fact his confession is based on a whole series of such concessions, allowing him the rhetorical advantage of being free, by his own work, of accusations he has already admitted.

However true this may be, Clamence is authentically serious even in the midst of irony, especially when he illuminates, in effect, what Josef K.'s problem really was by recounting his own analysis of such crises: "The question is to slip through . . . to elude judgment. I'm not saying to avoid punishment, for punishment without judgment is bearable. It has a name, besides, that guarantees our innocence: it is called misfortune. No, on the contrary, it's a matter of dodging judgment, of avoiding being forever judged without ever having a sentence pronounced." If Josef K. had been able to accept punishment without judgment, he would not have had to endure the final judgment which ultimately comes without punishment. For death in The Trial (as in "The Judgment" or "The Metamorphosis") is not punishment, life is; though "punishment without judgment is bearable," judgment without punishment is not. Perhaps this has misled some readers to consider Josef's death as literal suicide and Clamence's exile as symbolic death. Neither is the case, but Josef K. is judged, whereas Clamence, in judging others, delays his own judgment while enduring the punishment of that choice. Clamence chooses what the painter, Titorelli, describes for Josef K., as the second alternative, "postponement." In such a state the case is an ongoing matter and the "accused is never free"; his condition, as Titorelli describes it, fits Clamence very well: "For the case must be kept going all the time, although only in the small circle to which it has been artificially restricted." For Clamence that "small circle" is Amsterdam, a city of circles, as he insists, "concentric canals" described both as the "vestibule" and "hell." Of one thing Clamence is certain, whether that certainty is rationalized or not: "no one is ever acquitted any more."

Once having acquired memory (or consciousness), he finds self-accusation almost effortless: "I accuse myself up and down. It's not hard." But the fear of freedom, Nietzsche's view of which I have already quoted, equals the fear of judgment, so that self-accusation becomes a propitiatory gesture insured to keep Clamence in bondage. In bondage to what? "In short," he says, ". . . the essential is to cease being free and to obey, in repentance, a greater rogue than oneself." Such bondage to obedience and repentance has further rewards than merely keeping one from the stark and lonely vigil of personal freedom: "The more I accuse myself, the more I have a right to judge you." Therefore Clamence's "fall," like Adam's, has all kinds of fortunate consequences, not only for Clamence but for the *"mon cher compatriote"* interlocutor who, whether he exists or not, is a projected synecdoche for the rest of us, brought into the confession far more deeply than Hesse could manage and deliberately echoing that other judge-penitent, Baudelaire. If I had not fallen, Clamence says in effect, there would be no consciousness, no memory; without these, conscience is impossible; without conscience, and a bad one (that is, guilty), there would be no repentance, no confession; and without repentance to what law could man appeal? For "the keenest of human torments," he says, "is to be judged without a law."

So he may still await the detective from Paris who may some day come, mere symbol that he may be, for the stolen panel is his hostage against himself, the instrument of blackmail against his conscience, and always kept in readiness.

Again Hegel's conception of Socrates plays ironically against a contemporary situation. For Hegel Socrates was a kind of Adam-Eve, Athens a fallen Paradise: the Fall of Socrates would, however, bring a higher synthesis. "Knowledge brought about the Fall," writes Hegel, "but it also contains the principle of Redemption. Thus what to others was only ruin, to Socrates, because it was the principle of knowledge [consciousness], was also a principle of healing."[31] Hesse said this of *Steppenwolf*; but what had Camus in mind? He conjectured, perhaps ambiguously like the pigeons in the snow outside of Clamence's window, in possibilities. Adam's fall was "fortunate" because it prepared for the glorious redemption of Christ;[32] Clamence's fall is fortunate because it allows for the possibility of a redemption through man. That such a possibility seems to Clamence "always [to] be too late" is not merely defiant hypocrisy; rather it is Clamence's knowledge that in suspending the success of a "second chance," he keeps man in his fallen state still straining for what may be unattainable; the process, not the goal, seems important. That is why his fall is fortunate after all; that is why facing the unresolved second chance which seems to him to be too late evokes from him, a man used to the subjunctive, the tentative "Fortunately!"

The fundamental error in Clamence's desperate juggling act of being both judge and penitent is his illusion, though he barely preserves it, that he can in fact be his own adjudicator. Kant had warned that "as far as all man's duties are concerned, his conscience will have to suppose someone other than himself to be the judge of his actions, if his conscience is not to contradict itself."[33] In his unguarded moments even Clamence recognizes how self-evident that must be. But he falls into the trap of thinking (or pretending to think?) that one's self can be the judge, mete out the sentence, and serve it. In this he is a refinement of Lord Jim; but in both men their remorse, like all remorse, only "delays action, and it is action that ethics specifically requires." Otherwise remorse must ultimately "become its own object,"[34] just as Clamence, through ceaseless talk, turns remorse into self-serving reassurance. Clamence, of course, becomes his own object. That way, as Claudius said in *Hamlet*, his

> ... words fly up ... thoughts remain below:
> Words without thoughts never to heaven go.

Coleridge wrote a play called *Remorse* and one speech in it, while far from his best poetry, aptly defines the central problem of *The Fall*:

> ... Conscience rules us e'en against our choice.
> Our inward Monitress to guide or warn
> If listened to; but if repelled with scorn,
> At length as dire Remorse, she reappears,
> Works in our guilty hopes, and selfish fears!
> Still bids, Remember! and still cries, Too late!
> And while she scares us, goads us to our fate.
>
> (V, i, 288-294)

Hegel had scored the hypocrisy of a consciousness that undertakes to judge itself. In its superiority, he reasoned, it discovers only a twin, someone "the same as himself," and this identity allows the judged part of the double freely to unburden his sufferings to the judge, expecting, even demanding, a reciprocal confession from the judge.[35] Such a closed circuit permits Clamence to stay forever safe, forever outside the judgment of all fathers, a judgment he fully admits he must elude. Fortunately?

"Later times," wrote Hesse in 1935, "will in sport or also in earnestness read the seismographs of our epoch; and they will postulate a succession and rank of those symptoms of disquiet, shock, and despair which the collapse of Christianity brought to the surface in some thinkers and writers." There will be no lack of ruins and false idols, he observed wryly, but among the wasteland rubble, the future, he hoped, will be better able to sort out the genuine suffering from the mere preaching, the "usufructuary." But among those souls in whom the foreshadowing of great upheavals could be discerned, he was certain the name of Kafka would be counted.[36] Hesse was partially right on all counts, certainly that "later times" have made a sport of reading the seismographs of the recent past. By now the view that Kafka, Hesse, Camus, among many others, form a contiguous chain of disaffection and despair has become one of the vulnerable and vulgarized commonplaces of the criticism of the past twenty or thirty years. After the war Existentialism brought Nietzsche, Kierkegaard, Dostoevsky, and many others into that uneven chain; in addition a variety of dissociation theories (and dates) invited us to view whole centuries as constituting ages of the Wasteland, the breakdown of everything, from man to God.[37] It almost seems that the price of being counted modern is to disown a prescribed baggage list at the entrance; anything vaguely redemptive may be suspect contraband and subject to being confiscated. Truly the entrance into the circle of acceptability as a modern is guarded by the strictest gatekeepers (a la Kafka) and "revisionism" is quite as much a crime as in political arenas where dogmas prevail.

So despite Kafka's disclaimers, Hesse's palinodes, and Camus's ironic comments scattered through his works, fiction and nonfiction, these three (among others) have been kidnapped as once it was fashionable to kidnap John Donne[38] and the metaphysical poets. Clearly the view of these writers as wastelanders is not altogether off the mark, but it is an oversimplification which leaves much to be said. Basically we must acknowledge in all the writers and their works which I have discussed in this essay a sense of disaffection, sometimes despair, and very seldom an unambiguously hopeful resolution—not even in *Faust* or *The Prelude*. Indeed Hesse, in reviewing Kafka's *Trial* in the essay I have cited, sees in that "gloomy book" an "atmosphere of fear and loneliness," which he considers so heavy that it stifles not only the philistine but the empathetic reader. In addition he finds the book leaning towards a "fatalism" which negates every entry into the spiritual (*göttlichen*) "except a brave submission to the unalterable."[39] What we should question, however, are the reasons sometimes offered for such pessimism; causes and consequences in literary history are not always sequential, and an interplay or a dialectic may be a more useful metaphor. To me it appears that such a dialectic between conscience and consciousness as explored here has played a major role in the shaping of modern literature.

It would also seem that, after unsuccessful attempts to divide

conscience from consciousness, the painful truth of their insepara-
bility has once more confronted such writers as Kafka, Hesse, and
Camus. Each has given us a hero whose consciousness has resisted
assault unsuccessfully, and who has subsequently had to submit
himself to the function of an authentic conscience ("good" and
"bad" if we insist on the adjectives). That function is to make us
aware, whatever the risks and the consequences; the consciousness
of conscience is, as I indicated at the start, the inevitable, perhaps
the only state we can achieve, at least in this life. For Kafka,
consciousness activates conscience with results that devastate the
hero, confirming his worst fears; for Hesse, consciousness bares a
conscience that feebly attempts to slip away once more contritely
begging only for oblivion, succeeding, however, only in being condemned to live; for Camus, consciousness awakens conscience to
form the ultimate fusion, "judge [conscience]-penitent [con-
sciousness]." Memory floods the life of the hero and compels him
to acknowledge that innocence is merely everyone's wish fulfillment, guilt everyone's emergency exit. So, neither condition being
possible in the pure state, one must partake of both and avoid, in
the twilight of ambiguously descending birds, any commitment,
either to guilt or innocence. The concluding pages of *The Fall* bear
a haunting resemblance to the ending of Wallace Stevens's "Sunday Morning":

> And, in the isolation of the sky,
> At evening, casual flocks of pigeons make
> Ambiguous undulations as they sink
> Downward to darkness, on extended wings.[40]

Camus refuses to allow his hero the privilege of dying or living
with multiple selves. He makes of him the sojourner in the "vestibule" whose consciousness (memory may be a function of consciousness) operates conscience and vice versa, so that at last no
distinction is possible. For whatever Clamence becomes conscious
of is something he may call part of his conscience. Freud lucidly
described this process: "As long as things go well with a man, his
conscience is lenient and lets the ego do all sorts of things." It is

when "misfortune befalls him," that he then "searches his soul, acknowledges his sinfulness, heightens the demands of his conscience, imposes abstinences on himself and punishes himself with penances."[41]

Such is the course of Clamence's history, with one significant addition: being conscious of his conscience allows him a painful, if ironic, detachment and the dangerous opportunity to establish a new dualism, "judge-penitent." It is doubtful it can work any better than conscience-consciousness, and Camus seems to caution us against dualisms and dialectics, even his own. If we can be acknowledged bearers of guilt, he seems to say, that could become quite as equivocating a game for the future as any one of the old dualisms. It is in this area that Clamence's implicit appeal that we join him carries its true dangers. Imagine, Camus might be asking, a world full of judge-penitents! Imagine a world of men not heeding the great cries of distress but hearing them and acting, with delayed timing, like Jean-Baptiste Clamence?

Conclusion

It is still the great definition of humanity, that we have a conscience . . . an element of our being;—a conscience unrelenting yet not absolute; which we may stupefy but cannot delude; which we may suspend but cannot annihilate . . . .

—Coleridge

Beginning with such philosophers as William James, who denied the existence of consciousness (insisting that experience was mediated by pure perception—that it did not, in effect, reside anywhere—), the argument about consciousness took on some very behavioristic overtones at the turn of the century. These A. O. Lovejoy has charted in his complex study, *The Revolt Against Dualism.*[1] Such epistemological and phenomenological questions have preoccupied the minds of the greatest philosophers. Today, far more than when Lovejoy published his book, the solutions turn away from what Joyce called, more endearingly than one might think, the "scholastic stink": separations between mind and matter which would invest consciousness with as separate a life as matter. Whether or not consciousness exists, in philosophic terms, is far beyond the intent of this study. I have been content to deal with what men have said about consciousness (and conscience); how they feel and express that feeling, through fiction and in the cooling lava of fiction, discursive philosophy.

Curiously, consciousness nowadays is being treated in ways that suggest a revival, in different shape, of course, of the earlier conceptions of consciousness as an existing phenomenon, a *Ding an sich.*[2] Whether the pendulum is really swinging again it is difficult to say; and whether its swing is a welcome one is certainly in doubt. For all the recent emphasis on consciousness it is still con-

242

ceived behavioristically: actions cause consciousness; reactions make us conscious. To put it another way: consciousness in no way appears to exist as the process of *becoming* aware but rather as the phenomenon of *being* enlightened. What brings us to such consciousness varies: it may be the stimulant of drug; it may be the stimulant of rebellion; or it may be a kind of instant conversion. In any case it is quick and it has about it not the dawning of perception but the apocalypse of instant vision. Such speed eliminates not only process but, more disturbing, the conscience which consciousness has traditionally engendered. "No man," Coleridge said long ago, "can have the sensation of an approving conscience, in the nature of things, but as far as he has consciousness in himself that he did it [whatever the act] because it was his duty."[3] But "duty" too is now in disrepute, having become equated either with the false plastic values of a corporate society or the tyrannical canons of a corporate state. Such a view, though it may distort the truth considerably, cannot be dismissed simply by calling it injudicious or amoral. Like consciousness, duty needs to be redefined to make clearer how it responds authentically to man's actions. Still it seems scarcely conceivable that the concepts of duty are divisible from the newly emerging conceptions of consciousness. However we try, we come back to King Conscience holding court. It was a dilemma that Coleridge confronted all his life, desiring always the freedom of will he considered sine qua non for existence but bowing (always) to a certain *primum mobile* which, in his case, tended to emanate from divine sources (Kant acted much too often the role of God) in the shape of duty or conscience.

Coleridge, wisely I think, placed emphasis on the process of reaching an act, not on the act itself: "The more consciousness in our Thoughts and Words," he felt, "and the less in our Impulses and general Actions, the better and more healthful the state both of head and heart" (*I.S.*, p. 95). Morality, he believed, should be "grounded" in both "conscience and the common sense" (*F.*, p. 314); and "the conditional cause of Conscience" is reason "applied to *motives* of our conduct" which correspond with our "sense of moral responsibility" (*F.*, p. 159). Clearly the process of arriving at "moral responsibility" was a carefully guided tour, aided by reason, through the stages of consciousness, until we were brought face to face with conscience. That arbiter would then decide in its role as judge whence we had come from and wither we were headed. In fact conscience imposed upon us the duty of improving our judgment, of widening our judgment—of becoming, in effect, more conscious (*F.*, p. 290). Emanating from that consciousness Coleridge still saw the possibilities of what he called man's "free-agency": "Of so mysterious a phaenomenon [as conscience] we might expect a cause as mysterious. Accordingly, we still find this [that is, cause] . . . involved and implied in the fact, which it alone can explain. For if our permanent consciousness did not reveal to us our free-agency, we should yet be obliged to deduce it, as a necessary inference, from the fact of our conscience" (*I.S.*, p. 137). If, then, the process itself fails in convincing us of our ability to choose freely, then the inference may be drawn from the "mysterious phaenomenon" itself—from conscience, which is but the mirror reflecting consciousness itself, allowing us to work back to it as both the end of our journey into action as well as its cause.

One conclusion of this book is that we have apparently recognized the necessity for understanding conscience as a state of mind and spirit of which one must become conscious (consciously)—or else not possess at all. We have come some distance from Faust's liberties or Manfred's naïve distemper, from Werther's psychological provincialism or Lord Jim's enervating energies in the name of salvation. We have also learned about will, a disease Poe diagnosed and Mann described; we have begun to understand the contingencies of freedom; we have, I think, seen the dangers of Arnold's distinctions, and we have taken seriously the lesson of James's renunciation fables. Perhaps, in some strange way, the heroes of both James and Nietzsche, ascetics in different ways, chart the unlived life, which in Kafka and Hesse comes to haunt the hero. Goethe spoke earnestly not only for himself but for his time, which reached far beyond his octogenarian life, when he said that "the participant is always without conscience; no one except the spectator has a conscience."[4] Yet, being Goethe, he already anticipated Clamence, for is he not precisely correct regarding that future hero of a time he could only have guessed about? So long as Clamence participates, he in fact does not hear the great cry of distress, for, as Goethe suggests, the very ambiance of activity precludes the silence necessary to hear anything else. But when Clamence becomes a spectator, of himself as well as of life, when activity ceases and he has silence, then the laughter rings through the night leading him at last like a beacon to the cry he had forgotten. Conscience, we recall Schopenhauer saying, "is man's knowledge [*das Wissen*] concerning what he has done." Nietzsche agreed in essentials, but drew the lines a little finer, a little more ironically, and altogether more finally: "What is it that constitutes the history of each day for thee? Look at thy habits of which it consists: are they the products of numberless little acts of coward-ice and laziness, or of thy bravery and inventive reason? Although the two cases are so different, it is possible that men might bestow the same praise upon thee . . . But praise and utility and respectabil-ity may suffice for him whose only desire is to have a good con-science . . . not, however for thee, the 'trier of the reins' [*Nieren-prüfer*] who hast a *consciousness of the conscience*! [*Wissen um das Gewissen*!]"[5] This much cannot be denied Nietzsche, that conscience in the most authentic sense is beyond good and evil; nor is he wrong in scoring those who would seek only a "good conscience," thereby once again nullifying the authentic (not the "spurious") meaning of conscience which Nietzsche, we recall, rendered essentially as a sense of responsibility and obligation. "Consciousness of conscience," then, is the proper phrase: it was that state, achieved or not, which it was my aim to study. In the final three works we came, I think, progressively closer to that condition. And if Nietzsche again comes to mind at the close of this study, it is fitting in every way, for it is Nietzsche, often furthest from unifying conscience and consciousness, who is also sometimes closest to doing just that. Had insanity not overcome him he might well have overcome his hatreds to glimpse the "truth" to which he often was so close.

Of consciousness he wrote in *Ecce Homo*: "The whole surface of consciousness—for consciousness *is* a surface—must be kept free from any of the great imperatives."[6] This expressed his wary attitude towards consciousness which was consistent; Schopenhauer, we recall, also wished to keep *conscience* free from the imperatives. Both, however, were really looking for some mobility, because "imperatives" would always limit choices. Unamuno also attempted to rescue consciousness from "surface"; "Consciousness," he wrote "(*conscientia*) is participated knowledge, is co-feeling, and co-feeling is com-passion." All centers on Love personifying everything, even the universe. That universe becomes a suffering, pitying, loving consciousness which ultimately we call God, "the personalization of the All," the final consciousness.[7] Unamuno considered Nietzsche his enemy, but a final assessment may find them closer than he thought; in any case, though one might not expect it, he seemed suspicious of Hegel as well. "Participated knowledge," although it may lead to God, at least begins in man. And Blake played on the word conscience with characteristic dogmatism supported by a sense of complete reasonableness: "Innate Ideas are in Every Man, Born with him; they are truly Himself. The Man who says that we have No Innate Ideas must be a Fool & Knave, Having No Con-Science, or Innate Science." Innateness and co-feeling are also "co-knowledge." From the earliest philosophical considerations about conscience two conclusions have been almost universally acknowledged: that conscience is knowledge of self, and that it is essentially a consciousness the self has of its own certainty. "Conscience," to quote Blake again, "in those that have it is unequivocal."[8] It is, as the Germans would say, *gewiss.*

Despite the anger in a very lucid *Genealogy of Morals,* Nietzsche knew he could not destroy conscience: he did wish to remove it from the pit of fear and restore to it its original meanings. Those meanings, as we have seen, he struggled to express in different ways, but the eloquent English definitions I recorded in the first chapter would come close to expressing his intent: "Inward knowledge, consciousness: inmost thought, mind. Inward knowledge or consciousness; internal conviction." Conscience as "internal conviction" he would hardly have found "obsolete." Nor is Chaucer's use of conscience: "feeling, sensibility, pity, sympathy," words Nietzsche might have rejected polemically but agreed with in principle, for they have nothing to do with transgression or guilt but everything to do with human consciousness and obligation and response (responsibility), with which alone men can measure right from wrong.

No laws prescribe that literary history should or even can be "objective." History is by definition in part interpretive, and the addition of the adjective "literary" changes little. These days too much critical industry is invested without a personal commitment by those who expend that energy. This seems to me a waste of spirit: no book such as this should remain so detached that it precludes its author from making judgments. My own judgments have, of course, been implicit and explicit throughout. In the critique that follows I do not, however, speak merely the bent of personal opinion; I speak from having hopefully absorbed some of the lessons I have learned from writing about the men and works that make up this book.

What David Daiches has recently called the "non-conformist conscience" became an integral companion of the Victorian faith that endurance was its own reward. Such a test of endurance, says Daiches, was the hollow aspect of an imperialism that had already lost its raison d'être and was now playing out a role of "sceptical stoicism combined with sceptical activism"—energy expended with little or no conviction. Such endurance for its own sake became "a substitute for understanding," a mere ritual tinged with a tradition of "relished melancholy" extending from early Tennyson through Arnold to Hardy, Housman, Kipling, and Conrad. Duty became not a function of conscience but rather a function of boredom and, in some cases, of despair. To cling to irrational and indefensible ideals not for the sake of the ideals but for the sake of the clinging has always been a presentiment of a declining age. Such "duty" fulfills neither the needs of genuine conscience nor of realistic survival. In fact the consequences of aimless duty are self-serving and self-consuming. In nineteenth-century England, with few exceptions, the expression of such duty even lacked the justification of a truly ascetic Christianity. And, as Daiches suggests, the relationship between an exhausting asceticism and an exhausted aestheticism was perhaps no accident during *fin de siècle.*[9] In fact it was an unholy alliance which had led the continent towards Nihilism in the fifties and sixties, an admixture of stoic and skeptical attitudes already implicit in the earliest Romantics, as Hegel was quick to perceive. Some release from sheer duty was both urgent and justified, and Arnold was not alone in recognizing this need. It is only when such release becomes as aimless as the "duty" it proposes to replace that we should again become concerned.

The old connotations of "conscience" die hard, and hence misconceptions have plenty of room to crowd the issue, creating either confusion or simplifications. In a recent book called *The Development of Conscience* Geoffrey M. Stephenson opens his argument with this: "If we say of a person that 'He has no conscience', we are criticising his behaviour. We imply that he shows no consideration for others, that he is wayward or unprincipled. 'He has a conscience', on the other hand, means he behaves dutifully and morally. It is difficult to give a precise definition of conscience, for people behave morally for different reasons."[10] If conscience means behaving "dutifully and morally," then we have indeed begged the question, and that such a concept of conscience should still reign nearly eighty years after Nietzsche's *Genealogy* is testimony to his failure or to ours—or to both. However, such seems to be the case: while it is bravely invoked today (as we said at the outset), conscience is still coated with barnacles one thought, or hoped, had long since been scraped off by the bruised hands of the heroes (real or fictional) whom I have written about in this book. Alas, it seems not to be so. And as conscience remains misunderstood why should we be surprised when the word which derives from it, consciousness, is even in worse shape?

Today, once again, Arnold's "spontaneity of consciousness"— the whole spectrum of "consciousness"—illuminates our culture, in fact creates it. The new conceptions, by and large, would not have found approval from Arnold or Nietzsche or Freud.[11] Especially Freud would scarcely have dreamt of conceiving of consciousness as behavioral expressions or political-social attitudes. For him as for the tradition he inherited, consciousness was awareness of self that led this self to judgment. One of the first presences that consciousness discovered occupying its illuminated self was Old King Conscience. He had insisted on recognition all along. Those who failed, those who evaded, those who fought not to confront their conscience are the dramatis personae of some of the fictions I have discussed in this book. Everyone now wants freedom; it has been sought before. But without recognizing its contingencies imposed not by the corporate society (these are very real) but imposed by the very self for whom that freedom is intended, there can be nothing but disaster. In the end consciousness has no numbers and, except for scientific purposes, it cannot be divided. Only one consciousness matters, and it is indivisible, unnumbered, and never, certainly, a viable part of any dualism or dialectic.

I have long felt that the nineteenth century split itself into unrecognizable shapes by its almost maniacal fascination with "doubling" and dualisms—that subject has been the source of books and will continue to be a theme of investigation for some time to come. Here I have examined only one such contorting dualism: conscience-consciousness. It should be obvious that I consider the whole notion of a division—let alone a dialectic—between conscience and consciousness impossible. I have attempted to show the failure of all divisive attempts, not only or even primarily in the thinkers—Schopenhauer, Hegel, Arnold, Nietzsche, Freud—but as revealed in art. For the artist remains the principal guide: It is he who tortures his sensibility with the dualisms that beset his age—and ages to come, for the artist is always partly prophet. Within the majesty of his fictional world, it is he who can best illustrate the fate of an idea without invoking polemics. In his works we have witnessed the struggle of conscience and consciousness and will; and although the outcome may always be uncertain, what is certain is not only the abstract conscience, as the thinkers all insisted, but the necessity for possessing it. Conscience may indeed be a very uncertain place to search for and find certitude; but it is certain that only in becoming fully conscious can we even recognize that a conscience exists, whatever it may hold in its cards. We are indeed obliged, I think, to restore

conscience and consciousness to their original unity, freeing conscience once more not merely to judge but to feel. Such a change
might restore to conscience an immediacy and a humaneness
which it has long been without and which Goethe, despite his
Faust, considered essential to civilized life:

> Sofort nun wende dich nach innen,
> Das Zentrum findest du da drinnen,
> Woran kein Edler zweiflen mag.
> Wirst keine Regeln da vermissen;
> Denn das selbständige Gewissen
> Ist Sonne deinem Sittentag.
>
> (At once then turn to what is within
> For there you'll find the center,
> Which no noble mind can doubt;
> You'll miss no precepts there
> Because the independent conscience
> Is the sun of your moral day.)
>
> *(Vermächtnis* [Legacy]*)*

In her exhaustive study of the etymological evolution of consciousness, Gertrud Jung (Chapter I, note 1) points to the important moment in history when *syneidesis* and *conscientia* ceased to
mean merely knowledge of an action or even its value and took on
the additional power of judgment. That moment, it seems, occurred sometime between Roman Stoicism, with its heavy "ethical
undertow," and the advent of Christianity, the epistles of St. Paul.
It was a development that altered the landscape of ethics as permanently as the telescope was to alter the landscape of the cosmos; it
was the sort of moment Yeats envisioned in his "Leda and the
Swan" ("sudden") when he asks whether Leda, after being ravaged, became aware of the enormity of the event:

> Did she put on his knowledge with his power
> Before the indifferent beak could let her drop?

The emphasis, Gertrud Jung points out, becomes increasingly
centered on *deed* and on *judgment* of that deed. From Christian
Wolff she quotes the following (1733): "The judgment of our

deeds, whether they be good or bad, is called conscience [*Gewissen*]." That conscience, that power of judging deeds, is the father of what we now call, too often without pause, "consciousness." As all children do, this child too was predictably rebellious against its father. But the history of the nineteenth century and part of our own is, in one respect, the history of how that rebellion failed. It failed not because the father was stronger but because, as in Kafka's *Judgment,* he was inevitable and demanded his due and could not, *would* not be put to rest.

If we view literary tides from a generous aperture of time we might concede that only the thinnest line divides Hamlet—"Thus conscience does make cowards of us all"—from Kafka's Georg Bendermann—"dear parents, I have always loved you all the same." Hamlet survives his despair, his "ordeal of consciousness," only because Shakespeare invests him with extraordinary strength to withstand its shocks; George Bendermann (son of a now more hardened father than Hamlet's) cannot survive the moment of recognition, that revelatory instant when the enormity of his *hubris* (for it is that) illuminates his being. Some have merely called this "guilt"; Kafka, who knew something about guilt, preferred to call his story "The Judgment."

When philosophers and poets invested knowledge with value, when they pointed to an inevitable relationship between perception and judgment, they undertook to remove conscience from being merely the abstract *vox Dei,* a voice of God, transposing and transforming conscience so that it became the inner voice of man himself. Inevitably that led to *Existenzphilosophie,* the philosophy of existence. With this came all the risks of "freedom": dread, separation-anxiety, doubt. "Being" became a function of the consciousness of conscience; and nothingness remained what it always must have been—the horror of being able to conceive of it at all. By giving himself the power of judgment, by transferring to himself the responsibility to sort out values, man burdened himself only, it seems, to seek at once to unburden himself. It is, one suspects, a paradox of existence from which there may be, at this late hour, no turning back. As the Devil says in Thomas Mann's *Doktor Faustus*: "Certain things are no longer possible."

From Rousseau and Herder to our present antiestablish-mentarians, one of the consistent complaints has been that over-civilization has deprived us of sensitivity, spontaneity, feeling, simplicity—the "naïve" Schiller called it. This lament has governed much of our art and philosophy over the last two hundred years, and it cannot all have been prompted by mistaken perceptions: too many convincing voices have warned us that perhaps we have already passed the point of salvation. Yet possibly the protest itself hastens the fulfillment of prophecy; it will not have been the first time. There can be little doubt, for example, that introspec-tion ironically exacerbated what intuition had suggested; we have become heavy with the burden of history on our backs. To locate ourselves in the *here* and *now* only makes more painful the aware-ness of the distance from where we have come, from the *there* and *then*. Many, however, have now recognized the danger of perpetu-ating self-hatred and *ressentiment* by rejecting the present in favor of the past. Such a path only leads to an accelerated and self-imposed diminution: we will more quickly become the epigones we dread. Others have cautioned us not to reject the past in favor of the future. That path leads to the foolish comfort that progress is a matter of forward movement in time.

History may have disabused us of both choices only to strength-en our belief that together the two paths have already annihilated us. Today we often appear to reject the past and the future with only the illusion that we do so for the sake of the present. We yearn neither for the Golden Age nor for the millennium, but in truth the present pleases us even less. We seek to palliate the pain of the moment, not to drain its pleasure. Without artificial stimu-lation consciousness has become too risky, yet the risks of stimu-lating are, of course, often immeasurably more deadly. Of con-science we know only that, as students asked to define it in a high school class wrote (almost in identical language), "it is the feeling that we have done something wrong."

Clearly we must, at our peril, cease separating knowledge from value, without committing the error of confusing and identifying them as synonymous. I agree that words such as "knowledge" and "value" must not be played with fast and loose; but knowledge, whether perceptual or conceptual, is still a form of awareness; how much knowledge we can have and how we get it are the difficult questions. As for "value" it matters not how relative we treat its implications; in the end value is in part that which defines our survival—individually and together. Knowledge and value are therefore expressions of consciousness and conscience. "To be conscious of our conscience" is one way of saying that awareness (at the very least) alerts us to a judgment of our actions. It provides us with what Kant called *Urteilskraft*, literally the power of judgment. If we continue to delude ourselves that true awareness lies somehow always "beyond" the mundane process of living itself, we are indeed headed for a collision course. That may sound apocalyptic. Yet I suspect that we are seldom nearer the Apocalypse than when we confidently think we have already experienced it.

Notes
Index

Notes

Introduction

1. Dualisms are not always dialectical; but dialectics are apt to be expressions of dualisms. An important book on the subject with respect to German literature is Peter Heller's *Dialectics and Nihilism: Essays on Lessing, Nietzsche, Mann, and Kafka* (University of Mass. Press: Amherst, 1966). Heller's argument proceeds from the positive function of dialectics in Lessing, where the aims were synthesis, rational order, liberation, to the demise of dialectics in "ambiguity," "incongruity," "alienation," "despair," and, in Kafka, the absurdity of striving—i.e., "nihilism." On Mann, Peter Heller differs from Erich Heller (*Thomas Mann, The Ironic German* [Cleveland: World Publishing, 1961, rev. ed.]) who, Peter Heller feels, does not quite see the possibilities that await us at the end of dialectical collapse—at least in Mann (*Dialectics and Nihilism*, pp. 168-172). See also Masao Miyoshi, *The Divided Self: A Perspective on the Literature of the Victorians* (New York and London: New York University Press, 1969) and Maurice Beebe, *Ivory Towers and Sacred Founts: The Artist as Hero in Fiction from Goethe to James Joyce* (New York, 1964).

2. Because a writer's work deals with, say, the twentieth century, or because he writes in that particular time-span does not classify him irrevocably as "belonging" to that time. An author's temperament, in literary-historical terms, far more "places" him than arbitrary dates. There were certain lines of nineteenth-century thought which did not reach their climax until well into the twentieth century, developed by the writers I have mentioned. Conversely, some writers who either lived or wrote in or not very far beyond the nineteenth century may be considered "twentieth" century in their orientation. A good example of this sort of phenomenon might be the

late French *symbolistes* whose work culminated, in some respects, in the modernity of the early Eliot and Pound.

3. A.O. Lovejoy, *The Revolt against Dualism* (La Salle, Ill.: The Open Court Publishing Co., 1929 [1955]), pp. 1, 43. (See chap. I, pp. 1-41, for a detailed account of what Lovejoy considers to be the "revolt" against dualisms.)

4. Austin Warren, *The New England Conscience* (Ann Arbor: University of Michigan Press, 1966), "Conscience and Its Pathology," pp. 3-28.

I. Conscience and Consciousness

1. The most comprehensive investigation into the relationships and development of the German consciousness (*Bewusstsein*) from the Greek *syneidesis* and the Latin *conscientia* is an essay by Gertrud Jung, "ΣΥΝΕΙΔΗΣΙΣ, Conscientia, Bewusstsein," *Archiv für die gesammte Psychologie*, 89 (1933), 525-540. Its main point is to trace how the modern (i.e., Descartes and Christian Wolff) concept of consciousness evolved from the original concept of "with knowledge" by way of the Christian interpretations of "conscience." Interesting points along similar lines are made by R. J. Zwi Werblowsky in "The Concept of Conscience in Jewish Perspective," tr. R. F. C. Hull, *Conscience*, Essays by Hans Zbinden and others, ed. The Curatorium of the C. G. Jung Institute, Zurich, tr. R. F. C. Hull and Ruth Horine (Evanston: Northwestern University Press, 1970), pp. 81ff. In the same volume C. G. Jung begins his essay, "A Psychological View of Conscience," tr. R. F. C. Hull, by flatly stating: "The etymology of the word 'conscience' tells us that it is a special form of 'knowledge' or 'consciousness' " (p. 181). Further discussion of etymology and its problems may be found in the same volume in Hans Schär's "A Protestant View of Conscience," tr. R. F. C. Hull and Ruth Horine, esp. pp. 115ff. An early etymological discussion which I have not found in any bibliography is G. Carring's account in his interesting study, *Das Gewissen, im Lichte der Geschichte socialistischer und christlicher Weltanschauung* (Berlin-Bern, 1901), chap. ii ("Das griechische und das lateinische Wort Für den Begriff 'Gewissen' "), pp. 29-30. For further references see n. 7 below.

2. The title of a noted historical study by Paul Hazard, *"La Crise de la conscience européenne"* (Paris, 1935); the book was translated by J. Lewis May as *The European Mind: The Critical Years 1680-1715* (New Haven, 1953). Obviously the French "conscience" could not be translated without creating undue ambiguity. In a section on Zola entitled "Conscience and Consciousness" appearing in *The Gates of Horn: A Study of Five French Realists* (New York: Oxford University Press, 1963), Harry Levin discusses the "interrelated meanings" of the French *conscience* (p. 371). In his essay on "The Unconscious" (1915), Freud speaks of the *"double conscience"*

which is, as the editor points out, the French term for "dual consciousness," or in Freud's term *"Bewusstseinspaltung,"* literally "splitting of consciousness," *The Standard Edition of the Complete Psychological Works of Sigmund Freud,* 23 vols. ed. James Strachey, XIV (London: Hogarth Press, 1953-1966), 170 (hereafter referred to as *Standard Edition*). For purposes of collation with the original I have consulted the *Gesammelte Werke,* Imago Edition (London, 1946).

3. My thanks to my colleague Professor Andrée Collard for calling my attention to this. Her translation of selections from las Casas' book is now published, *History of the Indies* (New York: Harper & Row, 1971).

4. The English dictionaries used in the pages that follow (unless otherwise identified) are: *The Oxford English Dictionary,* unabridged (hereafter the *OED*); The *Middle English Dictionary* (hereafter the *MED*); J. Bosworth and T. N. Taller, *An Anglo-Saxon Dictionary.*

5. "Ayenbite" or "agenbite" is a neologism; its extension as "pricke of conscience" is fairly accurate. If the compound is broken down into agen/ ayen and bite, the stress is more literally the inner bite of "inwit," or conscience; the blow of conscience.

6. The original is quoted from *The English Text of the Ancrene Riwle,* ed. Frances M. Mack, Cotton MS Titus D. XVIII, Early English Text Society No. 252 (London: Oxford University Press, New York, Toronto, 1963 [for 1962]), p. 107, ll. 16-17. The translation is quoted from *The Nun's Rule, Being the Ancren Riwle Modernised* by James Morton with Introduction by Abbot Gosquet (New York: Cooper Square Publishers, 1966), p. 231.

7. The German dictionaries used in this discussion are: Friedrich Kluge (rev. Walter Mitzka), *Etymologisches Wörterbuch der Deutschen Sprache,* 20th edition; Hermann Paul (rev. Werner Betz), *Deutsches Wörterbuch.* However, the most comprehensive source for the etymological history of *Gewissen* is the entry in *Die Religion in Geschichte und Gegenwart, Handwörterbuch für Theologie und Religionswissenschaft,* 3rd rev. edition, IV, ed. Kurt Galling et al. (Tübingen [1958]), 1550-1558. The entry for *Bewusstsein* is in vol. VI (1957), pp. 1113-1116. Although the emphasis is different, some of the information both supplements and adds to Gertrud Jung's essay (see n. 1 above).

8. Arthur Schopenhauer, *On the Basis of Morality,* tr. E. F. J. Payne (Indianapolis and New York: Bobbs-Merrill, 1965), p. 104. The Greek word, like the Latin, is a compound: *syn* = with + *eidesis* = knowledge. According to Liddell and Scott (rev. H. S. Jones), in *A Greek-English Lexicon,* the Greek word "conscience" as used in the moral sense dates from the Christian era. Hegel says in several places that the Greeks had no word for conscience in the Golden Age, for they served with honor by instinct, without reflection. The Furies, on the other hand, did have a specific function: "They are meant to suggest that it is man's own act and his consciousness which torment and torture him, in so far as he knows this act to be something evil in him . . .

They [the Eumenides] represent what we call conscience." *Lectures on the Philosophy of Religion*, tr. E. B. Speirs and J. Burdon Sanderson (London: K. Paul, Tranch, Trubner & Co. Ltd., 1895), II, 258. For purposes of collation with the original I have consulted the Jubiläumsausgabe of *Hegels Sämtliche Werke* ed. Hermann Glocker (Stuttgart, 1959). However, Gertrud Jung's essay traces the Greek in greater detail (see no. 1 above).

9. *Deutsches Wörterbuch* (see n. 7). Most of these points are also made in the other sources cited (see nn. 1 and 7). Hegel made extensive use of the cognate connections between *Wissen*, *Gewissen*, and *Bewusstsein*. Some of his remarks in this connection are discussed in chap. IV.

10. *Hamlet, The London Shakespeare*, ed. John Munro, V (London: Eyre & Spottiswoode, 1958), p. 460; *Hamlet*, ed. G. L. Kittredge (Boston: Ginn & Co., 1933), p. 210. Since this Note was written a new essay has appeared on the subject, Harold Skulsky, "Revenge, Honor, and Conscience in *Hamlet*," *PMLA*, 85 (January 1970), 78-87. Skulsky's discussion indicates that he accepts "conscience" in *all* its appearances in the play as expressing the "moral sense" meaning—indeed he insists on it.

11. *Spinoza Dictionary*, ed. Dagobert D. Runes (New York: Philosophical Library, 1951), p. 121.

12. *New Essays Concerning Human Understanding* by Gottfried Wilhelm Leibnitz, tr. Alfred Gideon Langley (La Salle, Ill.: The Open Court Publishing Co., 1949 [1896]), 3rd ed., pp. 90-91.

13. John Locke, *An Essay Concerning Human Understanding*, collated and annotated with Prolegomena, Biographical, Critical, and Historical by Alexander Campbell Fraser (New York: Dover, 1959), I, 71.

14. Ibid., pp. 71-72, and Notes from *Marginalia Lockiana*.

15. David Hume, *The Philosophical Works, A Treatise of Human Nature*, ed. T. H. Green and T. H. Grose (Aalen: Scientia Verlag, 1964) II, 236, 290-291. See also p. 24.

16. Hume, *Philosophical Works, Essays, Moral, Political, and Literary*, IV, 172; 257; 171. For an interesting discussion of Hume and morality see A. Macbeath, "The Moral Good," in *Hume and Present Day Problems* (London: Harrison & Co. Ltd., 1939), pp. 123-143. Also helpful is Henry D. Aiken's Introduction to *Hume's Moral and Political Philosophy* (New York: Hafner Publishing Co., 1948).

17. De Jaucourt was a close collaborator of Diderot.

18. *Encyclopédie, ou Dictionnaire raisonne des sciences, des arts, et des métiers*, ed. Diderot and d'Alembert (Paris, 1751), III, 902-904. My thanks to Mr. Roger Hooper for helping me to translate some *Encyclopédie* French.

19. Hume had discussed "duty" prior to Rousseau's *Emile*; it is likely that Hume was the first pre-Kantian to assign an important role to duty as a moral-social imperative. See *Philosophical Works*, II, 252ff.

20. Paul Hazard, *European Thought in the Eighteenth Century from Montesquieu to Lessing*, tr. J. Lewis May (New Haven: Yale University Press,

1954), pp. 26ff. (The original *La Pensèe europèenne au XVIII ème siècle: De Montesquieu à Lessing* was first published in 1946.)

21. Locke, *An Essay Concerning Human Understanding*, I, 138.

22. Ernst Cassirer, *The Philosophy of the Enlightenment*, tr. Fritz C. A. Koelln and James P. Pettegrove (Boston: Beacon Press, 1955), pp. 157, 160.

23. *Emile, ou de l'éducation*. The discussion of duty and conscience is from a separate section, *Profession de foi du vicaire savoyard* (Profession of Faith of a Savoyard Priest). (This excursus resembles Goethe's *Bekentnisse einer schönen Seele* [Confessions of a Beautiful Soul] in *Wilhelm Meister's Apprenticeship*.) It is this "apostrophe" to conscience from the priest's creed which Lewis White Beck thinks might have inspired Kant's "apostrophe" to "duty." See his *A Commentary on Kant's Critique of Practical Reason* (Chicago: University of Chicago Press, 1960), p. 225n.

24. Kant, *Critique of Practical Reason and Other Writings in Moral Philosophy*, tr. and ed. with introduction by Lewis White Beck (Chicago: University of Chicago Press, 1949), p. 204.

25. "Foundations of Morals," ibid., pp. 61, 96.

26. Ernst Cassirer, *Rousseau, Kant and Goethe*, tr. James Gutmann, Paul Oskar Kristeller, and John Hermann Randall, Jr., (New York: Harper & Row, 1963), pp. 20, 41-42. (First published by Princeton: Princeton University Press, 1945.)

27. *Critique of Practical Reason*, p. 187.

28. Kant, *The Metaphysical Principles of Virtue*, tr. James Ellington with introduction by Warner Wick (Indianapolis and New York: Bobbs-Merrill, 1964), p. 59.

29. Ibid., pp. 60, 104.

30. Ibid., pp. 100-101.

31. Johann Gottlieb Fichte, *The Vocation of Man*, tr. William Smith (La Salle, Ill.: The Open Court Publishing Co., 1940), esp. pt. III, "Faith," pp. 93-176.

32. J. G. Fichte, *Gesamtausgabe*, Der Bayerischen Akademie der Wissenschaften, ed. Hans Jacob (Stuttgart-Bad Cannstatt, 1964), I, 1, 279. Fichte, like Kant, speaks of the "inner courtroom of conscience" ("das innere Richteramt des Gewissens," p. 375).

33. Søren Kierkegaard, *Fear and Trembling and the Sickness unto Death*, tr. with introductions and notes by Walter Lowrie (Garden City, New York: Doubleday Anchor, 1954), pp. 175, 211.

34. Geoffrey H. Hartman, "Romanticism and 'Anti-Self-Consciousness,' " *Centennial Review*, 6 (1962), 553n, 554-555, 557-558. (Inclusive page numbers are 553-565.)

35. See R. M. Adams, *Nil: Episodes in the Literary Conquest of Void in the Nineteenth Century* (New York: Oxford University Press, 1966).

36. The Baudelaire quotation is from *Intimate Journals*, tr. Christopher Isherwood with an introduction by W. H. Auden (London: Methuen & Co.

Ltd., 1949), p. 61. The De Quincey quotations are from *Confessions of an English Opium Eater and Other Writings,* ed. Aileen Ward (New York: The New American Library, 1966), pp. 61, 63-64, 70, 99.

37. See R. H. Super's fine recent study, *The Time-Spirit of Matthew Arnold* (Ann Arbor: University of Michigan Press, 1970). The quotation from Arnold is taken from vol. I of R. H. Super's *The Complete Prose Works of Matthew Arnold, On the Classical Tradition* (Ann Arbor: University of Michigan Press, 1960), p. 23.

38. A fuller discussion of Arnold will be found in Chap. V. The relationship between Arnold and Heine has been thoroughly discussed; that between Arnold and Nietzsche or Arnold and Hegel, whom he read, has scarcely been touched. For all quotations from the prose of Arnold, I have used *The Complete Prose Works of Matthew Arnold,* ed. R. H. Super (Ann Arbor: University of Michigan Press, 1960–). The present quotations are from I, 23, 28, 32. Studies relevant to Arnold's "Hebraism" and "Hellenism" will be found in the notes to Chap. VI.

39. *Aesthetic Paganism in German Literature: From Winckelmann to the Death of Goethe* (Cambridge, Mass., Harvard University Press, 1964).

40. *Inquiring Spirit, A New Presentation of Coleridge,* ed. Kathleen Coburn (Pantheon Books: New York, 1951), pp. 25, 31, 45. The remark beginning "Consciousness is the problem . . ." is quoted by Miss Coburn from *Notebook* 51. References to this edition will be incorporated into the text with the abbreviation *I.S.* and page numbers.

41. For the most recent discussion of Coleridge's relation to Kant and German Idealism see G. N. G. Orsini, *Coleridge and German Idealism* (Carbondale: Southern Illinois University Press, 1969). On the whole, Orsini agrees that Coleridge was an obedient disciple of Kant, though he concedes there were occasional rebellions. See esp. chap. I-V.

42. *The Collected Work of Samuel Taylor Coleridge,* vol. I: *The Friend,* ed. Barbara E. Rooke (Princeton and London: Princeton University Press and Routledge & Kegan Paul, 1969), p. 523n. All references from *The Friend* are from this edition and will be incorporated into the text abbreviated as *F.* with page numbers.

43. Cf. "CONSCIENCE—that law of conscience, which in the power, and as the indwelling WORD, of an holy and omnipotent legislator *commands* us." (*F.,* p. 112).

44. Schopenhauer, *On the Basis of Morality,* tr. E. F. J. Payne with an introduction by Richard Taylor (Indianapolis and New York: Bobbs-Merrill, 1965), p. 107.

45. *Three Short Novels of Dostoevsky,* tr. Constance Garnett rev. and ed. Avraham Yarmolinsky (Garden City, New York: Doubleday & Company, Inc., 1960), p. 209. All subsequent quotations are from this edition.

46. Arthur Schopenhauer, *Essay on the Freedom of the Will,* tr., with an introduction, by Konstantin Kolenda (Indianapolis and New York: Bobbs-

Merrill, 1960), p. 10. The essay was first published in 1841. For purposes of collation on all of Schopenhauer's work used in this study, I have consulted the Insel-Ausgabe of *Schoepnhauers Sämtliche Werke in Fünf Bänden* (Leipzig, n.d.). "Freiheit des Willens" appears in vol. III, *Kleinere Schriften.*

II. The Price of Consciousness

1. E. M. Butler, *Byron and Goethe: Analysis of a Passion* (London: Bowes & Bowes, 1956). See also Peter Larsen Thorslev, *The Byronic Hero: Types and Prototypes* (Minneapolis: University of Minnesota Press, 1962), and Bertrand Evans, "Manfred's Remorse and Dramatic Tradition," *PMLA*, 62 (1947), 752-73. Evans sees Manfred as "a transformed villain [from Gothic tradition] as hero" (p. 772). For a view of Manfred as an exponent of "Romantic egoism" see Masao Miyoshi, *The Divided Self: A Perspective on the Literature of the Victorians* (New York and London: New York University Press, 1969), pp. 62-63. For a translation of Goethe's review of *Manfred* (1820) and for Goethe's translation of Manfred's soliloquy, "The lamp must be replenished . . ." (I,i) and other passages, see Byron, *Letters and Journals*, ed. Rowland E. Prothero, V. App. II, 503-507. For an older but good general discussion of *Manfred*, see Samuel C. Chew, Jr., *The Dramas of Lord Byron* (Göttingen and Baltimore, 1915), pp. 67-84.

2. Friedrich Nietzsche, *Gesammelte Werke*, Musarion Ausgabe, I (München, 1922), 37, 44-45, 46. From "Ueber die dramatischen Dichtungen Byrons," Germania-Vortrag, Dezember, 1861, given when Nietzsche was seventeen. The translation is mine.

3. *Manfred* offers, in some respects, a view of guilt strikingly similar to that we find in Hawthorne, for Hawthorne, too, was by and large less interested in the nature of the unpardonable sin and more in the *operari* of its consequences.

4. *The Complete Works of Friedrich Nietzsche*, ed. Oskar Levy et al., 18 vols., VI, pt. 1 (London: Russell and Russell, 1909-1911), p. 112 (hereafter referred to as *Works*). The reference is to *Human, All-Too-Human*. Except for the long discussion of *The Genealogy of Morals* (chap. VI) I have used this edition throughout. For purposes of collation with the original I have consulted the Musarion Ausgabe (see n. 2 above).

5. Kant, *The Metaphysical Principles of Virtue*, tr. James Ellington with introduction by Warner Wick (Indianapolis and New York: Bobbs-Merrill, 1964), p. 120.

6. Thomas Mann, "Goethes *Faust*," *Essays of Three Decades*, tr. H. T. Lowe-Porter (New York: A. Knopf, 1948), pp. 28-29.

7. Georg Lukács, *Goethe and His Age*, tr. Robert Anchor (London: Merlin Press Ltd., 1968), pp. 181-182; 224; 227. We have recently become

familiar with the words of a military commander, "We had to destory the town in order to save it."

8. Erich Heller, *The Artist's Journey into the Interior and Other Essays* (New York: Random House, 1965), pp. 31, 36-37. Heller's essay is titled: "Faust's Damnation: The Morality of Knowledge."

9. Georg Lukács, "Thomas Mann," *Faust und Faustus* (Munich, 1967), pp. 211-278.

10. Cassirer, *The Philosophy of the Enlightenment*, tr. Fritz C. A. Koelln and James P. Pettegrove (Boston: Beacon Press, 1955), p. 93.

11. A very abbreviated list of critics who have taken a critical view of *Faust* would include: William Barrett, *Irrational Man: A Study in Existential Philosophy* (Garden City, New York: Doubleday, [1958], 1962); Erich Heller, *The Disinherited Mind* (Cambridge and New York: World Publishing, [1952], 1959), esp. the essay "Goethe and the Avoidance of Tragedy"; Walter Kaufmann, *From Shakespeare to Existentialism* (Garden City, N.Y.: Doubleday, 1960), esp. the following essays: "Goethe's Faith and Faust's Redemption" and "Goethe Versus Romanticism"; Morse Peckham, *Beyond the Tragic Vision: The Quest for Identity in the Nineteenth Century* (New York: George Braziller, 1962), esp. pt. II. I have benefitted most from the works of Heller and Kaufmann, two of the most stimulating critics writing in the past several decades, particularly on Goethe, Nietzsche, Mann, and Kafka.

12. Nietzsche, *Ecce Homo, Works*, XVII, 40.

13. *The Complete Writings of William Blake*, ed. Geoffrey Keynes (New York: Nonesuch Press, 1957), p. 42. (From "Then She Bore Pale Desire.")

14. The problem of the Romantic "I" is, of course, an enormously complicated matter, and I can but touch it briefly here. More will be said in the next chapter and, more indirectly, throughout the remainder of the book. For a recent and controversial discussion see Harold Bloom, "The Internalization of Quest-Romance," *Romanticism and Consciousness: Essays in Criticism*, ed. Harold Bloom (New York: W. W. Norton, 1970), pp. 3-24. The essay was originally published in the *Yale Review*, 58 (Summer 1969).

III. The Risks of Consciousness

1. Georg Lukács, "The Sorrows of Young Werther," in *Goethe and His Age*, tr. Robert Anchor (London: The Merlin Press Ltd., 1968), pp. 46-48. The entire essay is worth study, pp. 35-49.

2. Thomas Mann, "Goethes Werther" (1938), *Altes und Neues: Kleine Prosa aus Fünf Jahrzeiten* (Frankfurt-am-Main: S. Fisher Verlag, 1953), pp. 207-209. The translation is mine.

3. Friedrich Schiller, *Sentimental and Naive Poetry and On the Sublime*, tr. Julius A. Elias (New York: Frederick Ungar, 1966), pp. 105, 138, 137.

4. William Rose, *From Goethe to Byron; The Development of 'Welt-schmerz' in German Literature* (London and New York: G. Routledge & Sons Ltd. and E. P. Dutton & Co., 1924), pp. 21-22. The book is relatively old; the critical opinion of *Werther* has survived.

5. All quotations from *Werther* are from *The Sufferings of Young Werther,* tr. Harry Steinhauer (New York: W. W. Norton, 1970). Dates of letters have been used to simplify notations except when narrative replaces letters, in which case page numbers are in parentheses. Professor Steinhauer's Afterword in this book makes an excellent contribution to contemporary understanding of *Werther.*

6. Nietzsche, *The Joyful Wisdom, Works,* X, 47. This passage is quoted and discussed in an extended version in chap. V.

7. See Morse Peckham, *Beyond the Tragic Vision, The Quest for Identity in the Nineteenth Century* (New York: George Braziller, 1962), pp. 87-99.

8. *Goethes Gespräche mit Eckermann* (Leipzig, 1921), pp. 631-632. The translation is mine.

9. Freud, *Standard Edition,* XIV, 248.

10. Nietzsche, *Joyful Wisdom, Works,* X, 47-48. For one of the most stimulating recent essays on *The Prelude* see Arthur J. Carr, "The Mythic Substratum in Wordsworth's *Prelude,*" Papers of the Michigan Academy of Science, Arts and Letters, 51 (1966), 559-569. Carr convincingly presents Wordsworth's increasing realization that he could not consummate the Paradise he sought; indeed he sees in the narrator-protagonist "often terrifying discontinuities in the consciousness" (p. 564), which in effect force Wordsworth to consummate another vision—that of reality, a world that "unites the ordinary world of mixed feelings with the unfallen world of the first Paradise"—an experience that contains its share of "terror" (564-565). I agree with this view, and yet it is the very ability to overcome that terror that makes even the second vision possible, something Goethe denied Werther when he created his fanatical nature.

11. All quotations from *The Prelude* are from the 1850 edition, *Wordsworth's Prelude,* ed. Ernest de Selincourt, second ed. Helen Darbishire, ed. (Oxford, 1959). All quotations from *The Excursion* are from *The Complete Poetical Works,* vol. V (see n. 16).

12. See A. O. Lovejoy, " 'Nature' as Aesthetic Norm," in *Essays in the History of Ideas* (Baltimore: The Johns Hopkins Press, 1948). In the Capricorn paperback ed. pp. 69-77.

13. Richard Friedenthal, *Goethe, His Life and Times* (New York: World Publishing Co., 1965), pp. 128-132.

14. Geoffrey H. Hartman, *Wordsworth's Poetry, 1787-1814* (New Haven: Yale University Press, 1964). The discussion of "self-consciousness" from which most of my quotations are drawn is scattered throughout this book. The reader should consult the index, which is very thorough. For other

especially valuable discussions of *The Prelude* see David Ferry, *The Limits of Mortality, An Essay on Wordsworth's Major Poems* (Middletown, Conn.: Wesleyan University Press, 1959); Herbert Lindberger, *On Wordsworth's Prelude* (Princeton, N.J.: Princeton University Press, 1963); A. F. Potts, *Wordsworth's Prelude* (Ithaca, N.Y.: Cornell University Press, 1953); and consult Hartman's "Critical Bibliography," in *Wordsworth's Poetry, 1787-1814*, pp. 389-390.

15. For an annotated bibliography on "The Ode to Duty" see Hartman, *Wordsworth's Poetry*, p. 397. One of the specific issues is the possible influence of Kant and German Idealism as developed by Newton P. Stallknecht in *Strange Seas of Thought, Studies in William Wordsworth's Philosophy of Man and Nature* (Bloomington: Indiana University Press, 1958), esp. the argument that "The Ode to Duty" owes a good deal to Schiller's conception of *"die schöne Seele."* Stallknecht in general sees Wordsworth in the light of Kant and German Idealism. Like Hartman, who disavows any direct influences, Stallknecht is aware of René Wallek's original warning [*Immanuel Kant in England 1793-1838* (Princeton: Princeton University Press, 1931)] that such "influences" in Wordsworth are difficult to prove. I myself agree with Wellek but at the same time find Stallknecht's approach worthwhile. I would not feel it necessary to claim any direct influences, for the arguments in this case gain little either way. A concept like *"die schöne Seele"* had counterparts not only in France but in England. What one is interested in is not so much "influence" as trends of thought; here Stallknecht makes a valuable contribution.

16. *The Poetical Works of William Wordsworth*, ed. E. de Selincourt and Helen Darbishire (Oxford: The Clarendon Press, 1947), IV, 85 (variant reading of ll. 25-32).

17. See the definition in the *OED*.

18. Kant, *Critique of Practical Reason*, tr. and ed. with intro. Lewis White Beck (Chicago: University of Chicago Press, 1949), p. 61.

19. Hume, *Philosophical Works, Essays Moral, Political, and Literary*, ed. T. H. Green and T. H. Grose, II (Aalen: Scientia Verlag, 1964), 286.

20. Kant, *Critique of Practical Reason*, p. 193. Also Introduction, p. 21.

21. Willard L. Sperry, *Wordsworth's Anti-Climax* (New York: Russell & Russell, [1935], 1966), p. 12. Sperry specifically warns against the temptation to make Wordsworth a modern by lifting him out of historical context—a warning I hope I have heeded. Quite aside from the intellectual distortions such kidnapping always causes, Wordsworth no longer needs such special pleading.

22. *The Notebooks of Samuel Taylor Coleridge*, ed. Kathleen Coburn, II, pt. I (New York: Pantheon Books, Random House, 1957–[1962]), 2543/f67v. References to *Notebooks* will henceforth be incorporated into the text and identified by the entry number. Numbers run consecutively.

23. For further discussion by Coleridge on duty see *The Friend*, I, esp. 38, 290, 314, 324. (See chap. I, n. 42.)

24. See Paul Dietrichson, "What does Kant Mean by 'Acting from Duty?' " in *Kant, A Collection of Critical Essays*, ed. Robert Paul Wolff (South Bend, Ind.: University of Notre Dame Press, 1968), pp. 316ff.

25. *The Friend*, I, 430n.

26. The Underground Man and Hegel's view of *"die schöne Seele"* will be discussed in chap. IV. It was inevitable that the idealistic version of consciousness would be strongly challenged.

IV. Versions of Consciousness and Egotism

1. Konstantin Mochulsky, *Dostoevsky, His Life and Work*, tr. Michael A. Minihan (Princeton: Princeton University Press, 1967), pp. 155, 157.

2. On further documentation regarding Hegel's influence in Russia during the nineteenth century, see Edmund K. Kostka, *Schiller in Russian Literature* (Philadelphia: University of Pennsylvania Press, 1965) and, more recently, André von Gronicka, *The Russian Image of Goethe* (Philadelphia: University of Pennsylvania Press, 1968). I have been helped by both studies.

3. For one of the strongest statements on the subject see Edward Wasiolek, *Dostoevsky, the Major Fiction* (Cambridge, Mass.: M.I.T. Press, 1964), pp. 39-59. The chapter is entitled: *"Notes from the Underground* and Dostoevsky's Moral Dialectic."

4. I have used the text in *Three Short Novels of Dostoevsky*, tr. Constance Garnett, rev. and ed. Avraham Yarmolinsky (Garden City, N.Y.: Doubleday, 1960), pp. 179-297.

5. Joseph Frank, "Nihilism and *Notes from the Underground*," *Sewanee Review*, 69 (Winter 1961), 1-33. I hope my remarks do not in any way imply a lack of regard for this essay, for I consider Frank's contribution indispensable for any serious discussion of the *Notes*. René Girard also dismisses modern versions of the Underground Man, insisting indeed that Dostoevsky has described us without our realizing it: "you will recognize in almost every line of this great text a ferocious parody of the intellectual myths of our time," *Deceit, Desire, and the Novel, Self and Other in Literary Structure*, tr. Yvonne Freccero (Baltimore: The Johns Hopkins Press, 1965), p. 262. One of Girard's most interesting points is that Dostoevsky's hero, unlike the modern existential hero to whom he is so often likened, has "metaphysical desire." Girard also has relevant passages on "Master and Slave" (chap. iv) which relate to the notions in Hegel, Nietzsche, and Dostoevsky in relation to the "unhappy consciousness."

6. It was, of course, important to establish first of all that Dostoevsky used the word "consciousness" and second what its Russian linguistic profile was like. In this I have been helped by my colleague Robert Szulkin to whom

I express my gratitude. His suggestions were as invaluable as his information. Any errors are mine, but any I have not committed I have been spared by his aid. Consciousness in Russian is *soznanie*; conscience is *sovest'*. *Znat'* and *vest'* are both infinitive forms of to know. Knowledge is *znanie*. A key sentence of the offical definition reads: "It is precisely because man relates to the objects [of reality] *with knowledge* that the means by which he relates to the world is called *consciousness*." Conscience is defined, in part, as "an ethical category, expressing the capability of the personality towards self-control, toward moral *evaluation* of its own actions on the basis of understanding its own responsibility for the action undertaken ... Being an active response-action of man to the demands of society, conscience is a powerful inner force of the moral perfection of the personality and simultaneously expresses the level of its moral self-knowledge." *Filosofskii Slovar*, ed. M. M. Rozental and N. F. Yudin (Moscow, 1968). The definition of consciousness is from pp. 326-327; that of conscience from p. 323. The translation is Professor Szulkin's. As we can see, in Russian as in the other languages we examined (chap. I), both conscience and consciousness are closely related to knowledge, indeed to self-knowledge.

7. Dostoevsky's "knowledge" of Poe antedated the *Notes* by several years. See Vladimir Astrov, "Dostoievsky on Edgar Allan Poe," *American Literature*, 14 (March 1942), 70-74. Astrov's proof consists of an "anonymous" article, a not very convincing piece of evidence. Still Dostoevsky and Poe had much in common in their view of "perversity."

8. Arthur Schopenhauer, *On the Basis of Morality*, tr. E. F. J. Payne with an introduction by Richard Taylor (Indianapolis and New York: Bobbs-Merrill, 1965), p. 197.

9. G. W. F. Hegel, *The Phenomenology of Mind*, tr. J. B. Baillie, rev. and cor. second ed. (London: G. Allen Unwin Ltd., New York: Macmillan, 1949), p. 461. The parenthetical words in the above quotation are the translator's. The original reads: "... *Gewissen der seiner selbst gewisse Geist ist.*" All subsequent quotations from *The Phenomenology* are from this edition. In order to prevent crowding the text or the notes, here are the inclusive page numbers for the corresponding ideas from Hegel: 1) self-consciousness, including its development from master-slave to the "unhappy consciousness": pp. 215-267; 2) conscience; including the "beautiful soul" and "evil and the forgiveness of it": pp. 644-679. My understanding of *The Phenomenology* has been much aided by J. Loewenberg's *Hegel's Phenomenology, Dialogues on the Life of Mind* (La Salle, Ill., 1965).

10. Hegel's *Philosophy of Right*, tr. T. M. Knox (Oxford: Clarendon Press, 1942), pp. 88, 91. All subsequent quotations are from this edition.

11. *Oblomov* was published in 1859, five years before the *Notes*.

12. There is, of course, the "missing" material from "the next to last chapter," which the censor, to Dostoevsky's dismay, excised. From a letter to his brother, we can surmise that this missing material brings the Underground

Man to the brink of Christian transcendence: "Those swines of censors—where I mocked at everything and sometimes *blasphemed for form's sake*—that's let pass, but where from all this I deduced the *need of faith and Christ*—that is suppressed." Quoted in Mochulsky, *Dostoevsky*, p. 256. Though no one can afford to ignore this letter (and the new "chrystal palace" mentioned in the existing text), it is too little on which to build a case for an achieved transcendence. What we can say is that Dostoevsky brings his hero to a point where neither Romanticism nor nihilism will serve, a point from which he searches for a new ideal. And that ideal clearly was to be in Christ.

13. Mochulsky, pp. 260-261.

14. Kostka, *Schiller in Russian Literature* (see n. 2). Also illuminating is Walter Kaufmann, *Hegel: A Reinterpretation* (New York: Doubleday, Garden City, 1965), esp. chap. i.

15. The phrase is borrowed from William H. Gass's essay on Henry James, "The High Brutality of Good Intentions," *Accent* (Winter, 1958).

16. See Baudelaire, *Correspondance générale*, ed. Jacques Crepet (Paris, 1917), III, 76.

17. Jean-Paul Sartre, *Baudelaire*, tr. Martin Turnell (New York: New Directions, 1950), p. 31. Further references to this book will be incorporated into the text with page numbers in parentheses.

18. *Correspondance générale*, II, 77.

19. Ibid., III, 279-280.

20. I have used the Michael Meyer translation of *Peer Gynt* (New York: Doubleday, 1963).

21. Here is part of the translator's note to this passage: " '*Troll, be thyself—and thyself alone!*' The phrase . . . to be self-sufficent in a bad sense, was not . . . created by Ibsen. The danger of self-sufficiency was a problem which was occupying people during the middle of the nineteenth century far outside the boundaries of Norway . . . The absence in modern English of any pejorative equivalent of self-sufficiency makes this vital phrase peculiarly difficult to translate . . . In the final scene with the Old Man . . . I have used two variant translations, 'Look after yourself' and 'To hell with the rest of the world', in an attempt to clarify the meaning; no single English phrase quite suffices."

V. Consciousness and Will

1. The problem of process is an extensive one, and I wish only to indicate its presence here, and perhaps to suggest, here and there, how process governed much of the thinking in certain nineteenth-century (and early twentieth-century) writers. For a somewhat different but detailed discussion of process see Charles Feidelson, Jr., *Symbolism and American Literature*

(Chicago and London: University of Chicago Press, 1953). The index will supply the appropriate pages.

2. Edward H. Davidson, *Poe, A Critical Study* (Cambridge, Mass.: Harvard University Press, 1957), p. 46.

3. Adams, *Nil* (New York: Oxford University Press, 1966), p. 45.

4. For a balanced view of Poe as philosopher and artist, and how the function of the latter was hurt by that of the former, see the excellent essay by Charles O'Donnell, "From Earth to Ether: Poe's Flight into Space," *PMLA*, 77 (March 1962), 85-91.

5. *The Fall of the House of Usher* by Edgar Poe, illustrated by Alastair, introduction by Arthur Symons, Editions Narcisse (Paris, 1928), p. III.

6. For all quotations from the works of Poe I have used *Selected Writings of Edgar Allan Poe*, ed. Edward H. Davidson, Riverside Edition (Boston: Houghton Mifflin Co., 1956).

7. Arthur Schopenhauer, "On Death and Its Relation to the Indestructibility of Our True Nature," in *The Will to Live, Selected Writings of Arthur Schopenhauer*, ed. Richard Taylor (New York: Frederick Ungar, 1962, 1967), p. 157. The German title is "Zur Lehre von der Unzerstöhrbarkeit unseres Wahren Wesens durch den Tod," in *Parega und Paralipomenia*, Zweiter Theil.

8. Arthur Schopenhauer, *On the Basis of Morality*, tr. E. F. J. Payne with an introduction by Richard Taylor (Indianapolis and New York: Bobbs-Merrill, 1965), p. 197. The essays comprising this work were first published in 1841 under the title *Grundlage der Moral, Kleinere Schriften*.

9. Ibid., p. 104.

10. Freud, *Standard Edition*, XXI, 132. See also *Totem and Taboo*, *Standard Edition*, XIII, 67-70.

11. I have used the H. T. Lowe-Porter translation of *Buddenbrooks*, Vintage Books (New York: A. Knopf, [1924], 1952).

12. Erich Heller has commented on the music that Hanno plays in *The Ironic German* (Meridan Edition), calling the "adolescent version of Richard Wagner's music," "Hanno's swan song to the Will," an abandonment to bliss, and exhaustion, pp. 64-65.

13. Schopenhauer, *Essay on the Freedom of the Will*, tr. with an intro. by Konstantin Kolenda (Indianapolis and New York: Bobbs-Merrill, 1960), pp. 98, 9, 12, 96.

14. Mann, "Schopenhauer" (1938), *Essays of Three Decades*, (New York: A. Knopf, 1948), pp. 386-387.

15. *Hegel's Philosophy of Right*, tr. T. M. Knox (Oxford: Clarendon Press, 1942), p. 91.

16. Mann, *Essays of Three Decades*, p. 395.

17. Georg Lukács, *Essays on Thomas Mann*, tr. Stanley Mitchell (New York: Grosset & Dunlap, 1965), pp. 21-22.

18. Schopenhauer, "On Death and Its Relation to the Indestructibility of Our True Nature," *The Will to Live*, pp. 122, 125, 156-157.

19. One is reminded of that haunting poem of Frost's, "Neither out Far nor in Deep" which reads in part:

> The people along the sand
> All turn and look one way.
> They turn their back on the land.
> They look at the sea all day.
> . . . . .
> They cannot look out far.
> They cannot look in deep.
> But when was that ever a bar
> To any watch they keep?

20. Mann, *Altes und Neues* (Frankfurt-am-Main: S. Fischer Verlag, 1953), p. 569. The translation is mine.

21. Schopenhauer, "Free-Will and Fatalism," *The Will to Live*, p. 268. Many nineteenth-century writers, particularly the Russians, were preoccupied with fatalism in both its primitive and sophisticated versions. Pushkin, Gogol, Lermontov, Dostoevsky, and, of course, Tolstoy were all fond of writing on the subject of fatalism, and in some cases their debt was inherited from writer to writer, with possibly the original inspiration in E. T. A. Hoffmann. See Charles Passage, *The Russian Hoffmannists* (The Hague, 1963). Poe, too, fancied fatalism in some of his Tales, though his "System" was rigidly predictive if we take *Eureka* as its guide.

22. Lukács, *Essays on Thomas Mann*, pp. 19-20.

VI. The Tyranny of Conscience

1. See John Henry Raleigh, *Matthew Arnold and American Culture* (University of California Press: Berkeley, [1957], 1961), pp. 17-46, and Leon Edel, *Henry James, The Conquest of London, 1870-1881* (Philadelphia and New York: Lippincott, 1962), pp. 175-180.

2. David J. De Laura, *Hebrew and Hellene in Victorian England: Newman, Arnold, and Pater* (Austin and London: University of Texas Press, 1969), pp. 167, 170, 171. For the full discussion of Arnold in relation to Hebraism and Hellenism one should consult the whole book which, unfortunately, was published after the present chapter was written so that I have been unable to make the fullest use of this interesting study.

3. For a modern instance see my discussion of Yeats's "The Statues" in *The Vast Design, Patterns in W. B. Yeats's Aesthetic* (Toronto: University of Toronto Press, 1964), pp. 180-204.

4. William Barrett, *Irrational Man* (Garden City, New York: Doubleday, 1962), pp. 72, 82, 77, 78. (See pp. 69-91.)

5. All quotations from *Culture and Anarchy* are from R. H. Super, *The Complete Prose Works of Matthew Arnold* (Ann Arbor: University of Michigan Press, 1965), V, 87-229. The two chapters in *Culture and Anarchy* from which I quote directly are chap. IV, "Hebraism and Hellenism" (pp. 163-175), and chap. V, "Porro Unum Est Necessarium" (pp. 176-191). For useful books in relation to Arnold's Hebraism and Hellenism besides those already mentioned see William Robbins, *The Ethical Idealism of Matthew Arnold: A Study of the Nature and Sources of His Moral and Religious Ideas* (London: William Heineman, 1959), especially pp. 40-42; Warren D. Anderson, *Matthew Arnold and the Classical Tradition* (Ann Arbor: University of Michigan Press, 1965); William A. Madden, *Matthew Arnold, A Study of the Aesthetic Temperament* (Bloomington: University of Indiana Press, 1967); Frederic E. Faverty, *Matthew Arnold the Ethnologist* (Evanston, 1951), chap. vi; Miyoshi, *The Divided Self, A Perspective on the Literature of the Victorians* (New York: New York University Press, 1969), pp. 244-245. My comments on Arnold attempt to focus on the implications of "Hebraism and Hellenism"; no amount of quoting from other works can change Arnold's genuine belief that, for the moment, we must be done with brooding on conscience.

6. Heinrich Heine, *Ludwig Boerne, Eine Denkschrift, Erstes Buch Sämtliche Werke*, VIII (Leipzig, 1913), 359-361. The translation is mine. See also *Heinrich Heine, A Biographical Anthology*, ed. Hugo Bieber, tr. Moses Hadas (The Jewish Publication Society, 1956), pp. 360-361. For an example of the English side of the Arnold-Heine relationship see Stanton Lawrence Wormley, *Heine in England* (Chapel Hill: University of North Carolina Press, 1943); Sol Liptzin, *The English Legend of Heinrich Heine* (New York: Bloch Publishing Co., 1954); and E. M. Butler, "Heine in England and Matthew Arnold," *German Life and Letters*, n.s., 9 (April 1956), 157-165. For a German point of view see Walther Fischer, "Matthew Arnold und Deutschland," *Germanisch-Romanische Monatsschrift*, 35 (April 1954), 119-137 (cited in R. H. Super, *Complete Prose Works*, III, 435). Heine also expressed views of Hebrew and Hellene similar to those quoted from *Boerne* in *The Gods in Exile*: "The point . . . was to defend Hellenism itself or Greek methods of feeling and of thought, and to defeat the extension of Judaism . . . The real question was whether the dismal, meagre, overspiritual, ascetic Judaism of the Nazarenes, or Hellenic joyousness, love of beauty, and fresh pleasure in life should rule the world?" *The Works of Heinrich Heine*, tr. Charles Godfrey Leland, XII (New York: Croscup and Sterling Co., 1900), 306-307.

7. The influence of Hegel on Arnold needs to be further explored. At any rate Hegel, Heine, and Arnold agreed essentially in their judgment of Hellene *versus* Hebrew. For example: "The Jewish Idea that God essentially

exists for thought alone, and the sensuousness of the Greek form of beauty . . . ," Hegel, *Lectures on the Philosophy of Religion,* tr. E. B. Speirs and J. Burdon Sanderson (London, 1895), II, 255. For a general account of the Greek Influence on German thought see E. M. Butler, *The Tyranny of Greece over Germany* (Cambridge, England, 1935); a biased book, it is nevertheless useful.

8. "Heinrich Heine," Super, *Complete Prose Works,* III, 127-128.

9. From the preface to the Laurel Edition of *The Wings of the Dove* (Dell, 1958), p. 10. All quotations from the *Prefaces* are from *The Art of the Novel, Critical Prefaces by Henry James,* ed. R. P. Blackmur (New York: Scribner's, 1934), pp. 3-348.

10. The most recent study of *The Sacred Fount* is Jean Franz Blackall, *Jamesian Ambiguity and 'The Sacred Fount'* (Ithaca: Cornell University Press, 1965).

11. For a recent treatment of the artist in *Roderick Hudson,* see Maurice Beebe, *Ivory Towers and Sacred Founts, The Artist as Hero in Fiction from Goethe to James Joyce* (New York: New York University Press, 1964).

12. The present essay is not concerned with the textual problems of James's revisions. James first serialized the novel in the *Atlantic Monthly* (1875), first published it as a book in 1876, and then revised the novel for subsequent editions in 1879, 1882, and, of course, the New York Edition, 1907-1909.

13. "Dumas Fils and Goethe," *The Nation* (October 1873), reprinted in *Literary Reviews and Essays,* ed. Albert Mordell (New York: Twayne, 1957), pp. 110-118.

14. The New York Edition of *The Novels and Tales of Henry James* (New York: Scribner's and Sons, 1907-1909), I. All quotations are from this edition. In the New York Edition *Roderick Hudson* was published in 1907. Oscar Cargill, *The Novels of Henry James* (New York: Macmillan, 1961), offers the best review of opinions on *Roderick Hudson,* pp. 19-40. In his introduction to the Harper Torchbook edition of *Roderick Hudson* (New York, 1960), Leon Edel writes that "James [is concerned] with sex . . . Roderick allows his terrible passion to destroy his art" (p. vii). However, in *The Conquest of London,* Edel modifies this view slightly, insisting that a mere art-sex conflict ignores "the complexity of the story fabric" (p. 175). See also Lotus Snow, " 'The Prose and the Modesty of the Matter': James's Imagery for the Artist in *Roderick Hudson* and *The Tragic Muse,*" *Modern Fiction Studies,* 12 (Spring 1966), 61-82. Snow agrees with the view that *Roderick Hudson* demonstrates James's view that "an artist who will not sacrifice passion to art sacrifices art" (p. 82).

15. Henry James, *Autobiography,* ed. F. W. Dupee (New York: Criterion Books, 1956), p. 562, and notes, p. 609.

16. "In Matthew Arnold the young Henry James had found an intellectual kinsman," Edel, *The Conquest of London,* p. 123. The entire episode of the

meeting between James and Arnold is described on pp. 122-125. The reference to Arnold's letter is on p. 394.

17. Osborn Andreas, *Henry James and the Expanding Horizon* (Seattle: Greenwood, 1948), p. 53; see also William H. Gass, "The High Brutality of Good Intentions," *Accent* (Winter 1958), p. 67; Cargill, *The Novels*, p. 26, n. 32; p. 37, p. 31.

18. The question of "free will," or the lack of it, is interestingly explored by Viola R. Dunbar, "The Problem in *Roderick Hudson*," *MLN*, 67 (February 1952), 109-113. However she tends to place all the blame for failure on Roderick's passivity, not taking into account Rowland's role in the novel. In his final revision, James made changes which show that he wished to distribute blame among Roderick, Rowland, and fate as well.

19. Warren, *The New England Conscience* (Ann Arbor: University of Michigan Press, 1966), pp. 152-153, 156.

20. For the Conrad-James relationship see G. Jean Aubrey, *Joseph Conrad, Life and Letters* (New York: Doubleday, Page & Co., 1927), vols. I and II; *Letters from Joseph Conrad, 1895-1924*, ed. with an intro. by Edward Garnett (Indianapolis: Bobbs-Merrill, 1928); Jocelyn Baines, *Joseph Conrad, A Critical Biography* (New York, London, Toronto: McGraw-Hill, 1960).

21. Introduction, *The* Portable *Conrad* (New York: The Viking Press, 1947), pp. 1-47.

22. Mann, "Vorwort zu Conrads Roman 'Der Geheimagent," *Altes und Neues* (Frankfurt-am-Main: Fischer Verlag, 1953), pp. 493-506. The translation is mine.

23. For all quotations from *Lord Jim* I have used the Norton Critical Edition, ed. Thomas C. Moser (New York, 1968).

24. Schopenhauer, *On the Basis of Morality*, tr. E. F. J. Payne with an introduction by Richard Taylor (Indianapolis and New York: Bobbs-Merrill, 1965), pp. 127, 109, 197.

25. Dorothea Krook, *Ordeal of Consciousness in Henry James* (New York and London: Cambridge University Press, 1962), p. 21. See also pp. 16-25.

26. Super, *Complete Prose Works* (Ann Arbor: University of Michigan Press, 1960–), V. 180-181.

27. *Thomas Mann's Addresses*, delivered at the Library of Congress, 1942-1949 (Washington, D.C., 1963), p. 84. From an essay called in English "Nietzsche's Philosophy in the Light of Contemporary Events"; in German, "Nietzsche's Philosophie im Lichte unserer Erfahrung," first delivered at a Pen Club Meeting in Zürich on 2 June 1947. In vol. IX of *Gesammelte Werke* (Frankfurt-am-Main: Fischer-Verlag, 1960).

VII. Towards a Genealogy of the Modern Problem

1. Walter Kaufmann, *Nietzsche, Philosopher, Psychologist, Antichrist* Meridian edition (Cleveland: World Publishing, 1956), p. 189; other com-

ments on the relationship between Nietzsche and Freud are scattered through Kaufmann's *From Shakespeare to Existentialism*; Philip Rieff, *Freud: The Mind of the Moralist* (New York: Doubleday: Garden City, 1959).

2. *Standard Edition*, XX, 59-60.

3. *Standard Edition*, IV, pt. 1, pp. 36, 66, 90.

4. *Standard Edition*, XIV, 15-16.

5. *Standard Edition*, XX, 60.

6. Ernest Jones, *Sigmund Freud, Life and Work*, I (New York: Basic Books, 1954), 391, n. 1.

7. Ibid., II, 218.

8. Mann, *Essays of Three Decades*, tr. H. T. Lowe-Porter (New York: Alfred Knopf, 1948), pp. 412, 417. Mann's essays on Schopenhauer, Nietzsche, and Freud remain among the most exciting, partly because Mann made connections among these thinkers in the context of a certain continuum of German thought.

9. Schopenhauer, *On the Basis of Morality*, tr. E. F. G. Payne, with an intro. by Richard Taylor (Indianapolis and New York: Bobbs-Merrill, 1965), p. 104.

10. Ibid.

11. Nietzsche, *Human All-Too-Human, Works*, VI, pt. I, 61.

12. Nietzsche, *Will to Power, Works*, XIV (vol. I, bk. 2), 192.

13. *Totem and Taboo, Standard Edition*, XIII, 67-68. Strachey's note reads: "E.g. the French *'conscience'* which has both meanings. The German word for 'conscience' is *'Gewissen'*, which contains the same root as such words as *'wissen'*, 'to know', and *'bewusst'*, 'conscious', as well as the word . . . *'gewiss'*, 'certain' " (p. 68). Cf. Hegel's view, chap. IV above. See Ernst Blum, "Freud and Conscience," tr. R. F. C. Hull, *Conscience*, pp. 161-178. After making the point that Freud considered conscience a judge—*Richter*—which we have seen as part of a long tradition, Blum writes: "Freud, whenever he concerned himself with conscience—and he did so from his first work to his last—approached it very gingerly as a concept, considering it to be something probably belonging to man *a priori* [innate] but not regarding it as any kind of given psychological knowledge" (p. 163). Also indebted particularly to Freud is Grace Stuart's *Conscience and Reason* (London, 1951). Freud was very interested in the problem of "antithetical" words, as shown most notably in his essay on "The Uncanny," 1919 ("Das Unheimliche," *Standard Edition*, XVII) which contains the analysis of E. T. A Hoffmann's "Der Sandmann." In the essay Freud tries to show how, etymologically, "unheimlich" (uncanny) and "heimlich" (homely) share some identical meanings or sometimes exchange connotations. A much earlier interest in antithetical words appears in " 'The Antithetical Sense of Primal Words': A Review of a Pamphlet by Karl Abel, "Uber den Gegensinn der Urworte" (1884), 1910, Freud, *Collected Papers*, ed. Joan Rivere, IV (London: The Hogarth Press, 1949), 184-191.

14. Schopenhauer, *On the Basis of Morality*, p. 104

15. Freud, *Totem and Taboo, Standard Edition*, XIII, 68.

16. Freud, *Civilization and Its Discontents, Standard Edition*, XXI, 136-137.

17. Ibid., p. 131.

18. Schopenhauer, *On the Basis of Morality*, pp. 195-196.

19. Nietzsche, *Will to Power, Works*, XIV (vol. II, bk. 2), pp. 242-243.

20. Schopenhauer, *Essay on the Freedom of the Will*, pp. 9-10.

21. Nietzsche, *Will to Power, Works*, XIV (vol. I, bk. 1), p. 64.

22. See Kaufmann, *Nietzsche*, pp. 319ff.

23. Nietzsche, *Twilight of the Idols, Works*, XVI, 141.

24. Nietzsche, *The Joyful Wisdom, Works*, X, 299.

25. Ibid., pp. 47-48.

26. Ibid., pp. 260-261.

27. Freud, *Standard Edition*, XXI, 145.

28. Ibid., p. 134. Freud then quotes Hamlet's "Thus conscience does make cowards of us all." For a note on *Gewissensangst* see *Standard Edition*, XX, 128.

29. *Minutes of the Vienna Psychoanalytic Society, 1906-1908*, ed. Herman Nunberg and Ernst Federn, tr. M. Nunberg, I (New York: International Universities Press, 1962), 356-360. (See also Jones, *Freud, Life and Work*, III, 283-284.)

30. *Minutes of the Vienna Psychoanalytic Society*, 1906-1908, II (New York, 1967), 29-32.

31. For the *Genealogy of Morals* I have used *On The Genealogy of Morals*, tr. Walter Kaufmann and R. J. Hollingdale (New York: Random House, 1967), pp. 15-163. The *Genealogy* is part of a collection including aphorisms and *Ecce Homo* with commentaries by Walter Kaufmann.

32. See Nietzsche's *The Use and Abuse of History, Thoughts Out of Season, Works*, IV.

33. See Jones, *Freud, Life and Work*, III, 283-284. I have corrected a few minor errors in the transcription, using *Works*, XIII, 217-218.

34. These are the concluding words of *The Genealogy of Morals*. Adams, in *Nil*, supports Nietzsche's view, but there may be a danger in ascribing the "void" syndrome too inclusively to all major nineteenth-century writers. A strong countermovement was also in motion, and to remind ourselves of *Buddenbrooks*, the collision of the two movements—ennui and atavism—produced some significant literary works.

35. Mann, "Nietzsche's Philosophy in the Light of Contemporary Events," *Thomas Mann's Addresses*, delivered at the Library of Congress, 1942-1949 (Washington, D.C., 1949), pp. 69-103.

36. Nietzsche, *Human, All-Too-Human, Works*, VII, pt. II, 33.

37. Schopenhauer, *On the Basis of Morality*, p. 195.

VIII. A Case of Conscience

1. Schopenhauer, *On the Basis of Morality*, tr. E. F. J. Payne with an intro. by Richard Taylor (Indianapolis, New York, Kansas City: Bobbs-Merrill, 1965), pp. 105-108.

2. Nietzsche, *Human, All-Too-Human, Works*, VII, pt. II, 224.

3. Nietzsche, *Thus Spake Zarathustra, Works*, XI, 103; *Beyond Good and Evil, Works*, XII, 90.

4. I have found most helpful: Heinz Politzer, *Franz Kafka, Parable and Paradox* (Ithaca: Cornell University Press, 1962) and Walter Sokel, *Franz Kafka, Tragik und Ironie* (Munich, Vienna, 1964) and a drastically distilled version by the same author, *Franz Kafka*, Columbia Essays in Modern Writers (New York: Columbia University Press, 1966).

5. See Adrian Jaffe, *The Process of Kafka's "Trial"* (Lansing: Michigan State University Press, 1967).

6. I have used the so-called "definitive" English edition of *The Trial*, tr. Willa and Edwin Muir, rev. E. M. Butler.

7. Nietzsche, *The Joyful Wisdom, Works*, X, 260.

8. A paraphrase from Yeats's "Ego Dominus Tuus."

9. Nietzsche, *The Joyful Wisdom, Works*, X, 260-261.

10. *Hegel's Lectures on the History of Philosophy*, tr. E. S. Haldane, I (New York: Humanities Press, 1955), 431, 441-448.

11. Nietzsche, *The Joyful Wisdom, Works*, X, 161-162.

12. Both Politizer and Sokel (n. 4 above) see the ending as ambiguous.

13. *Kant's Critique of Practical Reason, and Other Writings in Moral Philosophy*, tr. and ed. with intro. by Lewis White Beck (Chicago: University of Chicago Press, 1949), p. 187.

14. Kierkegaard, *Fear and Trembling and the Sickness unto Death*, tr. with introd. by Walter Lowrie (Garden City, N.Y.: Doubleday), p. 182.

15. Theodore Ziolkowski, *Dimensions of The Modern Novel* (Princeton: Princeton University Press, 1969), p. 57.

16. See Klaus Wagenbach, *Franz Kafka, Eine Biographie Seiner Jugend, 1883-1892* (Bern: Francke Verlag, 1958), pp. 172-74, 102.

17. I have used the Modern Library edition of *Steppenwolf*, tr. Basil Creighton, rev. Walter Sorell (New York: Random House, 1963); I have also consulted the Rinehart edition, *Steppenwolf*, tr. and rev. based on the Creighton edition by Joseph Mileck and Horst Frenz (New York, 1963).

18. See n. 12 above.

19. Nietzsche, *Beyond Good and Evil, Works*, XII, 87.

20. Oskar Seidlin, "Herman Hesse, The Exorcism of the Demon," *Essays in German and Comparative Literature* (Chapel Hill: University of North Carolina Press, 1961), p. 210. I choose this quotation because it is fairly representative. The most stimulating recent work on Hesse I find in Theodore

Ziolkowski, esp. *Herman Hesse: A Study in Theme and Structure* (Princeton: Princeton University Press, 1965).

21. Freud, *Standard Edition*, XVII, 235.

22. Nietzsche, *Human, All-Too-Human, Works*, VII, pt. II, 48.

23. See Wayne Booth, *The Rhetoric of Fiction* (Chicago and London: Univ. of Chicago Press, 1961), pp. 294-296.

24. Nietzsche, *The Joyful Wisdom, Works*, X, 265-267.

25. Ibid., pp. 334-335.

26. I have used the Justin O'Brien translation of *La Chute [The Fall]*, Vintage Books (New York: Random House, 1956).

27. Søren Kierkegaard, *The Concept of Dread*, tr. Walter Lowrie, with intro. and notes (Princeton: Princeton University Press, 1957), p. 111.

28. Nietzsche, *Will to Power, Works*, XV (vol. II), p. 10.

29. Nietzsche, *The Joyful Wisdom, Works*, X, 87.

30. Clamence's ironic yet serious "slave-theory" and its debts to Nietzsche's "slave-morality" seem no accident, though I can only call attention to them here. I would characterize Clamence's position as a rhetorical critique of Nietzsche's.

31. *Hegel's Lectures on the History of Philosophy*, I, 447.

32. The idea of the "paradox of the fortunate fall," I have, of course, borrowed from A. O. Lovejoy's famous essay "Milton and the Paradox of the Fortunate Fall," *Essays in the History of Ideas*, (New York: Capricorn Books, G. P. Putnam's, 1960), pp. 277-295.

33. Kant, *Metaphysical Principles of Virtue*, tr. James Ellington with intro. by Warner Wick (Indianapolis and New York: Bobbs-Merrill, 1964), p. 101.

34. Kierkegaard, *Concept of Dread*, p. 105.

35. Hegel, *Phenomenology of Mind*, tr. J. B. Baillie, rev. and cor. second ed. (London: G. Allen Unwin Ltd., New York: Macmillan, 1949), pp. 673-674.

36. Herman Hesse, "Bemerkungen zu neuen Büchern," *Die Neue Rundschau*, 46 (June 1935), 667-668. The translation is mine.

37. There are far too many books to mention. Some I have already cited in previous notes. To these I would add several: Erich Kahler, *The Tower and the Abyss: An Inquiry into the Transformation of Man* (New York: Viking Press, 1957); William Hubben, [*Four Prophets of Our Destiny:*] *Kierkegaard, Dostoevsky, Nietzsche, Kafka* (New York: Macmillan, 1966); Geoffrey Clive, *The Romantic Enlightenment: Ambiguity and Paradox in the Western Mind* (1750-1920) (New York: New American Library, 1960); J. Hillis Miller, *The Disappearance of God, Five Nineteenth-Century Writers* [all English] (Cambridge, Mass.: Harvard University Press, 1963). For a critique of the "dissociation" theories see Frank Kermode's brilliant *Romantic Image* (London: Routledge and Kegan Paul, 1957), pp. 138-161.

38. My allusion is to the witty and pertinent essay by Merritt Y. Hughes, "Kidnapping Donne," *Essays in Criticism*, Second Series (Berkeley, 1934).

39. Hesse, *Die Neue Rundschau*, p. 668.

40. The subject matter of *The Fall* is not so far removed from "Sunday Morning"—it merely begins where Stevens attempted to leave off: man satiated with his natural world without a God but also beyond the reach of Zeus's "mythy mind," at evening, contemplating "ambiguous undulations."

41. Freud, *Standard Edition*, XXI, 126.

Conclusion

1. See Introduction, n. 3.

2. See n. 11 below.

3. *The Philosophical Lectures of Samuel Taylor Coleridge*, ed. Kathleen Coburn (London: The Pilot Press, 1949), p. 216.

4. Goethe, *Maximen und Reflexionen*, #241. The translation is mine.

5. Nietzsche, *The Joyful Wisdom*, *Works*, X, 241. "Nierenprüfer" is difficult to translate: one who exhausts all means of trying men with thoroughness.

6. Nietzsche, *Ecce Homo*, *Works*, XVII, 49.

7. Miguel de Unamuno, *The Tragic Sense of Life*, tr. J. E. Crawford Flitch (New York: Dover, 1954), p. 139.

8. Blake, *The Complete Writings of William Blake*, ed. Geoffrey Keynes (New York: Nonesuch Press, 1957), pp. 459, 385.

9. David Daiches, *Some Late Victorian Attitudes* (London: André Deutsch, 1969), 15-17, 29, 37-38.

10. Geoffrey M. Stephenson, *The Development of Conscience* (New York and London: Routledge & Kegan Paul, 1966), p. 1.

11. I allude to the current cause célèbre, Charles A. Reich's *The Greening of America* (Random House: New York, 1970). The word "consciousness" has become among the two or three chief terms of the new vocabulary. Recently, the *New York Times* Sunday Magazine section offered two essays on successive Sundays: Bruce L. Maliver, "Encounter Groups Up against the Wall," January 3, 1971; Vivian Gornick, "Consciousness," January 10, 1971. Both writers dealt with the new phenomenon—and faddism—of "consciousness" and both sounded some alarm. The high school students asked to define conscience were sophomores in several classes of World Civilization at Lexington High School. Their teacher was the author's wife; and the author specifically commissioned the definitions. Several were very imaginative, but Nietzsche would have been upset to see how many students merely equated conscience with guilt. On the other hand, Kant would have given high marks to the following definition (it was the most interesting): "[Conscience] is like

an abstract figure inside one's self that seems to be able to look at things objectively rather than subjectively. It tells you or makes you think about whether things are right or wrong. It is like a board you can argue with, but you usually lose." Almost all definitions spoke of conscience as being "something inside of you," strong testimony to the persistence of the conviction that conscience is innate.

Index

Abel, Karl, 275n13
Adams, R. M., 118, 261n35, 276n34
Adler, Alfred, 197
Aiken, Henry D., 260n16
Amour-propre, 6, 22, 24, 81; Peer Gynt as example of, 6, 111, 112; defined, 23; Kant on, 25; and duty, 78, 79; and the Undergound Man, 90-91. *See also* Egotism
Amour de soi, 6, 22, 23, 90. *See also* Egotism
Ancrene Riwle, 10
Anderson, Warren D., 272n5
Andreas, Osborn, 274n17
Aristotle, 207
Arnold, Matthew, 6, 144-154, 244, 249; dualism of, 10; on conscience and consciousness, 142-143; compared with Conrad and James, 144; influence of Heine on, 149, 150, 152-153, 262n38, 272n6; influence on James, 155, 160, 273n16; and Nietzsche, 205, 206, 262n38; and duty, 247, 248; influence of Hegel on, 262n38, 272n7
    "The Author of 'Obermann,' " 147 (quoted)
    Culture and Anarchy, 12, 148, 160
    Empedocles on Aetna, 145-147
    "Hebraism and Hellenism," 10, 12, 35-37, 135, 184-185, 271n2; discussed, 148-154; and James's *Roderick Hudson*, 155, 168-169; and Conrad's *Lord Jim*, 175-176

Arnold, Matthew (continued)
    "Literature and Science," 149
    "Memorial Verses," 147
    "Obermann Once More," 148 (quoted)
    "Rugby Chapel," 147
    "Stanzas from the Grand Chartreuse," 148
Astrov, Vladimir, 268n7
Aubrey, G. Jean, 274n20
Auden, W. H., 261n36; "September 1, 1939," 196 (quoted)

Babbitt, Irving, *Rousseau and Romanticism*, 23
Bacon, Sir Francis, 120
Baines, Jocelyn, 274n20
Bakunin, Mikhail, 89
Balzac, Honoré de, 75
Barrett, William, 151-152; *Irrational Man*, 264n11, 272n4
Baudelaire, Charles Pierre, 105, 147, 223, 224, 236; and drug-taking, 33-34; *correspondances* of, 69, 84; and nature, 71-72; and the Underground Man, 105-106
    "Au Lecteur," 110 (quoted)
    "De Profundis Clamavi," 106
    "Duellum," 108-109 (quoted)
    Les Fleurs du Mal, 36, 107-108, 110, 185
    "L'Irrémédiable," 106, 107
    "L'Irréparable," 109-110 (quoted)